THE NORTH CAUCASUS BARRIER

THE
NORTH
CAUCASUS
BARRIER

The Russian Advance towards
the Muslim World

ABDURAHMAN AVTORKHANOV
MARIE BENNIGSEN BROXUP *editor*
FANNY E. B. BRYAN
MOSHE GAMMER
PAUL B. HENZE
CHANTAL LEMERCIER-QUELQUEJAY

HURST & COMPANY, LONDON

CONTENTS

vii

MAPS

PHOTOGRAPHS

PREFACE

In June 1991, the leader of the national independence movement in Checheno-Ingushetia, General Dzhokhar Dudaev, declared that it was necessary to sign a peace treaty between Russia and the North Caucasian Chechen-Ingush Republic before any preliminary talks could be held on future political and economic relations between the respective leaderships. This statement referred to the fact that the North Caucasus had been at war against Russia, in an effort to preserve its independence, almost uninterruptedly since the end of the eighteenth century. This epic struggle, in comparison to which even Abdel Qadir's resistance to the French conquest of Algeria pales, is little known in the West and in most of the Muslim world.

This collection of writings, which gives only the highlights of this two-century-long struggle, is the final outcome of a symposium on the North Caucasus held in London in June 1988. The impetus, planning and advice for the conference were provided by Alexandre Bennigsen, for many years the leading specialist in the West on Soviet Muslim nationalities. Bennigsen died a week before the conference was held, and this book is a homage to his memory and his effort to bring the history of these resilient North Caucasian nations to the attention of scholars in the West. The authors of this work felt that the history of the conquest of the North Caucasus, which has played a predominant part in framing Russian colonial thinking, deserves to be known outside a narrow circle of specialists, and that this strategically important region and its turbulent, deeply Muslim peoples are destined to continue to play an important role in the shaping of Russian politics.

A crucial period for Russia has elapsed since the manuscript was first delivered to the publisher. This has made the present work relevant in a new light. In September 1991, I received documents from Chechnia-Ingushetia which prompted me to add an extra chapter, 'After the Putsch'. Then on 8 November 1991, only two days after it was written, the North Caucasian Chechen Republic became media news: President Yeltsin declared a state of emergency in the Republic which had been in turmoil since August 1991, dispatched troops to the Chechen capital, and ordered the arrest of General Dzhokhar Dudaev, newly elected president of Chechnia. Dudaev immediately counteracted: Chechnia was put on war alert, and the capital Groznyi became 'a fortress'. All warring factions in Chechnia rallied behind General Dudaev; the Daghestani mountain clans, which had traditionally fought against the Russian conquest

ix

along-side the Chechens, proclaimed *Ghazawat* – holy war – and pledged to help the Chechens repel Russian intervention. Mobilisation of volunteers began throughout the North Caucasus, even as far afield as Azerbaijan, after an appeal for support by General Dudaev. The Russian parliament went into emergency session and refused to endorse President Yeltsin's decision, amid accusations of dictatorial behaviour and mis-management of a political crisis – the first official rebuff to the post-putsch hero. Meanwhile the Chechen Parliament had sworn Dudaev in – the presidential oath was taken on the Qoran – and granted him emergency powers for one month.

The Caucasian wars of the nineteenth century drained Russian military power and contributed largely to Russia's defeat in the Crimean War. The example of the North Caucasian resistance under the leader-ship of Shamil became an inspiration to other subjugated nations of the empire, the Poles and the Ukrainians among them, while the atrocities and ruthlessness of the conquest irreparably tarnished the prestige of the Romanov dynasty. The present crisis in Chechnia is a logical conse-quence of two centuries of Russian onslaught on the North Caucasus, and may similarly discredit the Russian democratic leadership. The situation is strongly reminiscent of the 1917–20 Civil War period during which the North Caucasian peoples made a desperate bid for freedom. The subsequent reconquest by the Russian Bolsheviks was short and brutal. It is to be hoped, however, that this new conflict in Chechnia will not again lead to war. Unfortunately, most North Caucasians believe, rightly or wrongly, that the overwhelming majority of Russians would welcome a military crackdown in the Caucasus if this could be done with impunity. The history of this region helps to explain these attitudes. Ultimately, Moscow's heavy-handedness may well promote the long-held aspiration for a Pan-Caucasian confederation, referred to in the final chapter. The divided Muslim peoples of the North Caucasus have shown that they are quite willing to unite to fight for a common goal when faced with the real danger of a Russian military intervention, and quite capable of such action. Unity and independence in the North Caucasus could spur other feuding Muslim nations, such as the Tatars and Bashkirs and the Central Asians, towards closer political and economic coordination. Ultimately it could encourage the autonomous republics of the Russian Federation towards radical nationalism leading to a possible disintegration of the Russian Federation.

London   MARIE BENNIGSEN BROXUP
March 1992

THE AUTHORS

ABDURAHMAN AVTORKHANOV is a Chechen by birth. One of his first books, *Revolution and Counter-Revolution in Chechnia*, was published in Groznyi in 1933. He was arrested in 1937 during the Stalinist purges and accused of being 'an enemy of the peoples'. He was released in 1942 and emigrated to the West in 1943. His books, long forbidden in the Soviet Union, were read assiduously by Soviet dissidents. Among the most recent are *Strength and Weakness of Brezhnev: Political Studies* (1980), *The Enigma of Stalin's Death: Beria's Conspiracy* (1981), *The Origins of the Partocracy* and *Technology of Power* (1983) and *The Empire of the Kremlin* (1986). A hero in his native Chechnia, he has recently been rehabilitated.

MARIE BENNIGSEN BROXUP, editor of *Central Asian Survey* and director of the Society for Central Asian Studies, London, is co-author with Alexandre Bennigsen of *The Islamic Threat to the Soviet State.*

FANNY BRYAN is assistant professor of Russian history and fellow of the Center of International Studies, University of Missouri-St Louis.

MOSHE GAMMER teaches modern Middle Eastern history at the University of Tel Aviv. He is the author of·the forthcoming book *Muslim Resistance to the Tsar: Shamil and the Russian Conquest of Chechnia and Daghestan.*

PAUL HENZE has served on the US National Security Council from 1976 to 1980. He is a consultant to the Rand Corporation and author of *The Horn of Africa: From War to Peace* and *Soviet Strategy and Islam* (co-authored with Alexandre Bennigsen, George Tanham and S. Enders Wimbush).

CHANTAL LEMERCIER-QUELQUEJAY is *Maître Assistant* at the Ecole des Hautes Etudes en Sciences Sociales. She is the co-author with Alexandre Bennigsen of *Islam in the Soviet Union, Les mouvements nationaux chez les musulmans de Russie* and *La presse et le mouvement national chez les musulmans de Russie avant 1920.*

GLOSSARY

Abrek	Bandit of honour in the North Caucasus
Adat	Customary law
Agitprop	Department of Agitation and Propaganda
Alim (pl. *ulema*)	Muslim religious scholar
Aul	Mountain village or town
Cheka	Extraordinary Commission for the Fight Against Counter-Revolution and Sabotage (*Chekist*: member of this organisation)
Djigit	North Caucasian exemplar of equestrian and knightly virtues
GPU	State Political Directorate
Gaiour	Infidel
Ghazawat	*Jihad*, holy war
Ghazi	Slayer of the infidel
Gorkom	Communist Party City Committee
Haj	Pilgrimage to Mecca
Imam	Leader of the collective prayer, by extension leader of the community
Imamate	Theocratic state
Jadid	Religious reformist
Jami	Cathedral mosque
Kafir	Infidel
Kinjal	Caucasian ceremonial dagger
Kolkhoz	Collective farm
Komsomol	Youth organisation
Kraikom	Communist Party *Krai* Committee
Kurbam Bayram	The Feast of the Sacrifice
Madrassah	Religious high school
Mawlud	Birthday of the Prophet
Mazar	Holy place, tomb of a saint
Mufti	Canon lawyer
Murid	Adept of a Sufi order
Murshid	Master in a Sufi order
MVD	Ministry of the Interior
NKVD	People's Commissariat for Internal Affairs
Narkommnats	People's Commissariat for the Affairs of the Nationalities
Obkom	Communist Party *Oblast* Committee

Oblast	Administrative division, district
Qadi	Muslim judge
Padishah	Supreme Shah or 'king of kings'
Raikom	Communist Party *Raion* Committee
Raion	District, administrative unit and sub-division of an *oblast*
Revkom	Revolutionary Military Committee
Sadaqa	Voluntary contribution of the believers to the upkeep of a mosque or to a Sufi order
Samizdat	Underground literature
Shariat	Quranic law
Sheikh	Master, head of a Sufi brotherhood
Sovnarkom	Council of Peoples' Commissars
Stanitsa	Cossack garrison-type settlement
Streltsy	Archers' regiment
Tariqat	Sufi order
Ulu	Turkic word for nation
Uraza Bayram	Feast at the end of Ramadan
Uzden	Freeman
Voievod	Military commander
Zakat	Legal alms
Zikr	'Remembrance' of God, collective prayer

NOTE ON TRANSLITERATION

It is impossible to find a system which satisfies all scholars when transliterating from the Muslim languages of the Soviet Union, especially in the case of the North Caucasian languages which include Arabic, Turkic, Ibero-Caucasian and a russified vocabulary. For the sake of simplicity for the non-specialist reader, we have decide to use the generally accepted English spelling for well-known historical and political names. For geographical names, we have kept as far as possible to the modern phonetic rendering. For bibliographical references and surnames of the modern period, we have used the Library of Congress transliteration for Cyrillic. Thus one will read 'Dudaev' and 'Yeltsin'. Muslim surnames are usually spelt as transliterated from the Cyrillic alphabet, hence inconsistencies such as 'Husain Akhmadov'. We apologise for the irritation this may cause to the linguists.

MAPS

The CAUCASUS -
GEOGRAPHICAL SETTING

Tallinn
St. Petersburg
Riga
Kaliningrad
Vilnius
Warsaw
Minsk
Gorki
MOSCOW ■
Kazan
Kuybyshev
Kiev
Kharkov
Dnepropetrovsk
Volgograd
ROMANIA
Odessa
Rostov
Astrakhan
Bucharest
Krasnodar
BULGARIA
Black Sea
C A U C A S U S
Groznyi
Makhachkala
Istanbul
Tbilisi
Baku
Caspian Sea
Ankara
Yerevan
TURKEY
Tabriz
Mediterranean
Sea
SYRIA
IRAQ
IRAN
Tehran
Damascus
Baghdad

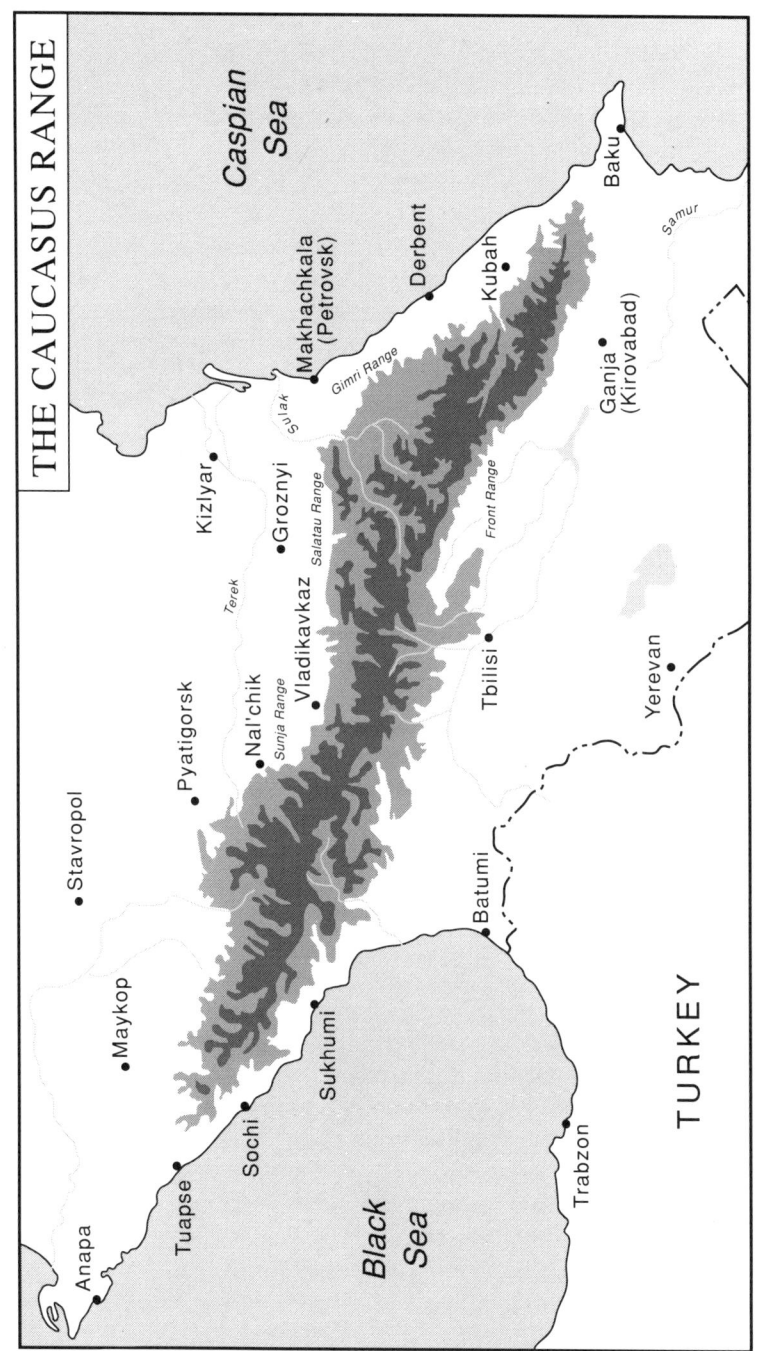

THE CAUCASUS RANGE

Caspian Sea

Baku

Samur

Derbent

Makhachkala (Petrovsk)

Kubah

Gimri Range

Ganja (Kirovabad)

Sulak

Front Range

Kizlyar

Groznyi

Salatau Range

Terek

Tbilisi

Yerevan

Pyatigorsk

Nal'chik

Vladikavkaz

Sunja Range

Stavropol

Maykop

Batumi

Sukhumi

TURKEY

Sochi

Tuapse

Trabzon

Anapa

Black Sea

INTRODUCTION
RUSSIA AND THE NORTH CAUCASUS

Marie Bennigsen Broxup

The Russian drive towards the warm seas began in the second half of the sixteenth century from the banks of the river Terek. Four centuries later the Russians had not moved further than the river Arax. The opening to the warm seas remains an unattainable goal. Turkey, Iran, Afghanistan still stand, and a count-down has begun for Russia's withdrawal from her colonies. External pressures from Great Britain, France, Germany, Turkey and the United States have often been advanced as an explanation for the lack of success of the Russian advance towards the Muslim world. Seldom have local resistance and opposition to the conquest been taken into account. However, the North Caucasus, which has been in a state of almost permanent warfare against Russia since the first *jihad* led by Sheikh Mansur in 1783 until the Chechen and Ingush uprising of 1943 has played a capital role in making any further Russian conquest southwards impossible. Today it remains the least sovietised and most staunchly Muslim of all the territories of the Soviet Union. This book focuses exclusively on the domestic factor.

The historical setting

We can identify roughly five different stages in the modern history of the North Caucasus:

1. Up till the middle of the sixteenth century the North Caucasus remained isolated from the international scene. It was inhabited by tribal clanic societies professing different religions — Christians in the west (Adyghes, some of the Kabardians and Ossetians), Muslims in the east (Daghestan), and pagans in the centre (Chechens and Ingush). There were no serious conflicts and no interest in this mountainous region from the main neighbouring states. Suddenly after 1556, with the conquest of Astrakhan by Ivan the Terrible, the North Caucasus became the object of a major international conflict and the centre of a 'great game' played by several powerful contestants: the Ottoman empire, the Crimean khanate and the Shaybanis of Turkestan in the east and west, Muscovy and the Great Nogay Horde in the north, and Iran in the south. The Caucasians

1

were unwillingly drawn into the contest. The dispute was not political; nobody was interested *per se* in annexing a territory with no resources. However, the North Caucasus was strategically of vital importance for trade and military routes. For Moscow, control over the Caucasus meant access to the warm seas and the Iranian market, also the realisation of a century-old Indian dream which had caught the Russians' imagination since the journey southward of the first Russian traveller Afanasii Nikitin;[1] for the Ottomans and the Crimean Tatars it provided a military liaison with Derbent and the possibility to outflank Iran through Shirvan; for the Shaybanis it opened the road to Haj from Bukhara and the last link between eastern and western Turks.

This first phase lasted approximately from 1556 to 1604. Moscow opened the game after the annexation of Astrakhan by trying to occupy first the western, then the central, and finally the eastern Caucasus. All cards were used: settlements, cooptation, christianisation and military conquest. The expansion, aimed at Kabarda and Daghestan, began with the occupation of the Lower Volga valley and the building of several fortresses. In 1587, the Russians had reached as far as the Terek in the Caucasian lowlands, and built the fortress of Terskii Gorodok which served as a springboard for further advance. In 1590, pushing further south, they built a fortress on the lower Sunja river and were thus ready for a major breakthrough into the Caucasus.

Realising the danger, the Ottomans and the Crimeans reacted vigorously by launching a major offensive against Kabarda, which was allied to Moscow, and razed it to the ground in 1587. The same year the *Shamkhal* of Tarku, the most powerful ruler in Daghestan, who had hesitated between Moscow and the Ottomans, finally sided with the Turks and became their staunchest ally in the Caucasus. In 1590 the Ottomans, in their campaign against Iran, occupied Shirvan and pushed northwards towards Derbent, and for a while a Turkish fleet roamed the Caspian sea. In 1591, after the Crimean Tatars had launched an unsuccessful expedition against Moscow, Russian troops reached the Sulak river where they built a fortress, only to be driven back three years later by a joint force of Ottomans and Daghestanis. In 1604, Tsar Boris Godunov undertook a major offensive aimed at breaking once and for all through Daghestan to link with his Iranian allies. It ended in a military disaster. The Muscovite army was routed by the Daghestanis, helped by the Ottomans. All Russian fortresses on the Sulak, Sunja and Terek rivers were destroyed, and the Russians forced to withdraw back to their frontline in Astrakhan.

2. The second phase lasted from 1604 to 1783, during which the North Caucasus disappeared from the arena of world politics. Russia turned towards Europe, Iran was not interested, the Ottomans and the Tatars defeated by Iran maintained a distant protectorate. There were no major conflicts during this period, except for the short and ill-fated expedition of Peter the Great against Iran and Derbent. However, three important changes occured which were to have long-lasting effects. First, religion became a major factor in the competition between the Ottoman Empire and Russia for the soul and alliance of the North Caucasus. Christianity retreated while Islam made steady progress in the western and central North Caucasus, thus laying the foundation for the future religious wars; secondly, the advance of Islam was paralleled by the steady growth of Russian peasant settlements in the piedmont of the east Caucasus with the establishment of Terek and Greben Cossack colonies; and thirdly, the decline of the mightiest Muslim military organisation in the area, the Nogay Horde, which until the end of the sixteenth century gave a certain equilibrium to the division of power in the region, and her replacement by more reliable allies and auxiliaries of Russia, the Buddhist Kalmyks.

3. The third phase lasted from 1783 to 1824 and marked the beginning of Russia's systematic offensive against the North Caucasus. In 1783 Azaq fell and the Crimean khanate was eliminated. The road was open for a face-to-face confrontation between Russia and the North Caucasus. Totally disunited linguistically and socially, the North Caucasus seemed doomed. However there was a swift response, this time from the North Caucasians alone. Sheikh Mansur Ushurma, a Chechen Naqshbandi sheikh initiated by a Bukharan *haji*, managed for a brief period, from 1785 to 1791, to unite most of the North Caucasus, from Chechnia and north Daghestan to Kuban, in a holy war against the Russians. In 1785, Mansur's warriors encircled an important Russian force on the bank of the river Sunja and completely annihilated it — the worst-ever defeat inflicted on the armies of Catherine II. However, the Naqshbandiya Sufi order had no deep roots at the time and the Russians were able to crush the North Caucasians when the Ottoman fortress, Anapa, fell in 1791. Sheikh Mansur was captured and confined in Schlusselburg prison where he died in 1793. The Naqshbandiya disappeared from the North Caucasus for almost thirty years but the *jihad*, a foretaste of the future *Murid* movement, left the memory that resistance as well as unity around Islam were possible.

The offensive went on after 1791 with all the piedmont occupied and inroads made deep into the mountains. Resistance by feudal lords was weak. It was easily overcome by Russia's army freshly victorious from the Napoleonic wars and led by her best generals such as Ermolov. Russian action was ruthless and for the first time genocidal tactics were applied against the Caucasians. The Ottoman Empire did not intervene, and once again the North Caucasus seemed doomed.

4. The fourth phase, from 1824 to 1922 was that of the *ghazawat* — the holy wars. During this period the North Caucasus underwent a total change: the feudal system was replaced by clans and free peasant societies (*uzden*), and the *tariqat* (the Sufi orders) provided a new ideology and became deeply implanted among the population. Unity was formed around the *Shariat* law as opposed to the customary law of the *adat*. Arabic language and culture spread from Daghestan to the western Adyghe territories and the last heathen Ingush *auls* were converted to Islam in the 1860s.

The period of *Muridism* and Shamil's imamate, 1824–59, is well known in the West thanks to the remarkable chronicle of the Englishman John Baddeley (*The Russian Conquest of the Caucasus*, London, 1908) and the dispatches of Karl Marx.[2] An overview of the military strategies used by the Russian commanders against Shamil is given by Moshe Gammer in the chapter 'Russian Strategies in the Conquest of Chechnia and Daghestan, 1825–1859'. After the fiercest and longest-ever armed resistance by a Muslim country to a foreign Christian invader, the North Caucasus was defeated but undaunted. The same ideology of *Muridism* — military *jihad* inspired by the Sufi orders combined with the age-old traditions of freedom of a 'democratic' clanic mountain society — brought the North Caucasians again to the well-trodden battlefields of Sheikh Mansur and Imam Shamil in 1877–8, and once more in 1920–1. In 1922, after the last great uprising inspired by the militant *tariqat*, the North Caucasus was finally subjugated and seemingly pacified. In fact all the problems remained.

5. The fifth phase, from 1922 to the present, witnessed several sporadic rebellions on which little information is available so far. However, as an iron curtain was drawn across the region, there followed the most brutal attempt yet by Russia to impose a final solution on her unruly Caucasian dominion — genocide through deportation of entire North Caucasian nations.

Russian strategies

Ever since the onset of the Russian advance towards the Muslim lands, from the conquest of Kazan in 1552 until the invasion of Afghanistan in December 1979, the Russian rulers and their Soviet successors applied the same political methods to subdue, pacify or win over the populations of the neighbouring Muslim states and colonies. Much simplified, this strategy can be presented as follows.

Settlement of Russian peasant colonies

Everywhere from the North Caucasus to the Volga region, Siberia, Kazakhstan and Central Asia, Russian military conquest was preceded, accompanied or followed by settlements of Cossacks (in particular in Terek, Greben, Kuban, Semirechie, Orenburg, and Yaik), and later, in the nineteenth century, by Russian peasants. Everywhere armed colonists provided dedicated militias who helped to expel the natives. Colonial settlement made the conquest final and irreversible. These lands became part of 'Russia'. This strategy was feasible only so long as Russia had a surplus rural population. It was impossible to apply in Afghanistan in the 1980s because of the Russians' demographic decline after the Second World War.

Assimilation

Under the tsars, two contradictory methods of assimilating the alien Muslim elements were used: conversion to Orthodox Christianity while retaining a national profile, without linguistic and cultural russification — a policy practiced with some success in the Volga region in the eighteenth and nineteenth centuries; or conversion followed by full assimilation by the Russian milieu, never a very productive policy for winning the Muslim masses because the russified converts were cut from their roots and lost the confidence of their people. The Soviets tried to apply the former method, merely replacing Orthodoxy with Marxism, with the slogan of 'national in form and socialist in content' with even less success than the tsars.

Cooptation of the élites

This was practiced from Kabarda in the North Caucasus in the sixteenth century to Afghanistan in the twentieth century. Cooptation of the feudal aristocracy proved only moderately successful if not counterproductive in the North Caucasus as argued by Chantal Lemercier-Quelquejay in the chapter on 'Cooptation of the Elites in the sixteenth

Century in Kabarda and Daghestan'. Cooptation of the Muslim religious élites, inaugurated by Catherine II in 1783 with the creation of the *muftiat* of Orenburg, on the other hand enjoyed a spectacular success. It gained the Romanov dynasty the loyalty and cooperation of the Tatar élites for more than a century. Stalin was inspired by Catherine's example when he instituted the Muslim Religious Boards in 1945, and seemed equally successful in endowing Soviet Islam with a cooperative and pliable official Muslim administration. However, the dramatic expulsion in 1989, through popular demand, of Mufti Shamsuddin Babakhanov in Central Asia and Mufti Mahmud Gekkiev in the North Caucasus, both reputed to be particularly subservient to Moscow, proved the limitation of this policy in the long term.

In the North Caucasus, the men who retained religious authority were the Sufi sheikhs, and for a short time during the Civil War and the 1920-1 war the Bolsheviks were able to play the religious card, undoubtedly counselled by Caucasian communists, such as Najmuddin Samurskii. Indeed, between 1918 and 1926, the Bolsheviks succeeded in dividing the Naqshbandiya *tariqat* by opposing the influential Sheikh Ali of Akusha in the Darghin region of Daghestan to the leader of the uprising, Imam Najmuddin Gotsinskii. Similarly in the Chechen-Ingush country they attracted to their side Ali Mitaev, the head of the powerful Bammat Giray *tariqat* who in 1920 led the Chechen Revolutionary Committee. The cooperation was short-lived — Ali of Akusha, expounded by early communist authors as a model of a modern enlightened Muslim leader, was executed in 1926, and Ali Mitaev in 1925.[3] The 1920-1 uprising is described in this writer's chapter 'The Last *Ghazawat*'.

Destruction of Islam

Serious efforts to destroy Islam as a religion under the old regime were only attempted under Tsar Feodor (the son of Ivan the Terrible), Peter the Great and Tsarina Anna (1738–55). In the Soviet period the anti-Islamic campaign in the North Caucasus was set in motion in 1924, earlier than in the rest of the Soviet Union where the full-scale attack on Islam was only launched in 1928. The reason for this was the predominant role of the Sufi orders in the political, military, cultural and social life of their country which set them up as competitors of the Communist Party. It was clearly explained by Najmuddin Samurskii, the leading communist in the North Caucasus in 1925, when he wrote that 'Revolution in Daghestan means above all a fight with the clergy'. He rationalised:

> Basically there is no fight against Soviet power as the bearer of Communism on the part of the religious intelligentsia. On the contrary *Muridism*, which in recent years has noticeably spread in Daghestan, willingly adapts to Communism. Contemporary *murids* who call themselves communists have indeed reasons to do so. In their predication there are undoubtedly some communist characteristics, but of a religious ascetic Communism, similar to that of the early Christian communities in the first century of our era.

Opposition to Soviet power was not due to the fact that it was communist but because of its 'Godlessness', its 'foreign, *giaour* character' as the bearer of a 'sinful and accursed Western civilisation'. Samurskii further commented: 'Dislike of European civilisation, sanctified by religion is more difficult to fight than religiosity itself. It is essential to avoid intimidation which would only confirm the clergy's preaching that European civilisation was always a weapon of oppression and enslavement of the Eastern people.'⁴ Samurskii himself, like most of the Muslim national communist leaders, was not in favour of the anti-Islamic campaign, at least not in the primitive and brutal manner in which it was implemented by the Russians. But in this he was overruled, as were his communist fellow-travellers in Tatarstan and Central Asia. Observing that in 1925 there were still 1,500 religious schools functioning with 45,000 students after four years of solid communist 'construction', as opposed to only 183 state schools, Samurskii prophetically forecast: 'To close the *madrassahs* is impossible. They will continue to exist whatever oppressive measures are taken against them. They will hide in the canyons, in the caves, and will then form a people who will be fanatical opponents of the Soviet power which persecutes religion.'⁵

After the deportation of the native Muslims in 1944, a unique experiment was tried in the Chechen-Ingush territory — the destruction of Islam through the total suppression of its official organisation. All mosques were closed until 1978. This radical experiment failed. The Sufi brotherhoods, which have been subjected to a ferocious persecution for over sixty years, continue to yield the same prestige today that they enjoyed before the Revolution, and Chechnia-Ingushetia remains one of the strongest bastions of Islam not only in the Soviet Union but in the whole Muslim world. In 1925, Samurskii wrote that the sheikhs and *ulema* of Daghestan and Chechnia belonged to the people and that their words were considered law. A modern-day believer gave a somewhat similar assessment of the religious leaders in an article comparing their activity to that of the Communist Party and government officials. The article was published by *Sovetskii Dagestan*, the journal of the Daghestani republican *obkom*, in 1989:

> The people know that the leaders who preach atheism have an ingrained habit of profiteering, money-grabbing and corruption. Their words do not correspond with their deeds . . . The mullahs are closer to the people and the believers. They are on the same level as other people, be they scholars, rich or poor. They have a common language with everyone, they do not offend or frighten, they only teach and preach. This is why all believers are equal, nobody demonstrates their superiority, nobody ingratiates themselves or grovels. Almost all believers are open with each other, speak the truth whatever it is, and do not give bribes to the mullahs . . . That is why believers are attracted to the mullahs, not to the Party workers. That is why the mullahs have great authority.[6]

Another good indication of the enduring character of the *tariqat* is provided by two almost identical assessments made by Tsarist and Soviet officialdom a century apart. The first, written in 1868 by A. Ippolitov, captain of the *gendarmerie* in charge of the repression of the Kunta Haji (Qadiriya) movement in Chechnia, proclaimed the final and irrevocable disappearance of the Qadiris. Ten years later the *tariqat* led a major uprising, 'the Lesser *Ghazawat*', which embraced the North Caucasus for two years. The second, written in 1968 by the Soviet author Tutaev, commenting on a particularly radical branch of the Qadiriya, similarly claimed: 'The sectarians now represent only an insignificant minority whose influence on the new Chechen generation is nil.'[7]

The chapter on 'Internationalism, Nationalism and Islam' by Fanny Bryan addresses the question of Islam in Chechnia and Daghestan before the failed *coup* in August 1991.

Expulsion, deportation and genocide

To preserve and expand her colonies Russia experimented with several more or less effective methods of genocide in the Muslim territories: genocide through extinction of a population completely cut off from external contacts and condemned to disappear. This policy was applied with some success in the Volga-Ural region from the sixteenth to the eighteenth century and in the Kazakh steppes in the late nineteenth and early twentieth century: genocide through slaughter attempted unsuccessfully by General Skobelev, the hero of the Slavophile movement, against the Turkmen tribes at Gök Tepe in 1881; and genocide through forced exodus, a crude but efficient policy, applied consistently in the North Caucasus against the Cherkess and the Chechens.

In 1834, a Russian civil servant, Platon Zubov, published a book entitled *A Picture of the Caucasian Region and Neighbouring Lands Belonging to Russia*,[8] a general historical, geographical, economic and anthropological description of the North Caucasus, both of the lowlands already under Russian rule and of the still unconquered high mountains. Zubov made an enthusiastic eulogy of Transcaucasia — an authentic Eldorado — unfortunately spoiled by its 'excessively lazy' and 'intellectually limited' population.[9] Moreover, this happy but underdeveloped land was constantly threatened by wild Mountaineers. It therefore fell to the Russians to conquer and pacify the Caucasus 'for the greater benefit of the Empire and of the Caucasians'. Zubov, obviously inspired by the French Encyclopaedists' vision of the 'noble savage', suggested a plan of pacification in several stages. During the first stage the Mountaineers had to be tempted through their women who would desire luxury goods not available in their own lands. These goods had to be offered to the Mountaineers by organised Christian missionary orders helped by the Russian government. They would turn the North Caucasus into an authentic dumping-ground in order to eliminate all foreign merchants from the area. Thus the missionaries would combine trade, proselytism and propaganda for the benefit of St Petersburg, which would become a friend of the natives. The Mountaineers would then 'look back in disgust at their wild and insecure life and beg to make their submission to the Emperor'.[10]

The second phase of the pacification plan would be the transfer of population. Natives from the lowlands which were easily controlled could remain in their villages where the Russian government would build them a 'superb church' which would be served by a missionary acting as a 'good father'. In order to develop their civic sense, children would be taken away from their parents and sent to special schools in St Petersburg. Those Caucasians who lived in the far-off mountains or in strategically important areas would have to be moved to the provinces of inner Russia and replaced by Russian settlers. The nobility had to be co-opted to serve in the army and the administration. All would be taught Russian which would become the dominant language; native non-written languages would be easily forgotten. Finally, the Mountaineers would be converted to Christianity, but only superficially, because, wrote Zubov, 'It is useless to try to teach these savages all the subtleties of our Christian faith.'[11]

This neat plan, however, could fail because some of the Mountaineers were too wild and fanatical to appreciate the benefits of mass transfer to the provinces of the Empire. This was particulary true of the Chechens, whom Zubov described as a nation 'remarkable for her love of plunder, robbery and murder, for her spirit of deceit, her courage, recklessness, resolution, cruelty, fearlessness, her uncontrollable insolence and unlimited arrogance. . . . The Chechens spend their life plundering and raiding their neighbours who hate them for their ferocity . . . Often punished by Russian arms, they are always ready to begin their crimes again.' Zubov therefore proposed: 'The only way to deal with this ill-intentioned people is to destroy it to the last . . . This', he added, 'would not be difficult because their total numbers have been greatly diminished. They cannot raise more than 4,000 warriors, their nation having been reduced to barely 15,000 souls.'[12]

Zubov's proposal regarding the first phase of the pacification programme was too naive in its arrogance and could never be implemented, although some efforts were made to revitalise Christianity among the Abkhaz and Ossetians. His advice regarding transfer of population, however, was followed, tragically, in the case of the Ubykhs and the Cherkess in the 1860s. After a Homeric struggle of thirty years, the Ubykhs left their ancestral lands in 1864 and sailed for Turkey, burning their villages behind them.[13] None remained in the Caucasus. The exodus of the Cherkess, the largest Muslim nation of the North Caucasus, had equally tragic consequences. Today they are dispersed in Turkey and the Middle East, where they have not assimilated entirely, and represent a weak minority in their national homeland in the Soviet Union.[14] In their case the genocide has been almost successful. The Chechens and Ingush, however, have proved remarkably resilient. They have survived the Second World War deportation during which half of their population died, and after Stalin's death they left their camps and returned to their homeland without waiting for the official permission to do so. Their will to survive is illustrated by their demographic progression immediately after their return — a 46.5 per cent increase between 1959 and 1970. One of the reasons for their extraordinary recovery and survival in the death camps, without any loss of national identity, was the strong organisational presence of the Sufi *tariqat* in their ranks.

The chapters on 'Circassian Resistance to Russia' by Paul Henze and 'The Chechens and Ingush during the Soviet Periods' by Abdurahman Avtorkhanov give an in-depth analysis of these nations' struggle against Russia.

Implications for the future

Today many Muslim countries are in the grip of wars, revolutions, and immeasurable suffering, often brought about by the arbitrary decisions taken at the time of decolonisation for the sake of short-term benefit and the convenience of *realpolitik*. One may wonder what interest, other than purely academic, a chronicle of obscure wars and repressions in distant lands may have for the modern reader immune to tales of war casualties and political terror. The answers are simple and are to be found, first, in the strategic position of the Caucasus, which remains as important today in the geo-politics of the region as it was in the past, and secondly, in the ambiguous attitude of the Russians towards the North Caucasians. Both factors may influence the course of events and the manner in which the Soviet empire is finally dismantled, whether peacefully or bloodily, and determine the future balance of power in the region.

For 200 years the North Caucasus has stood guard and protected the Muslim world, Turkey and Iran, from Russian designs. In the Soviet period alone, uprisings and wars in Daghestan and Chechnia-Ingushetia probably saved the territorial integrity of Iran by forcing Soviet Russia to abandon her plans for expansion and withdraw her armies from Ghilan in 1921 and South Azerbaijan in 1945. Today the Caucasus continues to provide the same defence. Furthermore the North Caucasus will play a decisive role in the political future of Transcaucasia as a whole. It is indeed difficult to imagine viable and effectively independent states in Georgia, Armenia or Azerbaijan without the active political coopera-tion of the North Caucasian autonomous republics, or at least their neutrality as buffer-states between Russia and Transcaucasia, and hence Turkey and Iran. Thus control over the North Caucasus remains stra-tegically as important today as it was in the sixteenth century, not to mention its significance for Russia as a trade route to oil-rich Azerbaijan and Chechnia.

Compared to the political ferment in other regions of the Soviet Union and in the neighbouring Transcaucasian republics, the North Caucasus remains deceptively quiet, as if gathering strength before the storm ahead. But the nationalist issues which are heatedly debated at ·

present are significant and all relate to the common struggle of the
Mountaineers to reject Russian rule and preserve their original identity:
the national liberation wars from 1783 to 1920, Shamil's *Muridism*, the
role of Islam and Arabic culture, the deportations of the 1860s and 1944.
Several pressing territorial disputes stemming from the 1944 deportations, still unresolved today, are of prime concern — between Chechnia
and Daghestan in the Novo-Lakskii district and between the Ingush and
the Ossetians over Vladikavkaz (Ordzhonikidze) among others. Unlike
their neighbours in Nagorno-Karabakh, Abkhazia, Ossetia and Georgia,
the Daghestanis, Chechens and Ingush, true to their tradition of independence, have had the wisdom to avoid calling in Moscow to arbitrate
over their internal problems. However, these questions need to be settled
before any serious concerted political action towards the centre can be
undertaken. Certain practical measures have already been taken to promote unity and reestablish 'horizontal' links which had been artificially
abolished during sixty years of Soviet rule: on 20 February 1990, representatives of *Gosplan* in four North Caucasian Muslim autonomous
republics — Daghestan, Chechnia-Ingushetia, Kabardino-Balkaria and
North Ossetia — met in the Daghestani capital Makhachkala to draw
up an agreement on long-term economic, scientific and cultural cooperation. The object of the agreement, which came into effect immediately,
was to integrate the economies of the four republics into a 'common'
market.

For the time being no strong national front movements and democratic political parties on the model of the Transcaucasian or Baltic
republics have emerged, except in Chechnia where these groups have
the implicit support of the Sufi *tariqat*. This is not the sign of a lack of
desire for independence or political maturity, but on the contrary points
to the fact that the North Caucasians remain faithful to a certain pan-
Caucasian ideal of a 'mountain confederation' where the uniting factor
was always Islam. You cannot have a 'national' front in Daghestan
where there are some twenty different nations. The 'democratic' plat-
form as interpreted in the European parts of the Soviet Union carries
little credit in the eyes of the North Caucasians in view of its European or
Russian centrism and because history has taught them that Russian
democrats easily shed their liberal skin when confronted with the nationalities' aspirations for freedom. This explains in part the passive voting
on the Union Treaty Referendum of 17 March 1991 in the North
Caucasian republics. The future struggle, when it comes, will not be
with an emasculated Soviet Union but with the RSFSR — the Russian

Federation — the Russian Republic, in short with the former Russian conquerors, whatever they choose to call themselves.[15]

Finally, because of their geographical position between Europe and Asia on the marches of Christendom and Islam, because of the widespread use of Arabic, the omnipresence of Islam, the existence of large diaspora communities and the *jihad* tradition, the North Caucasians have always been responsive, often in a turbulent manner, to events elsewhere in the Muslim world, more so than the Muslims of Soviet Central Asia. Thus their ability to influence Russian foreign policy towards the Muslim world is much greater than their modest numbers may presume.

Two examples can be given to illustrate this. One was a mutiny which occurred in June 1985 in Astrakhan when army recruits called up for army service, mainly Chechens, clashed with the military authorities when told that they would be trained for Afghanistan. The Chechen youths categorically refused to go to Afghanistan explaining that they did not wish to kill their Muslim co-religionists. The report from Moscow stated: 'In the course of a fierce clash, whose outcome was decided by the troops, there were wounded and killed on both sides, although of course not in equal numbers. This was probably the first act of anti-war protest in the Soviet Union suppressed with firearms.'[16] The other example is the strong empathy shown by some North Caucasians with Iraq, a brother Muslim state, during the Allied forces' bombardments in February 1991, after an initial strong condemnation of the Iraqi invasion of Kuwait.[17]

The Russians for their part have always despised their Muslim adversaries who were considered stupid, primitive, sly and treacherous, and were always treated as 'rebels' and 'bandits'. This was true for Sheikh Mansur, who fought Russia in a fair war at a time when the North Caucasus could in no way be considered a Russian dominion. And it was true for every Muslim military and political opponent of Russia ever since, including the Afghan *mujahidin* in the 1980s. The only exception was Shamil whose world-wide fame protected him from sharing the fate of his predecessor Mansur and his followers, Kunta Haji and many others, either languishing in Russian jails and Siberian camps, killed in battle or executed. Nevertheless, one cannot describe the treatment of Shamil, condemned to long years of dreary exile in Kaluga and denied permission to migrate to Mecca until old age by the liberal Tsar Alexander II, as in any way elegant. (Another rare exception consisted of the Kabardian noblemen who provided the Russian aristocracy with a model of knightly virtues.) As a result of such high-handed contempt, the

Russians were unable to understand their adversaries, their motivation, strategy and ideology. This explains the slow progress of the Russian conquest and the inability to pacify the territory and use imaginative thinking in articulating a colonial policy. One is struck by the repetition of the same recipes and mistakes in the military and political field for the last 200 years: in 1920 Todorskii, the general commanding the Red Army charged with quelling the Daghestani-Chechen rebellion, modelled his tactics on those of Prince Bariatinskii who accepted Shamil's surrender in 1859; the anti-religious persecutions of the Soviet period were not much different in spirit from the tsarist harassment of the Sufis in the second half of the nineteenth century; and Stalin's deportations, though on a wider scale, were inspired by the hounding of the Cherkess and Chechens forced to migrate to the Ottoman empire in the 1860s.

Important also is the psychological heritage of the Caucasian wars on the Russian mind. No other wars have left such a profound and long-lasting impression on Russian culture and folklore, not even the Napoleonic wars. The Romantic movement — the golden age of Russian literature and poetry — was imbued with the epic tales and pathos of the conquest. The most celebrated poems of Pushkin and Lermontov, and some of Tolstoy's fiction, were set in the craggy landscape of the Caucasus. Every educated Russian knows them by heart from childhood, and their impact runs much deeper than any of Kipling's tales of the North West Frontier for the British. Since 1783 Russian élites — grand-dukes, illustrious generals, famed poets and political exiles — have trodden the Caucasian mountain paths in battle or in search of poetic inspiration, both enthused and repelled by the Mountaineers' uncompromising and wild love of freedom, a freedom totally alien to the Russian sense of order. It was almost as if the grandeur of Russia had to be built on the ruins of the Caucasus. A Russian lullaby — a poem by Lermontov — sung by mothers to their newborn sons, depicts a cruel Chechen creeping along the bank of the Terek river and sharpening his dagger to kill the child. Perhaps more famous still is Pushkin's poem *The Caucasian Prisoner*, written in 1821 glorifying General Ermolov.[18] There he heralds the imminent downfall of the Caucasus and exhorts the Mountaineers to bow their heads in allegiance to Ermolov while shedding a sentimental tear for the doomed beauty of Circassian women. He predicts, mistakenly, that the sons of the Caucasus will betray the traditions of their ancestors and lay down their weapons without resisting, as nobody could doubt the power of the Russian sword. Four years later the North Caucasus was ablaze. He also proclaimed that shortly the Russian traveller would be able to explore the Caucasian mountains and canyons without danger. A century and a half later, from the 1970s onwards, thousands of Russians are emigrating from Daghestan and Chechnia unable to cope with the xenophobia of the local population. Pushkin had a magic tongue, his words flow with convincing ease, but he was not politically a discriminating judge, and one could well imagine him in other times writing eulogies of Stalin. To praise Ermolov to the Caucasians shows the same delicacy of feeling as someome today commending the prowess of Saddam Hussein to the Kurds. On the other hand, Tolstoy's novel *Haji Murat*, perhaps the bitterest judgment of Russian conduct during the war, was banned for many years under the tsars' regime. In 1988 a production of it by the Avar National Theatre was forbidden by Soviet censorship, an unwitting tribute to Tolstoy's talent.[19]

The legacy of two centuries of warfare is heavy. The North Caucasus remains a symbol both of Russia's political failure and its moral failure, the latter factor perhaps more difficult to come to terms with. This is why many Soviet official historians, even today under *glasnost*, continue to pretend that the Caucasian wars, the expulsion of the Cherkess and the Stalin deportations were all due to the misdeeds and banditry of the Caucasians themselves.[20] What is more, they try to impose their ideas on the North Caucasians. After all, it was only in 1990 that the decision to dismantle the statue of Ermolov in Groznyi was approved. It may therefore prove particularly difficult for the Russians to accept disengagement from the North Caucasus, more so than from the Baltic Republics, Transcaucasia and even Central Asia. Politically, the Mountaineers remained undaunted. In 1943, when the deportation of the North Caucasians was being planned by the Communist Party, the First Secretary of the Daghestani *obkom*, Danialov, felt confident enough to threaten Stalin with a general uprising in Daghestan if any attempts were made to banish his nation, a courageous action which probably saved the Daghestanis from the Siberian camps. The Chechens and Ingush have returned from exile, strengthened by their ordeal, many having shed all fear and shrugged off efforts to intimidate them. It is said that their vanguards, which left the camps immediately on Stalin's death to reclaim their villages, were preceded by a wind of panic among the Russian rural population. The Chechens proudly say that only in 1979 did the last *abrek*, bandit of honour, die in combat defending the freedom of his mountains with a rifle in his hand. This old man, Khazaki Magomedov, protected by the local population, had been fighting since the Second World War 'sowing death and terror' among Soviet officials. He was also a Sufi; when he was killed, a small Quran was found on his breast.[21] Perhaps this is the way others will fight and die before the Caucasus is free again.

NOTES

1. Afanasii Nikitin (died in 1472) travelled to India and Persia through the Gulf straits and wrote *Khozhenii za tri moria* (Travels Beyond Three Seas), a classic of old Russian literature.
2. Karl Marx, *The Eastern Question: Letters written 1853–1856 dealing with the events of the Crimean War*, edited by Eleanor Marx Aveling and Edward Aveling, London, 1897.
3. The cooperation of Ali Mitaev with the Communist Party is particularly questionable. Recent information from private Chechen sources indicate that Ali Mitaev had a regular 'army' of some 5,000–10,000 men ready to join Gotsinskii's uprising in 1921. It is rumoured that even today the *tariqat* of Ali Mitaev could still call 5,000 men to arms. For the Chechens membership of the Communist Party, in the 1920s as today, remains a purely tactical move, with no ideological commitment whatsoever. It is possible to belong to the Party and be an active member of a Sufi *tariqat*. If a split in loyalty occurs, the *tariqat* always wins.
4. Najmuddin Samurskii, *Dagestan*, Moscow, Leningrad: Gosudarstvennoe Izdatel'stvo, 1925, pp. 131–2.
5. Najmuddin Samurskii, *op. cit.*, p. 132.
6. Tazhuddin Aliev, 'Ispoved' veruiushchego', *Sovetskii Dagestan*, no. 3, 1989, pp. 26–27.
7. For A. Ippolitov's comments, see *Sbornik Svedenii o Kavkazskikh Gortsakh*, Tiflis, 1869, no. II, pp. 1–17, or the French translation provided by A. Bennigsen and C. Lemercier-Quelquejay in *Le soufi et le commissaire. Les confréries musulmanes en URSS*, Paris, Seuil, 1986, pp. 238–44. A.M. Tutaev was commenting on the Batal Haji *wird* of the Kunta Haji *tariqat* in *Reaktsionnaia sekta Batal Khadzhi*, Groznyi, 1968, p. 27.
8. Platon Zubov, *Kartina Kavkazskogo kraia prinadlezhashchego Rossii i sopredel'nykh emu zemel'*, St Petersburg, published by A. Vingeber, 1834, 2 vols.
9. Platon Zubov, *op. cit.*, vol. 1, pp. 12–13. Zubov explained the limitations of the native population of Transcaucasia, including the Armenians, by the fact that they had been submitted to Ottoman and Iranian despotism.
10. *Ibid.*, p. 87.
11. *Ibid.*, p. 92.
12. *Op. cit.*, vol. 2, pp. 173–6.
13. On the Ubykhs, see George Dumezil's remarkable book, *Documents anatoliens sur les langues et les traditions du Caucase*, Paris, Institut d'Ethnologie, 1965, published for the centenary of the Ubykhs' exodus.
14. The Cherkess are divided between three national territories: the Adyghe Autonomous Oblast (AO), the Karachay-Cherkess AO, and the Kabardino-Balkar ASSR.

For more information, see Alexandre Bennigsen and S. Enders Wimbush, *Muslims of the Soviet Empire*, London: C. Hurst, 1985.

15. This of course was already noted by Lenin who stated that the degree of Russian liberalism must be tested on the nationality question. With the exception of the North Caucasian Mountaineers the only other Muslim nation of the Soviet Union which has similar misgivings about the Russian democrats' ultimate national policy are the Volga Tatars.

16. Information provided in an article by Sergei Khovanski, 'Afghanistan: The Bleeding Wound', featured in *Detente*, Spring 1986 (published by Leeds and Birmingham Universities).

17. It should be remembered, however, that the coverage of the Gulf war in the Soviet press was extremely uneven and that the North Caucasians had no possibility of assessing the situation. Many articles and radio broadcasts dwelt at length on the supposed destruction of the holy places of Najaf and Kerbela by the Allied forces. While the central Moscow press carried fairly objective analysis from time to time, this was not so with the reports published in the republican press of the Soviet Muslim republics, all reproduced from TASS or other Soviet official agencies' sources. One could venture that Moscow deliberately manipulated public opinion in the Muslim republics to provoke a strong reaction in favour of Iraq in order to justify its post-war support of Saddam Hussein with the Allies as bowing to popular pressure.

18. Lermontov's lullaby is entitled *Kazach'ia kolybel'naia pesnia* (A Cossack Craddle Song), *Spi mladenets moi prekrasnyi . . .* ; and Pushkin's *Kavkazskii plennik*.

19. Mentioned by A. Khalilov in his article 'Shamil' v istorii i pamiati naroda', *Sovetskii Dagestan*, 1988, no. 5. pp. 31–7.

20. Vinogradov, Bliev and Bokov, to name only a few.

21. See Dimitri Bezuglyi, 'S pozitsii boitsa', *Zhurnalist*, (Moscow), no. 1, 1981, pp. 46–8; and Alexandre Bennigsen's comments in *Mystics and Commissars Sufism in the Soviet Union*, London: C. Hurst, 1985, pp. 101–2 (co-author S. Enders Wimbush). The pride in this event was conveyed to the author in private conversations with independent Chechen informants.

CO-OPTATION OF THE ELITES OF KABARDA AND DAGHESTAN IN THE SIXTEENTH CENTURY

Chantal Lemercier-Quelquejay

The co-optation of political, economic and even religious indigenous élites in the areas coveted or already conquered by the Russians is an old strategy modelled partly on the Byzantine and partly on the Mongol tradition. It was applied with great success in the fourteenth and fifteenth centuries to the Tatar feudal nobility of the Golden Horde and to the successor states Crimea, Kazan, Astrakhan and Sibir. Since then, the cooptation of the élites has been a constant of Russian diplomacy in the Muslim world. For centuries it followed the same pattern with little or no change. The Soviets preserved the tradition and managed to apply it with obvious success during the Civil War in 1918–20, especially to the nomadic aristocracy of the Kazakh steppes and the merchant class in the Tatar territory of the Middle Volga. In 1980, they tried to use the same method in Afghanistan, but this time with little success.

Cooptation was, and still is, a complex if not always sophisticated strategy. It presupposes the granting of economic and political advantages to individuals, social groups and even entire tribes; delegation of power to a local ruler who becomes the representative of the Russian sovereign; cultural and linguistic assimilation, with or without conversion to Orthodox Christianity; and even marital strategy — a practice unknown to the Mongols but widely used by the Byzantines. When the Grand Prince of Moscow married the daughter of a local ruler, the latter became *ipso facto* the vassal and local representative of his Russian son-in-law.

Every élite group or class of the native society could become subject to co-optation — nomadic and landed aristocracy, merchants, the religious establishment, intellectual élites, and so on. All these groups have been approached and courted by the Russian administration in various areas and at different periods.

The Muscovite state and its Russian and Soviet heirs have invested heavily in the strategy of cooptation and spent an enormous amount of effort, money and time on it. Curiously, the results have been mixed. In

18

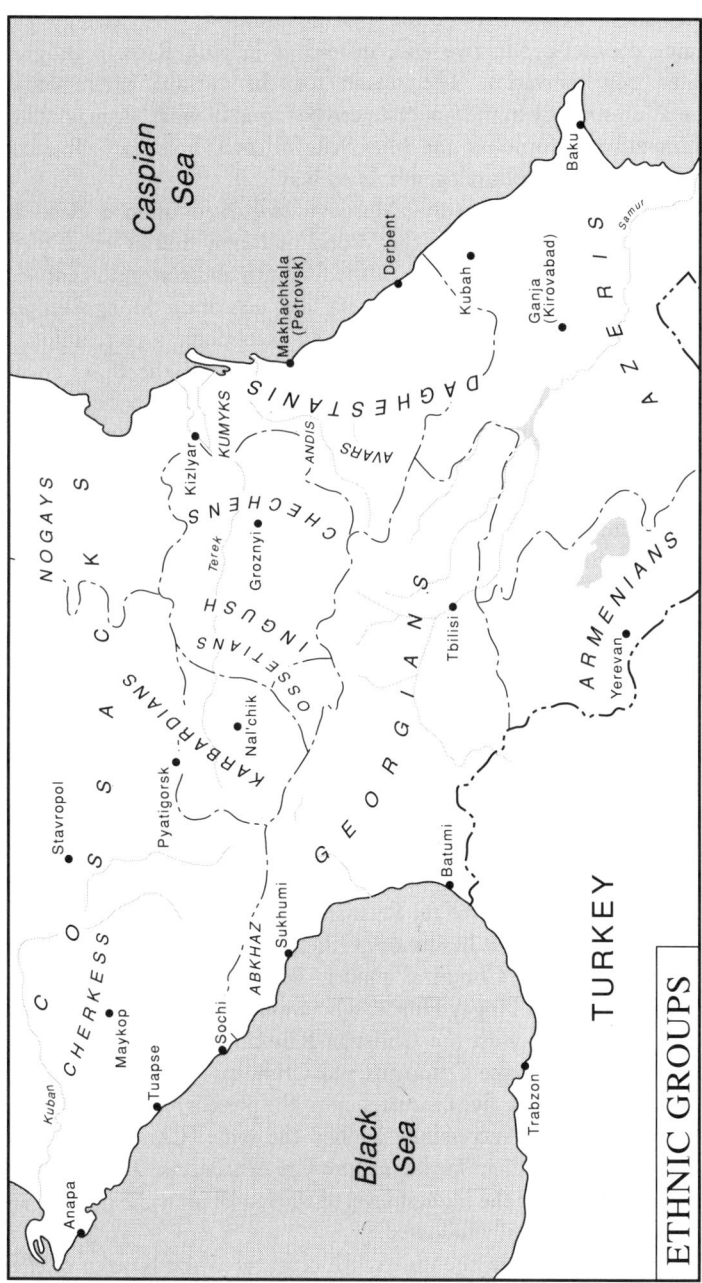

ETHNIC GROUPS

some cases — especially in the North Caucasus, the strategy even became counter-productive and, instead of helping Russian progress, created new obstacles. The reason for the curious failure of the cooptation strategy in the Caucasus can be found in what we may call the 'Chingizid syndrome' of the Muscovite oriental diplomacy. It can be summarised in the following simplified way.

In the fourteenth century, Muscovy embarked upon a close and permanent relationship with the World of Islam, first as vassal of the Golden Horde khans and later, in the fifteenth and sixteenth centuries, as the rival and heir of the Western (White) *ulus* of the Mongol empire, the '*ulus* of Batu'. These contacts had an exceptional aspect, unique in world history: in 1446, the Grand Prince Vasili II the Blind created the small kingdom of Kasymov for the benefit of a Tatar prince, Kasym, son of Ulugh Mohammad, the Khan of Kazan. The rulers, who bore the title 'tsar', were vassals of the Prince of Moscow. They all belonged to the House of Chingiz and were Muslims. The tsardom of Kasymov survived until the eighteenth century. It served as a 'reserve', a refuge for a great number of Chingizid princes of various origins: Great Horde, Kazan, Crimea, Astrakhan and Sibir. They came to serve Moscow with their *ulus* and they played a distinguished role, especially in the fifteenth and sixteenth centuries, sometimes as supreme army commanders of Muscovite armies.

To understand why this initial and seemingly excellent relationship between the Russian state and the Mongol-Tatar nobility became counter-productive elsewhere, we must remember the unique charismatic prestige enjoyed by the members of the House of Chingiz in all Muslim Asia. The Chingizid alone were supposed to rule, and their decisions were never discussed by their followers. When a Chingizid prince decided to go over to the Russians, his family, clan, tribe and even horde followed without hesitation. Other Turkic tribes of non-Mongol origin followed the Chingizid model. For instance, when a Nogay *mirza* of the Greater Nogay Horde, who was a descendant of Edighe and not Chingiz, sided with the Christian Russian rulers against his own Muslim brethren — the Ottomans and Crimeans — his tribe accepted his decision. Thus, for five centuries up to the present, the Russians have constantly and very successfully applied the same 'Chingizid' pattern when dealing with their Turkic neighbours or subjects. The important step was to win over the highest level of the feudal nomadic nobility and the people automatically followed.

This was still true in the nineteenth century, when Kazakh intellectuals of Chingizid descent, like Chokan Valikhanov, were staunch supporters of Russian rule in the steppe area, and even after the October Revolution. In 1918, when Dzhangildin, head of the Kipchak clan of the Middle Kazakh Horde joined the Bolshevik party, his entire clan went over to the Reds. Similarly in 1919, when Ahmed Bukeykhanov, a Chingizid prince of the Bukey Horde, leader of the nationalist liberal party, the *Alash Orda*, finally decided to abandon Kolchak and side with the Bolsheviks, the *Alash Orda* accepted his move and defected to the Reds.

In the sixteenth century, when the Russians in the North Caucasus came across other Islamic (or semi-Islamised) societies, they quite logically maintained the Chingizid strategy of courting and coopting the indigenous elites into the fabric of the Muscovite state. The strategy had been tried and found to be sound when applied to the highly hierarchical and disciplined Turko-Mongol society. But it was shown to be of little use in the anarchic context of the North Caucasian mosaic of nations and religions.

In spite of its drawbacks and failures outside the Turko-Mongol world, Russian rulers from Ivan the Terrible to Gorbachev persistently used this strategy towards the native aristocracy — from Kabarda in the sixteenth century to Afghanistan in the 1980s with the same lack of success.

Let us now revert to the North Caucasus.

Until the sixteenth century, this region, like Afghanistan until 1979, was a 'happy' territory, ignored and by-passed by the great powers of the time, by the Ottoman empire, the Safavi empire, the Crimean khanate, the Muscovite tsardom and the Shaybani empire in Turkestan. Then suddenly Moscow appeared on the scene, beginning its southward drive, and the North Caucasus, from the Taman peninsula to the Caspian Sea, became the focus of world politics and fierce rivalry. Two hostile blocks were formed, each endeavouring to set up its authority over this territory of vital strategic importance: on the one hand, the Ottoman Porte and the Crimean khanate, supported by the Shaybanis of Turkestan, and on the other Muscovy with its natural allies Transcaucasia, Christian Georgia and, further south, the Safavi Shia empire.

The objective pursued by both factions was to establish connections by every possible means — be it matrimony, religious conversion or vassalage — with Caucasian principalities or tribes in order to secure control over two military and commercial roads of primary importance:

from west to east: Taman (or Azaq)-Derbent-Baku-Tabriz, and from north to south: Astrakhan-Derbent-Tabriz. However, to establish their authority, the great powers had to find valid partners able to take the oath of allegiance and willing to convert to the religion of their nominal suzerain. These oaths and conversions rarely corresponded to real and lasting conviction. The small Caucasian princes and feudals changed their protectors and religious faith readily enough and did not hesitate to apply simultaneously for the patronage of the Ottoman Padishah and the Muscovite Tsar.

These partners could be either small sovereigns or feudal landlords. This was the case in Daghestan, in Kabarda and among certain Cherkess tribes (Adyghe), in particular the Besleneys (Besneys), the Temirgoys (Kemirgoys) and the Janeys. In the sixteenth century the gentry in certain regions — Daghestan for instance — belonged exclusively to the Muslim religion. Elsewhere, some were Muslims while others professed a very degenerate Christian Orthodox rite and even an ancient animist religion (Kabarda and Western Cherkess tribes). As to the popular masses, they were generally animists.[1] In other regions, there were only small tribes with a clanic, pre-feudal structure. To this category belonged the Chechens, certain groups of Upper Daghestan, the Muslim Ossetians, and some large Cherkess mountain tribes, such as the Abadzekhs, the Hatukhays and the Abkhaz.[2] Almost all were pagans 'with no chiefs and no religion', as stated in the Ottoman documents of the time. Thus they completely escaped the ascendancy of great powers.[3]

Moscow's first move was a decisive success: the cooptation of an entire nation, the Nogay Horde, the main military force in the steppe area north of the Caucasus, able to put an army of 100,000 horsemen into the field. Without the help or at least the neutrality of the Nogays, neither the conquest of the khanate of Astrakhan in 1556 nor that of Sibir in 1580, nor the Russian advance toward the Caucasus, would have been possible. The cooptation of the Nogays was the result of a rare combination of economic and marital strategy, a unique, highly successful case in Russia's Muslim policy. It started in the late 1520s, when the centre for the Nogay trade in horses, their sole but very important financial resource (in 1534 alone, the Nogays brought 50,000 horses to Moscow), was relocated from Constantinople to Moscow. It was Nogay horses that were instrumental in transforming the former feudal Muscovite infantry army into a modern one, corresponding to the era of 'gunpowder empires'. Without cavalry, the Russians could never have launched the conquest of Muslim territories.

In exchange, the Nogays received from Moscow all the commodities they needed: weapons including some firearms, cloth, paper, dyes, metals and even spices. The Nogay Horde was thus firmly tied to Moscow economically, at least for a while; firmly but not completely, because the Nogay House of Edighe lacked the charisma and the discipline of the House of Chingiz. Already in 1549 the Horde had split into two sub-hordes: the Greater which remained more or less loyal to the Muscovite orientation, and the Lesser Horde which migrated to the Crimea and became a vassal of the khanate.

In 1563, the connection between Moscow and the Greater Nogay Horde was reinforced by marital ties when Mirza Din-Ahmed, head of the Horde, married the daughter of Prince Temruk of Kabarda and thus became the brother-in-law of Tsar Ivan. Religious considerations did not play any role in Russian-Nogay relations. (Apart from the case of the Nogays, the cooptation of an entire minority, of an 'alien body', was seldom practised with success by the Russians. Neither in Central Asia nor in Afghanistan, which was *a priori* the perfect ground for such a strategy, did the despised minorities — the Shia Hazaras, the Turkmens, or even the Ismailis — agree to side with the *Soviets*.)

With their rear solidly protected by the Nogay nomads, the Russians moved towards the Caucasus.

Social, ethnic and religious structure of the North Caucasus in the sixteenth century

In the middle of the sixteenth century, the Caucasians had no centralised power, and only in two areas, Kabarda and Daghestan, did they succeed in creating more or less stable states. Logically, according to the Chingizid strategy, the first Russian contacts with the North Caucasus were directed towards the two areas where the feudal structures were strongest: towards Kabarda in 1557, and later towards Daghestan. To understand why the cooptation policy failed, it is necessary to study the social, political and religious structure of this region.

THE KABARDIANS

The Kabardians occupied the central sector — the most important one — of the North Caucasus: the region where the highway from Kefe to Derbent connected with the road from Azaq to Derbent and crossed the Daryal pass, from Terek to Georgia. This unique strategic position enabled them to play the role of arbitrators in the political arena of the entire Caucasus and gave them supremacy over their eastern and western neighbours. For over a century the Kabardians were courted and over-whelmed with honours by Muscovy, the Crimean khanate and the Ottoman Porte, as an alliance with them made it possible to exercise control over the entire Caucasian range, from the Black Sea to the Caspian.

Kabardian feudal lords, whose religious convictions were anything but firm, did not hesitate to change their creed and to pass constantly from the Muscovite camp to that of the Ottomans, thus making their history difficult to unravel. The difficulty is further increased because of the confusion in Russian and Ottoman sources between the Kabardians, Abazas and the western Cherkess. Moreover, the only distinction between them was in the dialects they spoke. The expression used by Russians to designate them — *kabardinskie cherkesy* (Kabardian Cherkess) — could apply equally to Kabardians and Besleneys. Ottoman documents also frequently misuse the term *kabartay* for Cherkess and Cherkess for Kabardians.

During the sixteenth century, the area inhabited by Kabardians stretched much farther than the present-day boundaries of Kabarda. It covered the whole of the foothills and lower mountain range bordering the valleys of the left-bank tributaries of the Terek — Cherek, Chegem, Baksan, Kuban — and the plains extending between the Terek and Sunja. In the preceding century, Kabardians could be found even further east, in the middle and lower valley of the Terek. They had been progressively forced from this territory by the Kumyks of Tumen and Enderi. In the west, between the valley of Malka and the high valley of Kuma, there is a region of low mountains that Russian sources call Pyatigorsk — 'the country of five mountains' (in Turkish *Beshtau*). This region was inhabited by the Kabardians and by the Cherkess Besleney tribe. Russians referred to both as 'Pyatigorsk Cherkess'. Beshtau was a territory of vital strategic importance — the object of rivalry for centuries between the Kabardians, the Crimean khanate, and the Nogays of the Lesser Horde, to whom, since the beginning of the seventeenth century, were added the Buddhist Kalmyks. Vanquished in the south, the Kabardians retreated slowly towards the mountains, and in the middle of the seventeenth century Pyatigorsk was entirely domi-nated by the Nogays.

In the sixteenth century, the ever-changing boundary of the Kabardian country was drawn approximately between the valleys of the

Kuban and Laba. From there bordered the country of the Besleneys, one of the tribes of western Cherkess (Adyghe) which seemed to have broken away from Kabarda in the fifteenth century.

The Kabardian country was the richest in the Caucasus thanks to agriculture and horse and cattle breeding in the plains and sheep herding and exploitation of silver, iron and lead mines in the mountains. The local production of weapons was famous throughout the East. (In the fourteenth and fifteenth centuries, trade had thrived mainly thanks to the sale of slaves in the Crimea, trade with the Genoese Italian merchant colonies on the Black Sea such as Kefe and trade in horses and weapons with Astrakhan through Persian and Bukharan merchants.) Finally, Kabardians acted as intermediaries and valuable guides for caravans in transit between Russia, Georgia and Shirvan by way of the Daryal passes. Kabarda was the most densely populated country of the Caucasus and could probably mobilise 1,500 horsemen.[4]

The social structure of the Kabardians was the most sophisticated of the Caucasus. According to Soviet historians it consisted of a 'feudal pyramid' that preserved the survival of the clanic system. At the top of the hierarchy was the *pshi*, a title first denoting 'elder' and 'oldest member of the clan'. However, at the end of the sixteenth century this title corresponded more to 'prince'. Children of the *pshi* — when both parents were of the same rank — had the honorific title of *mirza*. Princely clans owned their lands and their serfs collectively. They were not divided into nuclear families, and all obeyed the eldest member of the clan. Inheritance was devolved from brother to brother not from father to son. The clan's power was based on a number of 'burgs' (small fortresses) and the Kabardian *pshi* could be compared to the western barons of the high Middle Ages. They differed from western Adyghes, who had no fortresses and whose feudal lords were not as powerful as those of the Kabardians. Children of a *pshi* and of a woman of a lower status, though noble, received the title of *tuma*.

Next to the princely family came the 'gentry' composed of the vassals of the *pshi* — the *uork*. Russians usually translated this appellation by 'courtiers'. They were subdivided into two ranks: the most noble (in Russian *imenitye*, in Kabardian *tlakotle*) and the less noble (*dezhenugo*). These nobles were endowed with the privilege of changing their patron (the *pshi*) or even enlisting with the Crimean Khan, the Ottoman *padishah* or the Muscovite tsar. Social cohesion between princely families and vassal gentry was secured by a custom common to Adyghes and Kabardians: the *ataliq*, whereby children of princes were given to their vassals to be instructed by the latter in the military art. In this way, children of the vassals became 'foster brothers' of *pshis'* sons and later, when adults, their brothers in arms. Kabardian feudal society was numerous, war-like, with strict rules of military honour being obeyed, and comparable on a lesser scale to the Japanese *bushido*.

In the middle and at the foot of the social scale was the most populous class, that of free peasants (*tlofoqotle*) grouped in 'associations', *jemaat*. Next came the peasants obliged to perform various chores (*og* and *loganapit*, called 'black men' by Russian sources); then slaves (*azat*).

The strength of the feudal organisation explains why there could be no central authority in Kabarda during the sixtenth century: no princely family was strong enough to force the others to submit to its authority. The ancient tradition, whereby the assembly of the gentry 'of the entire Kabard land' elected the 'great princes of Kabarda', choosing each of them in turn among princely families, had no basis in reality. The 'Great Prince' did not yield any real authority and was only a *primus inter pares* among the Kabardian *pshis*. The Ottomans understood the situation well enough and were content to deal with the *pshi* and the *mirza*. The Russians, on the other hand, endeavoured throughout the sixteenth century to impose the authority of a unique chief upon the entire country. In the 1560s they supported Temruk, son of Idar and father-in-law of Tsar Ivan IV, then another son of Idar, Qanbulat (died in 1588), and at the end of the sixteenth century a son of Temruk, Mamstruk. All Russian efforts failed because of the opposition of other princely families. Undoubtedly, the absence of central power in Kabarda created a climate of permanent anarchy which their neighbours, the Crimeans, the two Nogay Hordes and, later in the seventeenth century, the Kalmyks took advantage of.

The situation of Kabarda was further complicated by the absence of religious allegiances among the governing classes (*pshi* and *mirza*) while peasants and *uork* practised mainly the ancestral animist religion with traces of Christianity inherited from the Alans. Most Ottoman documents refer to the Kabardian chiefs as Muslims, but Russian archival documents assembled in the two first volumes of *Kabardino-Russkie, otnosheniia v XVI-XVIII vekakh* and in Belorokov's *Snosheniia Rossii s Kavkazom 1578-1613* show a more complex situation. Kabardian nobles were lukewarm and superficial Muslims. As a general rule, some members of the princely *pshi* clan, the eldest ones, remained in the Caucasus while the younger ones went abroad to seek their fortunes. Some travelled to Baghchesaray or Istanbul, others to Moscow or even Poland and

Lithuania. Those who remained in Kabarda or engaged in the service of the Sultan or the Crimean Khan were (or became) Muslims while those who served the Tsar converted to Orthodoxy.

Thus the family of Temruk, his sons Mamstruk, Beberuk and Domanuk, who remained in Kabarda, were Muslims, while another of his sons, Sultanqul, accompanied his sister, the future Tsarina, to Moscow and was baptised, taking the name Mikhail.[5] Kanshov, grandson of Temruk, son of the Prince Mamstruk, originally a Muslim, also came to Moscow, was converted to Orthodoxy and became a *boyar*. All the other members of the Temruk clan remained Muslim. In July 1563, at the time when Prince Temruk protected by the Tsar was fighting his rivals, the princes Siboq and Qanuq of Beshtau (who were in the Tsar's service and known in Moscow by the Christian names Aleksei and Gavriil) fled to Lithuania and thence to the service of the Khan of the Crimea. Thus the pro-Russian party was headed by a Muslim whereas Christian Kabardians were in the Tatar camp. The co-existence in the same family of Orthodox Christians and Muslims was practically a unique phenomenon in the history of Islam.[6]

THE WESTERN CHERKESS (ADYGHES)

Western Cherkess tribes were more primitive and more divided than the Kabardian tribes and, judging from Russian and Ottoman accounts, they were little known to their neighbours.

The earliest documents date from 1555. As a rule, they refer only to the two great tribal formations nearest to the Crimea: the Janeys (inhabiting the peninsula of Taman south of the Kuban[7]) and, more rarely, the Besleneys. The latter lived in the middle valley of the Kuban and its southern tributaries Belaia, Laba and Urup. There is also some information regarding the Kemirgoys (or Temirgoys) and the Natukhays. As to the great tribes that were implanted further south and in the mountains — the Abadzekhs, Shapsugs and Hatukhays — Russian documents mention them only collectively, calling them 'Free Cherkess' while Ottoman documents speak of them as 'Unsubdued Cherkess'. The Abkhaz (Abaza), related to the Cherkess and speaking a distinct language, lived between the Kuban and Kabarda. These tribes came originally from the region of Bzib in the south of the Caucasian mountain range, and crossed the mountains in the fifteenth century. Similarly to the Western Adyghes, the Abazas had reached a fairly advanced stage of feudal development. At the top of the feudal ladder were the princes, or rather the clans' chiefs (*akha*). Then came the 'great nobles' (*amistadi* or *tawad*); then the 'small nobles', vassals of the former (*amista*); then the free peasants (*akavi* or *tefakashau*). Lower down the social ladder were the freed serfs forced to perform certain chores (*azat-lig*); then the serfs (*lig*), and finally slaves (*unavi*). Like the western Adyghes and the Kabardians, feudal Abazas hesitated throughout the sixteenth century between, on the one hand, the Crimean allegiance coupled with Islam and, on the other, Muscovite suzerainty and Christianity. Islam was finally implanted among the Abazas only in the eighteenth century.

The territory of western Cherkessia was rich and fertile. The plains were devoted to agriculture and horticulture, the mountains to stock breeding. There were important fisheries in the Kuban region. Commercial exchange was limited to the slave trade, in the Turkish ports of Taman and Temruk. The social structure of the Cherkess of the plains (Janey, Kemirgoy, Abaza, Besleney) was different from that of the 'free' Cherkess of the mountains. The feudal organisation of the former could be compared to that of the Kabardians, but less rigid with princes at the top (*pshi*), then nobles, free peasants (*tekhoqotle*), serfs (*pshitle*) and slaves (*unatle*). The mountain Cherkess had no feudal hierarchy and no gentry but consisted of free peasants, equal in rights, grouped in *jemaat*.

The religious situation in the Adyghe country was even more complicated and transient than that of Kabarda. The Adyghe gentry was, till approximately 1560, partly Christian and partly Muslim and might even have included a relatively important minority of pagans. Adyghe feudals had no scruples about changing their religion and did so even more frequently than the Kabardians. As to the masses of free peasants or serfs, they were almost all animists. In general, as with the Kabardians, those Cherkess princes who came to Moscow to engage in the service of the Tsar became Christians. The most ancient record of baptism of a Cherkess goes back to 1550 when an Abaza noble, Alqlich, son of Ezbuzluqo, came to Moscow where he was baptised and given the name Ivan. We also know that another Abaza, Qazii (Vasilii), son of Qardanuqo, of the Duduruqo clan, lived at the same time at the court of Ivan the Terrible.

In 1555, Siboq, prince of the tribe of Janey, son of the Khan Mohamed II 'Semin', though connected by ties of *ataliq* to Sultan Safa Giray, sent his son Kudadek to Moscow. There he was baptised and given the name Aleksandr, and admitted to the Tsar's court.[8] The same year, another son of Siboq, Prince Tutariq, was converted to Christianity under the name Vasilii. The case of the Qanuqo clan of the Besleney tribe was an even more striking example of the volatile character of the Adyghe aristocracy in matters of religion. According to Italian sources,[9] the first wife of Sultan Suleyman the Magnificent was '*una donna circassa*' probably belonging by birth to the princely clan Qanuqo. A member of this family, Maashuq, lived at the court of the Ottoman Sultan.[10] Despite eminent connections with the Sublime Porte, the son of that same Maashuq came to the Tsar's court in 1557–60 where he was baptised. He was the founder of the Aga Masukhov Cherkasskii family.

Religion did not determine the political allegiance of the Cherkess gentry. Thus in 1556–60, the chiefs of the Janey tribes (some of whom were Muslims) actively participated in the efforts of Prince Dimitrii Vishnevetskii to take possession of the Ottoman fortresses of Azaq, Taman and Temruk. Some of them were Muslims, though Turkish sources generally refer to them as 'unbelievers', *kafir*, a term which could apply to animists as well as Christians.[11] We are also informed that in February 1560, during Vishnevetskii's last offensive against the Crimea, the Tsar sent him a great number of Cherkess living in Moscow (consequently Christians) as well as Orthodox priests in order to 'convert the Janeys to Christianity'. One of the Janey chiefs, Tsuraq Mirza (who seems to have been a Muslim) took part in the battles against the Ottomans on the side of Vishnevetskii and later became a Christian, possibly through military solidarity.[12]

After 1560, when Vishnevetskii's efforts to seize Azaq with the help of the Cherkess tribes finally failed, Islam made progress among the Adyghes and the entire Janey country gradually converted to the Muslim faith. Thus in 1560 the Crimean Khan advised the Sublime Porte of the allegiance of the two sons of the supreme chief of the Janey tribe both of whom bore Muslim names: Mehmed and Daud. In 1565, the *beylerbey* of Kefe informed the Ottoman government that a Cherkess chief wished to come to Istanbul in order to become a Muslim, adding that 'certain Cherkess tribes had hoisted the banner of the Sultan, paid tribute and had submitted to the Porte', but that 'the Janeys were in a state of revolt and threatened Azaq'. However, this was no proof that they were not Muslims. At the same time, the governor of Kefe advised the authorities in Istanbul that an Adyghe chief, named Anqotoqo, wanted to come to Istanbul in order to convert to Islam but that 'all the Halyoqo clan was still plunged in revolt'.[13]

It would seem that the Ottoman authorities did not have a clear picture of the changeable religious situation among the Adyghe tribes. Thus in 1565 the Great Imperial Council ordered the *bey* of Azaq to supply an exact report on the Cherkess tribes, 'both those who had made acts of submission and on those on the enemy's side'.

In 1574 an order addressed to the *qadi* of Samsun permitted the sale of Cherkess slaves (consequently non-Muslim), and in 1562 an order addressed to the *beylerbey* of Batum refers to the Abkhaz and the mountain Cherkess who plundered the region as 'kafir'.[14] After 1590, there is a growing number of Ottoman documents concerning 'Christian' Cherkess chiefs who wished to come to Istanbul to take the oath of allegiance to the Sultan and convert to Islam.[15] It is probable that by the end of the sixteenth century all the western feudal tribes were already completely Muslim. However, an Ottoman chronicler of the seventeenth century, Hezar Fenn, wrote:

> The most western of the Cherkess, the Janeys of the Taman *sandjaq*, acknowledge the *Shariat* law and receive judges [*qadi*] appointed by the Sublime Porte. Therefore it is not permitted to take prisoners there. But east of the Janeys and as far as the Kabartay Cherkess territory, extends *Dar ul-Harb* ['the world of war'] and it is permitted to take prisoners.[16]

It follows from the above that western Adyghe tribes, including the Besleneys, were still considered as 'infidels' by the Ottomans.

THE DAGHESTANIS

Daghestan had already been converted to Islam by Arabs during the eighth and ninth centuries. Like the Arabs, the Daghestanis belong to the Shafei rite. The last traces of Christianity disappeared from Daghestan in the course of the tenth century. The Muslim Sunni religion was solidly established there in the sixteenth century and, for lack of other means, served as cultural cement between the various small tribes belonging to three main ethnic and linguistic groups:[17]
— the Turkic group comprising Kumyks and Nogays in the steppes of the northern foothills and the Azeris in the extreme south of the country;
— the Persian-speaking group composed of Muslim Tats and Jews established on the coast between Derbent and Baku;
— the Ibero-Caucasian group of the medium and high mountain range. This group was subdivided into several sub-groups: Avars in the high valleys of the rivers Andi Koisu and Koisu Avar extending from north to south; Darghins, Laks and Kaytaks in central Daghestan; Lezghins and a

mosaic of small tribes, the most important of which were the Tabasarans in southern Daghestan.

The social structure of the Daghestanis was greatly diversified. Kumyks had achieved a very complex feudal system, almost as complicated as that of the Kabardians, represented by a rigid pyramid of social classes upheld by the *adat*. The top of the pyramid consisted of the princely clan comprising the *Shamkhal*, the princes, the khans and their relatives (*mirza* and *beg* or *bey*) who could not accede to the supreme power. Then came the middle class, that of *chanka*: children of members of the princely clan and of women who belonged to the nobility of an inferior rank (*chanka* or *uzden*). The third rank consisted of *uzden*: free, noble agriculturists, vassals of the *Shamkhal*. They were divided into several groups, the highest being the *sala-uzden*, overlords of other, less noble *uzden*.

Below the *uzden* was a large group of various subordinates also sub-divided into several groups: (*a*) free but not noble agriculturists — peasants — who made up the mass of the population assembled into 'free societies' (*jemaat*); (*b*) serfs (*cagar* or *rayat*), peasants compelled to perform certain chores; (*c*) and finally, at the bottom of the social ladder slaves (*yasir* or *qul*), in most cases Russian, Georgian, Turkestani and Chechen former prisoners of war, or else purchased in the slave markets of Enderi, Derbent and Shemakha.

In the sixteenth century, the small Ibero-Caucasian tribes of the high mountains of Daghestan had not yet reached the level of social development of the Kumyks living in the plain. There was still no division into classes among them; in principle, all members of their community were considered as free and equal. They were grouped into *jemaat* ruled by the 'elders'. Neither the Russian archives nor the Ottoman texts of the time mention these little-known communities, destined two centuries later to form the hard core of the resistance of Shamil's Naqshbandi *murids*.

The political organisation of Daghestan did not correspond to its social, ethnic and linguistic structure. The country was divided into a number of diminutive multilingual and multi-ethnic principalities, with ever changing boundaries. Its most important principality was the *Shamkhalat* which derived its name from the fancy etymology of *Sham* — 'Syria' because its sovereigns, the *Shamkhals* claimed Arab lineage. The territory of the *Shamkhalat* covered the northern and north-eastern part of Daghestan. It included the foothills, a rich sedentary country irrigated by numerous rivers flowing into the Caspian — Terek and Sulak among them — and mountains of medium height with grassy

plateaux. The *Shamkhalat* owed its power and prosperity to its favourable situation on the great commercial road leading from north to south
and to the diversity of its economy: stock-breeding with transhumance
in the mountains, agriculture in the plains, fisheries on the Caspian.

From the Mongolian period onwards, the *Shamkhals* were considered
the masters of Daghestan. The khans of the Golden Horde granted them
the title of *vali* (governor), and the *Shamkhal* had the function of *basqaq*
(tax collector), like the grand princes of Moscow at the same time.

Until the end of the fifteenth century, the capital of the *Shamkhalat*
was the *aul* of Ghazi-Qumukh (spelt thereafter in its Russian form,
Kazi-Kumukh) situated in the mountainous Lak country in the upper
valleys of Samur and Kumukh Koisu. At the beginning of the sixteenth
century, the small market-town of Tarku in the southern part of Sulak
became the capital of the *Shamkhalat*. Situated in the plain of the Kumyk
country, Tarku was an important caravan centre at the crossroads of the
highways Astrakhan-Derbent and Taman-Derbent. As a result of this
transfer of the capital, and of its strategic position, the *Shamkhalat*
became one of the most important states of the Caucasus, coveted by all
those with whom it was in touch: Muscovy, the Khanate of Crimea, the
Ottoman Empire and Safavi Iran.

The principality's population was mainly Kumyk with a Lak minority in the mountains and some Chechen, Avar and even Nogay free
'associations' *jemaat* and clans. Turkic Kumyks were in a dominant
position, but the Laks, converted earlier to Islam, were endowed with a
particular prestige: they were viewed as propagators of the faith
throughout Daghestan. They also claimed Arab ancestry.[18] The political
structure of the *Shamkhalat* presented some rather curious archaic pecu-
liarities that influenced, up to a point, the relations of this state with its
neighbours: supreme power belonged to a princely clan, and it was a
member of this clan (not necessarily the oldest but judged to be the best)
who was elected to the high function of *Shamhal* by an assembly of
nobles and mullahs. Traditionally, the election took place in the *aul* of
Kazi-Kumukh.[19]The principality was divided into *yurts* (apanages), each
governed by a branch of the princely clan; the most important *yurt* (after
that of the *Shamkhal*) was that of the heir presumptive, the *Yarim-
Shamkhal*.[20] His capital was the *aul* of Buinaksk .

The names of princes who ruled over the *Shamkhalat* in the sixteenth
century are little known; Russians do not seem to have known them
while the Ottomans often mistook the title *Shamkhal* for a name. We are
informed that the principality remained unified until 1574, the year of

the death of *Shamkhal* Surhay whose authority extended over the entire territory of Northern Daghestan. After him the *Shamkhalat* was divided between his five sons into *beyliks*, and these were soon to become small rival principalities often fighting each other and uniting only when threatened from abroad. This happened, for instance, during the Russian campaigns of 1594, 1604 and 1605. At the end of the sixteenth century the *Shamkhalat* was divided again into *beyliks* — called Qaraqach, Qarabudagh, Erpeli and Djengutay — whose rulers took the pompous title of *sultan*. Djengutay later became an independent state called the Khanate of Mekhtulin. The 'atomisation' of the *Shamkhalat* continued, and by end of the seventeenth century the *Shamkhalat* had lost its control over the mountains.

Most of the Kumyk principalities were very small, some consisting of a single *aul*.[21] It is not surprising therefore that, voluntarily or not, the Ottomans and Muscovites ignored these divisions and negotiated only with the *Shamkhal* of Tarku even when the latter could no longer impose his authority upon his cousins. Ottoman Turks gave him the title of *hakim* (lord) of Daghestan and seemed to ignore the very existence of *Yarim-Shamkhal*. The Muscovites were a little better informed: they made a distinction between the *Shevkal Shamkhal*, the '*Krim-Shevkal*' and the '*Sultan of the Andreevo Village*' (Enderi). This ignorance of the constantly changing situation and particularly of the fractional rivalry between the *Shamkhals*[22] explains the confusion and the errors of Russian, Tatar, Ottoman and Iranian policy in Northern Daghestan.

To the north of the *Shamkhalat*, in the lower valley of Terek and its tributary the Tumenka, there was another Kumyk principality, the khanate of Tumen. Already in the middle of the sixteenth century, after the conquest of Astrakhan by the Russians, this small principality situated in the vicinity of Russian possessions had accepted Moscow's suzerainty. After the construction of Terskii Gorodok fortress, in the centre of the Tumen khanate, Russia dominated this territory completely.

The medium and high mountain range, whose population had not reached the stage of feudal development, was divided into several principalities, ranging from north to south as follows:
1. The Avar khanate in the high valleys of Koisu Avar, Kara Koisu and Andi Koisu with its capital in the *aul* of Khunzakh. The population of the principality was more or less homogeneous, consisting of Avars and small Andi and Dido tribes which had converted to Islam in the eleventh century. The khanate was a formidable power but, being far

from major highways, it did not have the same political importance as other states of Daghestan. The Avar prince, who had the title of *nutsal*, was chosen among members of the princely clan and elected by the assembly of elders and the gentry. At the end of the seventeenth century the dignity of *nutsal* became hereditary, and with the decline of the *Shamkhalat*, the khanate became the most powerful principality of Daghestan.

2. The principality of Kaytak, to the south of the Avar country. Its sovereign had the title of *utsmi* — fancy etymology of the Arab word *ism* (name) and *ismi* (famous) — who is often mentioned in Ottoman sources, which mistook the title of *utsmi* for a name.[23] The Kaytak population was heterogeneous, the majority being Darghins, Laks, Kaytaks, Lezghins and Mountain Jews *(Dagh Chufut)*. Kaytak was a rich flourishing country, renowned for its handicrafts *(Kubachi* weapons); it was near the sea and controlled the coastal Tarku-Derbent highway. The *utsmi* was deemed the most powerful and respected sovereign of the mountain range. According to Kusheva,[24] the population of this principality at the beginning of the sixteenth century numbered 40,000–60,000. The *utsmi* was able to mobilise 500 horsemen and about 1,000 infantrymen. He was elected from 'among the elders', but it would seem that this was governed by no precise rule.

3. The little principality of Tabasaran, in the extreme south of Daghestan in the high and medium valley of Samur. It was governed by two sovereigns, one of whom had the title of *ma'sum* and the other that of *qadi*. We do not know what the rules were for the election of these two sovereigns. The population was composed of Lezghins and Tabasarans and small tribes in the high mountains: Tsakhurs, Rutuls and Aguls. Ottoman documents underline its importance due to its strategic position close to the Derbent-Shirvan highway. Tabasaran could mobilise 500 cavalry horsemen.[25]

THE CHECHEN TRIBES

During the sixteenth century, the Chechen tribes lived mainly in the valley of the Terek and of its southern tributaries Sunja and Argun, and on the northern slopes of the great Caucasian mountain range, to the west of the Kumyk principality of Enderi and north-west of the Avar Khanate. Ottoman archives give no information on the situation of the Chechen tribes.[26] Russian and Georgian sources used by Kusheva are a little more informative,[27] but they also fail to give a precise picture of the social and political structure. In Russian documents, the word 'Chechen' does not appear for this period. It might be because they were designated simply as 'Mountaineers' or were given local names corresponding to their villages: Michkizi, Mezegi, Shubut, Otchan, Erokhan, Osoki, Okokhi, Okochani, Tshan, Galgay and Kalkantsi.

According to Soviet sources class society was not yet formed in the Chechen and Ingush mountains: there was no feudal aristocracy and Chechen communities were made up of large undivided families and clans whose members considered themselves free, noble and equal to each other — 'equal and free like wolves' according to their own saying. During the seventeenth century certain clan formations could assemble 1,000 warriors.[28]

In the sixteenth century, the overwhelming majority of the Chechen clans were animists. Islam was slow to penetrate into the eastern Chechen mountains, and it was only at the end of the eighteenth century, thanks to the activity of the great Sufi brotherhood, the Naqshbandiya, that the Chechen country became one of the strongholds of Islam in the North Caucasus.[29] The Chechens, the Ingush and the Daghestanis are the only Sunnis of the North Caucasus who belong to the Shafei rite: all others are Hanafis.

THE OSSETIANS

The Ossetians lived in the high valleys of Terek, to the west of Chechnia. They were the remains of the great Alan nation that dominated the North Caucasus in the Middle Ages, and lost their power when Timur's armies passed through their territory. Unlike the Chechens, the Ossetians possessed a feudal structure, though one less rigid than that of the Kumyks and of the Kabardians. It comprised the nobles (*aldar* and *badilat*), free peasants (*farsalag*), serfs (*kavsadar*) and slaves. Pushed back into the barely accessible high mountain range, the Ossetians played no part in the history of the Caucasus during the second half of the sixteenth century, and they are not mentioned by Ottoman or by Russian sources. No information is available either for that period regarding the Turkic groups — Karachays and Balkars — who lived in the region west of the Ossetians in the high valleys of Cherek and Chegem. It would seem that the Ossetians' religion was a derived form of Christianity, stamped with animist elements, remainders of an ancient primitive creed. Islam began to penetrate into this region only at the end of the seventeenth century both from the west (from the Kabardians) and from the north (the Nogays). But the process of Islamisation was never completed, and even now three-quarters of the Ossetians (the Tual and Iron groups) are nominally Christians. It is only the Digor group that is Sunni Muslim of the Hanafi rite.

THE COSSACKS

Confronting the indigenous Muslim, Christian or animist population were two groups of Christian Cossacks who appeared in the mid-sixteenth century: the Greben and Terek Cossacks.

Between the Terek and its southern tributary, the Sunja, lies a region of high hills, inhabited by the Greben Cossacks. Their origin is uncertain. It is known that the first settlers appeared along the Sunja at the beginning of the sixteenth century. Their numbers grew by the middle of that century with the addition of small groups of Don Cossacks who settled in the same neighbourhood. Russian sources mention them in 1559, in connection with the first campaign against Astrakhan. In 1563 they are cited as auxiliaries of the troops brought by the *voievod* Pleshcheev to assist Prince Temruk of Kabarda. They appeared again in 1568 in Kabarda as part of the Russian army placed under the command of the *voievods* Babishev and Protasiev. In 1577, they formed the garrison of the new fortress built by Novoseltsev at the confluence of the Terek and Sunja rivers. The Greben Cossacks consisted mainly of outlawed elements, and their relations with Muscovite *voievods* were not always easy or friendly. They served sometimes under Russian command as auxiliaries entrusted with the task of defending the Muscovite vanguards. But frequently they could not be controlled and started their own campaigns, plundering Caucasian, Tatar and Ottoman units on their way from the Crimea to Derbent. It was the Greben Cossacks who in the autumn of 1583 attacked Özdemir Oglu Osman Pasha in the Sunja pass on his way back from Derbent to Kefe. The Khan and the Sublime Porte blamed Moscow for the Cossacks' plundering, but Russian ambassadors in the Crimea rejected the responsibility stating that the Cossacks were not the 'Tsar's people' but plain bandits.[30]

Along the lower Terek lived another Cossack 'army' called the Terek Cossacks. It had been formed during the second half of the sixteenth century by Cossacks fleeing the lower Volga, a region which had become too well controlled for their rebellious taste after the construction of the fortresses of Samara, Saratov and Tsaritsyn. At the beginning, the Terek Cossacks rejected all attempts to govern them, but submitted after 1586 when a fortress was built along the lower Terek. Hence they were used as auxiliaries in defensive and offensive operations against the *Shamkhalat*. However, like their neighbours of the Grebni, they remained undisciplined, often attacking the Muslim population whom Moscow wished to conciliate.[31]

The first encounters — diplomacy and war

The first embassies between the Kabardian feudal princes and Moscow were exchanged in 1552. In 1557 the Princes Temruk and Siboq, heads of the two most powerful clans, offered their 'submission' (in Russian *shert*) and asked Moscow to protect them against the Crimea and Daghestan. However, their act was purely symbolic; it was meaningless because at the same time they were offering submission to the Tatar Khan and to the *Shamkhal* of Daghestan. Only Russian and Soviet historians have considered 1557 to be the date of the official annexation of Kabarda to the Russian empire, but in reality this was a simple misunderstanding, since a *shert* was not an act of allegiance but merely a gesture of politeness with no practical meaning.

On 20 August 1561, the Tsar Ivan married Altynjan, daughter of Prince Temruk (baptised Maria before her marriage). The Tsar gave Temruk the title of 'Great Prince of Kabarda' and invited members of the Tsarina's clan to join his court. Simultaneously the *voievod* of Terek was ordered to bring Orthodox priests to start building fortresses and churches in Kabarda. Thus the triple Muscovite offensive was aimed at: making one of the Kabardian princes a supreme 'khan' of the principality, co-opting the upper level of the feudal nobility, and converting the masses to Christianity. It was a triple error with disastrous results because the Ottoman empire and the Crimean khanate reacted vigorously, consolidating their alliances, and providing the Caucasians with weapons.

First, the Russians, ignorant of the traditional anarchic and chaotic state of Caucasian society (as they were ignorant in 1980 of the real situation of Afghanistan), mistook a clan chieftain for a 'prince' endowed with real authority. In fact, the authority of Temruk was immediately challenged by other Kabardian *pshis*. From 1563 onwards, the central and western Caucasus was torn between two camps, the pro-Muscovite camp led by Temruk and the pro-Crimean and pro-Ottoman camp led by Temruk's rivals. When, in 1567, the Ottoman army and the Crimean cavalry intervened directly in the Caucasus, Russian influence collapsed completely.

The second error was to co-opt the nobility, because those Kabardian noblemen who joined Moscow usually became Christian and migrated to the court of the Tsar. But in settling in Moscow they became Russians and completely cut ties with their homeland. Their influence on the domestic affairs of the North Caucasus ceased.

The same error of russifying the co-opted aristocracy was made later when dealing with other Muslim groups of the empire. In the eighteenth century, about one-third of the Russian aristocratic families had Turkic names — Turgeniev and Karamzin, Suvorov and Kutuzov, Yusupov, Shirinskii or Veliaminov — yet they were completely Russian, barely aware of their origin, and they played no part in the colonial policy of St Petersburg. Nor were they acknowledged as relatives by their kinsmen who had remained Muslims.[32]

Finally, the building of churches and the arrival of Russian priests, together with the construction of Russian fortresses with *streltsi* garrisons, appeared to the Kabardians and to the Adyghes as an insufferable intrusion into their domestic affairs. Documents from Ottoman archives show after 1570 a rapid expansion of Islam among the upper strata of the Cherkess communities. Conversion to Islam was also the only way to escape Tatar slaving expeditions. Around 1580, the competition between Christianity and Islam in the western and central Caucasus was decisively won by Islam. Consequently the entire Russian strategy in the area began to collapse. The first round of the Ottoman-Crimean competition with Muscovy ended with a Russian defeat. The conquest of this area was to take another two-and-a-half centuries.

The second Russian attempt to break through the Caucasian barrier to join with their Iranian ally was aimed at Daghestan. The high barren mountains of Daghestan were the only passage to the prosperous Transcaucasian Georgian kingdom, the khanate of Shirvan and beyond, the Safavi Shia empire of Iran and the Persian Gulf. This campaign was better prepared. The Russians already possessed an excellent springboard with fortresses garrisoned by the *streltsi* and colonies of Terek and Greben Cossacks. Their move was preceded by a series of genuine alliances with Georgian kings and local chieftains. Once again Moscow decided to play the 'Chingizid' strategy. This was the last time this policy was applied in the North Caucasus and coincided with the beginning of a long Ottoman-Safavi war in 1578.

Before attempting the military conquest of the territory, the Russians played a sophisticated game of courting the local rulers, initially from 1584 to 1590, by using a Chingizid Giray and later, from 1590 to 1604, by playing one ruler against another. Allied to the Georgian kings, who in turn were tied by marriage to some of the Daghestani rulers and to the powerful Safavi empire (the Great Shah Abbas acceded to the throne in 1587), they almost succeeded. If they failed it was because, unlike in Kabarda and the Adyghe country of western Caucasus, Islam played a major role in the outcome. The war of 1604–5 had a curious and anachronistic flavour of *jihad*, precursor of many other *jihads* in the following centuries.

To present a more or less coherent picture of the first Russian intervention in Daghestani affairs, one must considerably simplify a very complicated picture. The basic facts are as follows.

In 1584 a crisis of succession arose in the Crimea. The Khan Mohammad Giray II, who had refused to join an Ottoman expedition against the North Caucasus, was removed by the Turks and later killed. A civil war broke out in the Crimea ending in the victory of the pro-Ottoman faction. The three sons of the late Khan escaped to Muscovy. The eldest, Saadet Giray, was recognised by Moscow as the Khan of Crimea; another, Murad Giray, became the central figure of a grandiose Russian plan to conquer all the North-Eastern Caucasus.

To cut a long story short, Murad Giray married the daughter of the *Shamkhal* of Daghestan and became the focus of the anti-Ottoman and anti-Crimean coalition grouping Muscovy, Iran, *Shamkhal*, Georgia (Kakhetia), the Prince of Tumen and even some high mountain Daghestani clans. The aim of the alliance was to cut Ottoman garrisons in Derbent and Shirvan from the Crimea. Russians were offering money, firearms and, their greatest mistake, direct military assistance with advisers and troops. In Daghestan, an alliance of Sunni Muslims, Christian Georgians, Russians and Shia Iranians against the Sultan Khalif could not last long. The Chingizid khans refused to play the role of catalyst, Saadet Giray and Murad Giray died in 1590 (probably poisoned by the Russians), and the *Shamkhal* returned to the Ottoman camp.

A second attempt was made to co-opt Daghestani feudals. This time the Russians chose the *Yarym-Shamkhal* as their puppet. The *Yarym-Shamkhal* had married the daughter of Levan, the Georgian King of Kakhetia, and in 1552 a second anti-Ottoman coalition was established consisting of Moscow, Iran, Kakhetia and some Kumyks. However, by this time the Russians had lost confidence in the loyalty of the Muslim élites and decided to intervene directly. In 1594 an important expedition led by Khvorostynin (including 2,500 *streltsi* and Terek Cossacks) was launched against the capital of the *Shamkhalat*, with the aim of replacing the *Shamkhal* by the *Yarym-Shamkhal*. At the last moment, Islamic solidarity came into its own. The *Yarym-Shamkhal* abandoned the Russians whose forces were completely routed by the Kumyks.

Ten years later, in 1604, the Russians renewed their attempt. The moment was well chosen. In 1603, the Safavis had launched their offensive against the Turks in Transcaucasia and in 1604 had taken Tabriz and Erevan. But this time the alliance was limited to the Christians — Russians and Georgians — and the Shia Safavis. Henceforth the political and military cleavage in Daghestan would always be along religious lines. One could say that the era of the *jihads* began in 1605. A large Russian force of 10,000 men, *streltsi* and Cossacks under the command of Buturlin, took Tarku, but surrounded by the Kumyks, jointly led by the *Shamkhal* and the *Yarym-Shamkhal* (forgetting their traditional rivalry for the occasion) and reinforced by Janissaries from Derbent, they were unable to hold out. They tried to retreat to the Terek but were encircled and massacred almost to the last man. After this major defeat Russia practically disappeared from the North Caucasus until the early eighteenth century, when Peter the Great engaged in a short but successful campaign against Derbent and Mazanderan.

The Ottoman empire, though victorious in this first round, derived no benefit from its success. In the seventeenth century it was Safavi Iran, allied to Muscovy, which became the dominating power in the region. The conflict was resumed at the end of the eighteenth century after the treaty of Kuchuk Kaynardji, with the advance of the armies of Catherine II. Neither the Ottoman empire nor Iran, both weakened, was able to oppose Russian conquest.

During the long period of Russian absence, there were two important developments in the North Caucasus. First, the entire area of the foothills facing the central and eastern part of the region was colonised by Terek and Greben Cossack settlers who pushed the native population into the mountains and played an important role in the future conquest. And secondly, thanks to the organised missionary work of the Ottomans, the Nogays and the Crimean Tatars, and later the Sufi *tariqat* from Central Asia and India, Islam became firmly established in the mountains, something which would make the ultimate conquest infinitely more difficult. In the early nineteenth century, the only remaining non-Muslim Caucasians in the area were the Christian Ossetians and the heathen Ingush.

Later, during their conquest of the North Caucasus and after its occupation, the Russians did not abandon their practice of co-opting the local élites. Attempts were made in the nineteenth century to co-opt Muslim 'clerics', especially those hostile to the Naqshbandis in Daghestan and to the Qadiris (Kunta Haji) in Chechnia in order to use them against the *Murid* movement. They were usually unsuccessful and short-lived. The renewed effort in the nineteenth century to win over the feudal nobility in Kabarda and in North Daghestan (among the Kumyks) by accepting local feudal families into the Russian nobility was a strategy that was of little consequence, even when successful, because by then the backbone of the *Murid* movement fighting the *Ghazawat* was not the landed aristocracy but the *uzdens* who completely escaped all Russian attempts to control them.

Paradoxically, the only successful cooptation of the Daghestani nobility was accomplished by the Russian revolutionaries, especially the Social-Democrats. The majority of the first generation of Daghestani Bolsheviks — Korkmasov, Dakhadaev, Samurskii-Efendiev and others — belonged to the local aristocracy.

NOTES

1. 'Pagan' masses, whose religion was an intimate mixture of ancient animist rites and degenerate Christianity, were finally converted to Islam only at the end of the 18th century and during the first half of the 19th century thanks to the missionary activity of the Naqshbandiya brotherhood. The Ingush of Central Caucasus were converted at the end of the 19th century as a result of the efforts of Qadiri missionaries. The majority of Ossetians (the Iron tribes) remained semi-Christian till the end of the 19th century. They were re-christianised by the 'Society for the Restoration of Christendom in the Caucasus.' The same was the case of the Abkhaz minority who remained Christians of the Georgian rite.

2. The great rival powers displayed little interest in these 'primitive' social groups. This is proved by the fact that the names of Chechens, Abadzekhs, Natukhays and Ossetians are practically absent from Ottoman documents. As to the Abazas their name is often mentioned but always accompanied by offensive epithets such as 'bandits', 'accursed', 'impious', 'reprobates'.

3. An Ottoman chronicler Ebubekir bin Abdullah, the author of the narrative entitled '*Özdemir-zade sadr-i eskak Osman Paşanın Dagıstan ve Sirvan ve Iran muharebatı*' (Battles of Özdemir oglu Osman Pasha in Daghestan, Shirvan and Iran), written at the beginning of the month of Redjeb 992 (9–18 July 1584, folio 12b) in which he states: 'All the tribes of this region, Tumen, Kumyk, Kabartay, Cherkess, Abaza [Abkhaz] and others are infidels.' Further on, in folio 13b, the Ottoman chronicler

writes that the tribe of Kore (Kurin) — that is the present-day Lezghins — living near Tabasaran are all heretic *Cümlesi rafzilerdir*. Probably this expression indicates Shia Muslims. As a matter of fact, all the Caucasian tribes listed by Ebubekir bin Abdullah with the exception of the Abkhaz and — partly — the Cherkess and Kabardians were Sunni Muslims of Shafei rite. This error goes to prove that the Ottomans did not have a very correct idea at the time of the situation in the North Caucasus. On the other hand, it shows that one cannot put absolute trust in chronicles.

4. E.g., in 1567, according to Russian chronicles, the *qalgha* Mohammed Giray brought 20,000 prisoners from a raid in Kabarda. This figure is certainly exaggerated but it gives an idea of the large population in Kabarda (Cf. *Kabardino-russkie otnosheniia v XVI-XVIII vekakh*, Moscow, 1953, I. pp. 16–17). In 1775, 15,000 horsemen were mobilised by all the Kabardian feudals: *ibid.*, II, pp. 19, 316, 318. It is probable that in the 16th century levies were even more important.

5. The Muscovite career of the poor Sultanqul-Mikhail was to come to a tragic end. He was accused of having poisoned the third wife of Ivan IV, Maria Sobakina, and impaled. In 1578, the prince Qanbulat, brother of Temruk, a Muslim, also came to the Tsar's court to ask for Moscow's protection. He took with him his son Khoroshay, who was baptised taking the name Boris. He was the first of the princely lineage of Cherkasskii. Another son of Qanbulat, prince Kudanet, remained in the Caucasus but Kudanet's son Uruslan, who lived in Moscow became a Christian, taking the name Iakov.

6. A similar situation is to be found only in Serbia in the 16th century.

7. Russian sources call them *tamanskie* or *atamanskie cherkesy*, also *adinskie cherkesy*. This name is also found in Turkish documents: *Ada Cerakesi*, 'Cherkess of the Island' (or peninsula).

8. In 1563, this same Aleksandr fled to Lithuania and from there, it would seem, to the Khan of Crimea (where he probably converted or re-converted to Islam). Cf. *Kabardino-russkie otnosheniia, op. cit.*, p. 390, n. 5.

9. D'Ascoli, Russian translation: *Opisanie Chernogo moria i Tatarii. Zapiski Odesskogo obshchestva istorii i drevnostei*, vol. XXIV, 2nd part, p. 125.

10. E.N. Kusheva, *op. cit.*, pp. 150–1. The princely Adighe families were also related to the Girays, possibly because of the renowned beauty of the Cherkess women. The first wife of the Khan Devlet Giray was the daughter of the Adyghe prince Tarzatiq. His fourth wife was also a Cherkess, *ibid.*, p. 151.

11. Cf. my article 'Un condottiere lithuanien du XVIe siècle le prince Dimitrii Vishnevetskii et l'origine de la Sec Zaporogue d'après les archives ottomanes', *Cahiers du Monde Russe et Soviétique*, no. 2, 1969, pp. 258–79.

12. N. Belokurov, *op. cit.*, pp. 48–9.

13. *Name-i Humayun* to Devlet Giray, Khan of Crimea, of 21 Rebi' II, 973/3 December 1565, *Muhime Defteri* (thereafter *MD*) 5, *hukum* no. 505.

14. Undated order to the *beylerbey* of Batum (middle of Safar 990 — end of Zilhidjdja 990/beginning March — end 1582), *MD* 47, *hukum* no. 192. The *kafir* Cherkess correspond here to the 'Free Cherkess' of the Russian documents. They were probably Shapsugs or Abadzekhs.

15. In particular order to Bilaq (or Buvaq) Oglu of the Sozumuqo family (clan), described as 'paragon of notables of the Christian people' dated 3 Ramazan 999, *MD* 68, *hukum* no. 96; also *MD* 70, *hukum* no. 273 (undated, 1592?) and *name-i*

humayun to the Tatar Khan of 16 Rebi' I 1000/12 November 1592, *MD* 72, *hukum* no. 75.

16. Quoted by N. Belokurov, *op. cit.*, p. 37.

17. There also remained an important colony of 'Mountain Jews', *Dagh Chufut*, formerly a military Jewish colony implanted in the vicinity of Derbent by Sassanid kings to protect Transcaucasia from the raids of the northern nomads, particularly the Khazars whose sovereign and nobility belonged to the Jewish religion. The Jews of Daghestan spoke at the time, and still speak today, a dialect of southern Iran.

18. Cf. S.S. Gadzhieva, *Kumyki*, Moscow: Daghestani branch of the Academy of Sciences of the USSR, Institute of History, Archeology and Ethnography, 1961, p. 48. Towards the end of the 16th century or the beginning of the 17th, the mountainous part of the principality — the Lak region of Kazi-Kumukh — broke away from the *Shamkhalat* and formed a small purely Lak state whose chief, the *khalqavch*, was elected (cf. E.N. Kusheva, *Narody severnogo Kavkaza i ikh sviazi s Rossiei v XVI — XVII vekakh*, Moscow: Academy of Sciences, Institute of History, 1963, p. 47).

19. According to an old custom, the candidates were grouped in a circle on the green of the *aul* and the mullah threw an apple to the one who had been chosen as *Shamkhal*. On the election of the *Shamkhal*, see the work of B. Aliev, S. Akhmedov, M.S. Umakhanov, *Iz istorii srednevekovogo Dagestana*, Makhachkala: Daghestani branch of the Academy of Sciences of the USSR, Institute of History, Language and Literature named after G. Tsadasa, 1970. In practice, according to E.N. Kusheva (*op. cit.*, p. 43), it was almost always the next eldest brother and more rarely the eldest son who succeeded to the *Shamkhal*. In the course of the 17th century, the order of succession from father to son began to prevail.

20. Called inaccurately by the Russians *Krim-Shamkhal*

21. The most important of these principalities was Enderi (in Russian: *Andreevskaia derevnia*), situated in the most fertile region of the Caucasian piedmont between the Terek and the Sulak, on the strategic road from the Crimea to Derbent. Its first sovereign was the Sultan Mahmud, a *chanka*, son of a *Shamkhal* and of a Kabardian woman. It was Mahmud of Enderi who in 1605 united temporarily all the Kumyk *beyliks* against the Russians. The other principalities were Buinaksk, Kazanishchi, Kafir-Kumuk and Gelli. One appreciates how small these *beyliks* were by the number of armed horsemen they could mobilise. According to E.N. Kusheva, *op. cit.*, p. 45, Enderi: 200 horsemen, Kazi-Kumukh: 500, Shamkhal: 200, Erpeli: 400, Kafir-Kumukh: 150. However, in case of necessity the Kumyks could mobilise up to 5,000. In 1604 when fighting the Russian army of *voievod* Buturlin, the Sultan Mahmud of Enderi, who led the resistance of Daghestan, had at his disposal 13,000 horsemen — Kumyk, Nogay, Lak, Avar and Lezghin, not counting the infantrymen provided by the *jemaat* from the mountains.

22. Thus, for instance, around 1580 King Levan of Kahkhetia married the daughter of *Yarim-Shamkhal*, Kara Musal, while the *Shamhal* was at war with the Georgians. Also in 1559, the *Shamkhal* asked for the help of the Russian army against the *Yarim-Shamkhal* (R.M. Mokhammedov, *Istoriia Dagestana*, Makhachkala, 1968, pp. 136–7.

23. The *utsmi* of Kaytak was, with the *Shamkhal*, the only Daghestani chief entitled to receive from the Sublime Porte an 'august letter', *name-i humayun*.

24. E.N. Kusheva, *op. cit.*, p. 48.

44 Chantal Lemercier-Quelquejay

25. R.M. Mokhammedov, *Istoriia Dagestana*, Makhachkala, 1968, p. 86.
26. It was not so in the 18th century, when the 'Chachan' occupied the foremost place in the Turkish diplomatic documents.
27. Cf. in particular, the archives of the Russian fortress of Terskii Gorodok founded in 1588. These archives were preserved in the *Posol'skii prikaz* of Astrakhan (E.N. Kusheva, *op. cit.*, p. 60).
28. E.N. Kusheva, *op. cit.*, p. 80.
29. Cf. on this subject A. Bennigsen, 'Un mouvement populaire au Caucase au XVIIIe siècle. La "guerre sainte" du sheikh Mansur (1785-1791), page mal connue et controversée des relations russo-turques', *Cahiers du Monde Russe et Soviétique*, No 2, 1964, pp. 159-205.
30. The Russian ambassador Boris P. Blagovo, who travelled to the Crimea and Turkey from December 1584 to July 1585, had been received on the 26th March 1585 at Sinop by the Vizir Özdemir Oglu Osman Pasha. The vizir questioned the ambassador about the Cossacks of Terek (in reality of Grebni) who had attacked him. Blagovo replied, 'I told you already several times that it is not in obedience to an order of our sovereign that the Cossacks dwell on the Terek and the Don. They are bandits and runaways. And our sovereign had never given orders to his men to act against your sovereign. Also in the kingdom of your sovereign there are many bandits and our sovereign has given orders to find them and drive them away from Terek' (Report of Boris Blagovo, in *Kabardino-russkie otnosheniia, op. cit.*, pp. 39-40).
31. A *gramota* (a message) of the *voievod* Andrei Khvorostynin of 7 Sept. 1589 describes the trade between the Lesser Nogay Horde *Kazievskii Ulus* and the Kumyks of the *Shamkhalat* that Moscow wanted to attach at the time. The *gramota* notes that in spite of absolute prohibition the Terek Cossacks plundered the Nogays who traded with the Kumyks (N. Belokurov, *Kabardino-russkie otnosheniia, op. cit.*, p. 78.)
32. Today the same process could be seen throughout the Soviet Union, when the few 'russified' Muslims (Turkestanis and Caucasians) who married Russian women migrated to live in Moscow. They became 'Soviet' and ceased to act as middlemen between the Moscow rulers and their 'colonised' kinsmen. In this limited field, the Soviet Union was still a melting-pot although this concerned a particular elite.

RUSSIAN STRATEGIES IN THE CONQUEST OF CHECNIA AND DAGHESTAN, 1825–1859[*]

Moshe Gammer

The Caucasus may be likened to a mighty fortress, marvellously strong by nature, artificially protected by military works, and defended by a numerous garrison. Only a thoughtless man would attempt to escalate such a stronghold. A wise commander one would see the necessity of having recourse to military art; would lay his parallels; advance by gap and mine and so master the place. The Caucasus, in my opinion, must be treated the same way, and even if the method of procedure is not drawn up beforehand, so that it may be continually referred to, the very nature of things will compel such action. But in this case success will be far slower owing to frequent deviation from the right path.[1]

This passage, written in 1828 by Veliaminov,[2] was considered as prophetic by all pre-revolutionary Russian writers. Regarding it as the best definition of what they called 'the Ermolov System', generations of Russian writers used it as a yardstick for the activities of successive Russian commanders in the Caucasus. The use of this system by Ermolov, they claimed, was the reason for his success. Its abandonment by his successors caused their greatest failures, and its re-adoption by Vorontsov led to the final defeat of Shamil. Here we propose to re-examine this thesis.

The 'Ermolov system'

The Russian offensive into the mountains was connected with Ermolov, though some mountain tribes had been subjugated before his time.[3] Aleksei Petrovich Ermolov was nominated in 1816 as Governor and Chief Administrator of Georgia and the Caucasus, Commander-in-Chief of the separate Georgian Army Corps, and Ambassador Extraordinary to the court of Fath Ali Shah.

[*]This chapter is dedicated to the memory of Professor Alexandre Bennigsen, pilot of the study of the Muslims in Russia and the Soviet Union in the West and doyen of the growing number of Western scholars studying the North Caucasus and Central Asia.

Only forty years of age at the time of his Caucasian appointment, Ermolov had already made a brilliant career for himself. He had been decorated on the field by Suvorov while still in his teens; at twenty he was a colonel. At the fall of Paris in 1814 he commanded both the Russian and Prussian Guards, and with the death of Kutuzov and Bagration he became the most illustrious and popular soldier in the Empire.[4]

Enjoying the full confidence and backing of Alexander I, Ermolov had, in fact, a free hand, and soon acquired the nickname 'Proconsul of the Caucasus'. One of his first moves was to secure the nomination of Veliaminov as his chief-of-staff.

One year younger than Ermolov, [Veliaminov] never achieved one-tenth of the latter's popularity or fame: yet his career was almost equally brilliant and his merits in some respects greater. The reason is not far to seek. A man of great parts, assiduously cultivated, a zealous student of military history, who brought the teaching of the past to bear on the problems of the day, yet with a mind ever ready to profit by the circumstances of the moment and adapt tactics and strategy to immediate requirements; prompt to conceive and quick to strike, of an iron will and invincible determination; an able organiser; absolutely fearless in battle and no less richly endowed with moral courage, he possessed in a superlative degree all the qualities that command the respect of soldiers, but few that excite enthusiasm, more that enlist their affection. Calm, cool, silent, impenetrable, he was inexorably severe to his own men, merciless to the foe, and he was feared, admired, and hated by both.[5]

As far as can be ascertained from the existing sources, Veliaminov seems to have been the originator of the 'siege strategy'. This was, however, adopted by Ermolov and thus became associated with his name. Using the Caucasian Line as the first parallel, Ermolov established a second parallel along what became known as the Sunja Line and the Sulak (or Kumyk) Line. Three fortresses, the axes of the lines, were erected: Groznaia ('Menacing') on the Sunja in 1818; Vnezapnaia ('Sudden') near Enderi in 1819; and Burnaia ('Stormy') near Tarku in 1821. Many of the Chechens living between the Sunja and the Terek were expelled and Cossack *stanitsas* established on their lands.

The rulers of Daghestan, alarmed by the building of Groznaia 'together with what was known of Ermolov's intentions',[6] formed an alliance against the Russians. Instigated by Said al-Harakani, the most prominent *alim* in Daghestan,[7] they declared *jihad* but were beaten. The rulers of Avaristan and Kazi-Kumukh were replaced, and those of Mekhtuli, Kara-Kaytak and Tabasaran deposed and their lands annexed. The powerful confederation of Akusha, which had defeated Nadir Shah,[8] submitted, accepting a Russian-nominated *qadi* and giving twenty-four hostages. 'The subjugation of Daghestan', reported Ermolov to Alexander I, 'begun last year is now complete; and this country, proud, warlike and hitherto unconquered, has fallen at the sacred feet of Your Imperial Majesty.'[9] Ermolov was sure that the subjugation of the parts hitherto untouched would follow without great efforts and mainly by means of economic blockade or siege. In this belief, however, he was mistaken. 'He did not note that although the crater of the volcano had been cleansed, the internal fire was far from extinguished,' wrote a Russian source.[10] In 1825 the volcano erupted in Chechnia.

'Nothing has any influence on Ermolov,' wrote the head of the Tsar's secret police, 'except his own vanity.'[11] In his arrogance, Ermolov set himself the following aims: 'I desire that the terror of my name should guard our frontiers more potently than chains of fortresses, that my word should be for the natives a law more inevitable than death.' To achieve this aim, Ermolov acted with extreme cruelty and brutality. 'He was', wrote a Russian admirer, 'at least as cruel as the natives themselves.'[12] In fact, he was much more cruel. When rebuked by his master for his excesses, Ermolov replied that 'condescension in the eyes of Asiatics is a sign of weakness, and out of pure humanity I am inexorably severe. One execution saves hundreds of Russians from destruction and thousands of Muslims from treason.'[13] However, the executions were not necessarily confined to the guilty. On one occasion at least, the house of a suspect was blown up, with Ermolov's approval, killing all the family inside. When he decided to push the Chechens south of the Sunja, he surrounded a village and slaughtered all its inhabitants — men, women and children. On other occasions, captured women were sold as slaves[14] or distributed to Russian officers, so that in winter quarters 'for the officers, at least, the Commander-in-Chief setting the example, the time passed pleasantly enough in the company of native wives.'[15]

Ermolov was not an exception in his methods. 'The whole art of Russian government', wrote an Austrian diplomat, 'is in the use of violence.'[16] This was no less true in the Caucasus than in Russia proper. The great majority — the 'Suvorov school', as Baddeley called them — held firmly to the view that 'Asiatics' could understand only force.

The very few who tried to promote another view, namely that 'coercion and brute force cannot achieve what the love and trust of the people can',[17] were treated 'with scorn', condemned 'in no measured terms' and 'stigmatised as both weak and incapable'[18]. From the very beginning, Russian rule in the Caucasus was based on the premises that 'fear and greed are the two mainsprings of everything that takes place here' and that 'these people's only policy is force.'[19] In this respect, Ermolov was well within the existing consensus. If he exceeded it, he did so only in the severity of his measures, in the amount of force he used, and in his brutality and cruelty.

While the 'Ermolov system' was at least partly successful in Daghestan, it failed to subdue the Chechens. All Ermolov's efforts in a series of devastating 'punitive expeditions' served only to exasperate the Chechens rather than bring them to submission. But the last straw for the Chechens was Grekov, the new commander of the (newly built) Sunja Line, who surpassed even his superior in arrogance, brutality and cruelty. Nikolai Vasilievich Grekov 'looked at the natives from a very mean point of view and in speech as well as in official reports had no other name for them than rascals, and [called] any of their representatives either robber or cheat.'[20] No wonder, therefore, that he 'devoted himself heart and soul to the carrying out of Ermolov's policy and instructions', that is to say 'to destroy *auls*, hang hostages and slaughter women and children . . . Whatever the faults of the Chechens', observed a British writer sympathetic to the Russians, 'no impartial reader of the Russian accounts of this period — and we have no other — can doubt that they were cruelly oppressed.'[21]

In 1825 an uprising engulfed all of Chechnia. Soon it was joined by the Ingush, the Kabardians, the Aksay Kumyks and some Ossetians and Daghestanis. The Mountaineers captured one Russian fort, laid siege to another, and killed both Grekov and his immediate superior, Lisanevich.[22] Ermolov himself had to rush to Vladikavkaz, where he spent several months in relocating the line, destroying some forts and building others. Having completed this, Ermolov criss-crossed the country twice and 'punished the rebellious Chechens, burning their villages, destroying their forests, beating them in skirmishes that never developed into battles and, occasionally, even seeking to win them over by an unwonted display of clemency.'[23]

As the revolt collapsed in the summer of 1826, Ermolov returned triumphant to Tiflis. 'To outward appearances his success was complete.'[24] A closer examination of the events, however, discredits the

'Ermolov system' completely. It is true that the revolt subsided, but this had very little to do with Ermolov's movements. It collapsed from within, mainly because of poor leadership. But this fact was not realised then. Nor was it for many years to come. The final collapse of the 'Ermolov system' came on 31 July 1826 when a Persian army invaded the Caucasus. After more than six months of intrigues and mutual accusations Nicholas I dismissed Ermolov and nominated Count (later Prince) Paskevich in his stead.

Ermolov left Tiflis on 9 April 1827 but his gigantic figure continued to cast its shadow over the Caucasus. His dismissal served in the long run to enhance his reputation and increased the number of his admirers to the detriment of his successors who had to compete with a living legend. More important, his legacy proved to be particularly damaging in two respects: his extreme cruelty not only generated an enormous hatred of the Russians among the Mountaineers, but it actually made them immune to terror. Having already experienced the worst, they were no longer afraid of the Russians because they could expect nothing that would exceed it. Furthermore, it was instrumental in the spread of the Naqshbandi order all over Daghestan and Chechnia. Ermolov practically pushed the Mountaineers into the arms of the Sufi order, which would unite and lead them in a thirty-year-long struggle against the Russians.

The 'One Blow' approach

Paskevich[25] was in most respects Ermolov's opposite. A strict disciplinarian, pedantic and with an 'accuracy of eyesight in detecting a fault in the buttons and button-holes of the uniform', [26] he was never popular with his troops. Like Ermolov in his time, however, Paskevich enjoyed the full confidence of the Tsar, Nicholas I,[27] and consequently a free hand in the Caucasus.

Having successfully concluded the wars with the Qajars and the Ottomans, Paskevich turned towards the Mountaineers. His impression was that both 'the frequent punishment' of the Mountaineers 'by small expeditions and raids' and 'measures of gentleness and trust' brought 'little success'[28]. He therefore suggested:

> . . . . to carry out a general and concentric offensive against the Mountain tribes, to take possession of all the most important points in their land . . . to fortify them in order to protect the garrisons and, by securing communications, to make them into bases for further campaigns.[29]

On the surface this appeared a good method for the rapid conquest of the Caucasus, and Nicholas I adopted it wholeheartedly. Such an approach perfectly suited his temperament, outlook, self-image and pocket. Fourteen years later, for example, using very similar terms, he instructed his then Commander-in-Chief, Aleksandr Ivanovich Neidhardt, to 'enter the midst of the Mountains, defeat and scatter all of Shamil's hordes, destroy all his military institutions, take possession of all the most important points in the mountains and fortify those, the retention of which may seem necessary'.[30]

Unlike Nicholas I, Paskevich seems to have begun to develop some doubts about his proposed strategy. In March 1830 he started the implementation of his plan by the conquest of Chartalah (known in Russian sources as the district of Dzharo-Belakany). The conquest itself was easy and quick, being completed in a week, but it was followed by a series of uprisings assisted by considerable forces from Daghestan. Not until 1832 did the Russians finally establish their rule in Chartalah, and even then it remained precarious for many years to come.[31]

By then, however, Paskevich had departed. In 1831 a rebellion broke out in Poland and the neighbouring provinces which had been part of that kingdom before the partition. Paskevich was nominated by the Tsar to quell the rebellion and left the Caucasus on 10 May. He was succeeded by Baron Grigorii Vladimirovich Rosen, who had served for many years under his command.[32]

Rosen arrived in Tiflis on 20 October 1831. Unacquainted with the Caucasus, he initiated a lengthy process of re-thinking. Following hints of change in Paskevich's views, Rosen tried to suggest new schools of thought: 'It is difficult', he wrote, 'to pacify free and warlike tribes by force only.' Rather, Rosen suggested subduing the Mountaineers 'by way of peaceful relations and commerce', coupled with 'gradual consolidation in [important] points wherever the circumstances and our resources will allow us' and with 'exemplary punishment of tribes most hostile to us'.[33]

These suggestions were rejected by both St Petersburg and 'old Caucasian hands'. 'The Mountaineers', stated Veliaminov scornfully, 'have next to nothing to sell and almost no money.' Nicholas I, on the other hand, expected 'the final pacification of the Mountaineers [to be accomplished] singularly by way of a general offensive', and instructed Rosen to carry out Paskevich's plan 'without alterations'.[34] Although correspondence on this subject continued for five years, it had little to do with the events of those years, because the situation had changed dramatically by the time of Rosen's arrival. The conquest of Chartalah gave the final inducement to the various Chechen and Daghestani communities to form a united resistance to the Russians. Part of the leadership of the Naqshbandi-Khalidi *tariqat* played a central role in this process, and brought it to culmination by proclaiming Ghazi Muhammad imam (Kazimulla in the Russian sources).

Ghazi Muhammad was an able and energetic leader. During 1830 his authority spread rapidly throughout Daghestan and among the Chechens, Ingush, Kumyks and even the Nogays. The confused and feeble Russian reaction added to his growing fame and might. In 1831 he took full advantage of the long interregnum and the depleted number of Russian troops. At the beginning of June he captured Tarku and besieged Burnaia and Nizovoe. Later that month he also besieged Vnezapnaia and in late August Derbent. In November he threatened Groznaia and then carried out a devastating raid on Kizliar. Whatever his outlook, Rosen concluded soon after his arrival that first of all he had 'to reestablish peace as soon as possible and to defuse the general irritations of the Mountaineers'.[35]

Soon planning began for a major campaign to destroy Ghazi Muhammad once and for all. Rosen himself took command over it. Starting on 24 July from the Georgian Military Highway, the Russians crossed all of Chechnia with sword and fire. Then passing through Salty and Temir Khan Shura, Rosen approached Gimri where the Imam had decided to make his final stand. On 29 October the Russians stormed Ghazi Muhammad's fortified position. The Imam and about fifty followers were surrounded in a nearby house and all but two were killed.[36]

The complete success of Rosen's campaign seemed to have put an end to the problems in Daghestan. It was decided, therefore, to concentrate the main efforts in the western Caucasus. The conquest of that area achieved priority for the following reasons. First, unlike Chechnia and Daghestan, which were officially ceded to Russia by the Qajars, the Russian claim to sovereignty over the western Caucasus was equivocal at best, and the other great powers — most significantly Britain and France — refused to recognise it. Secondly, the tribes inhabiting that area, the Circassians, seemed to be much more numerous, powerful and fierce. Thirdly, their geographical position, due to the long shore on the Black Sea, enabled them to maintain contacts with the Ottoman empire and other foreigners, most notably the British. These contacts strengthened the Circassians militarily and morally and fortified their resolve to resist Russian penetration. Because of the diminished resources of the

Caucasian Corps since the revolt in Poland, the Russians had no choice but to adopt the 'siege strategy' during their operations in Circassia. In Chechnia and Daghestan the 'one blow' strategy remained in force both because there were no reasons to attempt anything else and because Rosen's success gave a resounding proof of its validity.

Soon after Ghazi Muhammad's death, Hamza Bek was proclaimed Imam. By the autumn of 1833 his growing power began to alarm the Russians,[37] and they started to contemplate an expedition against him. By the time this was carried out — in October 1834 — Hamza Bek had conquered Khunzakh and killed the Avar ruling house, but had himself been assassinated in revenge and very recently succeeded by Shamil. Thus the Russians met almost no opposition. They marched into Avaristan and appointed Aslan Khan of Kazi-Kumukh as temporary ruler. Thus a pattern was established. Whenever there was trouble, the Russians would mount an expedition and put everything in order. In the summer of 1837, when the death of Aslan Khan and Shamil's rising power seemed to threaten instability, a Russian force marched unopposed to Khunzakh and nominated Ahmad Khan of Mekhtuli in Aslan Khan's place.

In the summer of 1837 another expedition was undertaken to put an end to Shamil and his growing power. Major-General Fesi conquered Ashilta (Shamil's place of residence) and besieged Shamil in Tilitl, but was compelled to sign an agreement with him and retreat.[38] Being, however, 'a great master of the pen',[39] his expedition was hailed as a great victory and his agreement with Shamil as the Imam's submission to Russia. When, in October that year, Tsar Nicholas made an inspection tour of the Caucasus, Shamil naturally refused to come and make a formal submission to him. Once again, it was decided to launch an expedition and put an end to the Imam once and for all. A new Commander-in-Chief, Evgenii Aleksandrovich Golovin,[40] was charged with its implementation.

In 1837 and 1838 the Russians were preoccupied with a series of revolts in the eastern part of Transcaucasia (now Azerbaijan). The expedition against Shamil was therefore postponed until 1839 by which time the Russians had become so alarmed by the Imam's growing power that this expedition became the first priority in the entire country. It was led by Baron Grabbe, the commander of the Caucasian Line,[41] and the second most important general in the Caucasus. Grabbe led a force of about 10,000 into the mountains. He captured two villages defended by Shamil and after an eighty-day-long siege conquered Akhulgo, Shamil's fortified residence. The Imam escaped with only his family and a few confidants, leaving his eldest son Jamal al-Din as hostage in Grabbe's hands.[42]

The matter [is] finished even if the rebel, against all odds, succeeded in escaping. He no longer enjoys any trust in the Mountains, or a haven any more . . . ; nowhere can he find a place more inaccessible than his previous nest Akhulgo, or followers braver than those who sacrificed their lives for him. His party is finally destroyed; his *murids*, abandoned by their leader, perished . . .[43]

This view proved premature. In the spring of 1840, the whole of Chechnia was in arms again. Unlike the Russians, Shamil and his lieutenants learnt the lessons of previous campaigns. Taking full advantage of the fact that he was operating from internal lines of communications, and using classic guerrilla tactics, the Imam '. . . threatened the enemy north, east, [west,] and south, kept them continually on the move, dispersed his commandos to their homes, gathered them again as if by magic, and aided by extraordinary mobility of mounted troops who required no baggage, nor any equipment or supplies except what each individual carried with him, swooped down on the Russians continually when least expected.'[44]

The Russians' solution again was to mount expeditions to try and beat Shamil. The Mountaineers, however, 'thanks to their amazing speed, almost always successfully avoided pitched battles with our forces.' Thus, 'our columns were brought to extreme exhaustion.'[45] Resorting to the usual solution of mediocre generals, the Russians sought to gain success by increasing the size of their expeditions, but achieved adverse results. By the end of 1841 Shamil's rule had spread over the whole of Chechnia and most of Daghestan.

At the beginning of 1842, the Tsar became impatient for rapid result and decide to mount an expedition against Dargo, now the Imam's residence. Grabbe agreed to lead the campaign and was given command of both the Caucasian and northern Daghestan Lines independently from Golovin. In return, however, he had to accept close supervision of the expedition by the War Minister, Prince Chernyshev. In June 1842 Grabbe launched his expedition with 10,000 men and twenty-four guns. After three days of constant fighting in the forests, he had to retreat. In this campaign the Russians lost sixty-six officers and 1,700 men, one field-gun and nearly all their provisions and stores. 'The picture was terrible and it created a strong impression on Prince Chernyshev.'[46] This was an accurate image of the realities of the Caucasus, and not only of Grabbe's expedition.[47] Chernyshev suggested a change of policy. 'The system of our activity, being based exclusively on the use of the force of arms, has left political means completely untried,' he wrote. 'The English have been able to consolidate their power in India by political means. They thus preserved their forces and gained time in subduing that country. Should we not try this system as well?'[48]

The Emperor shared Chernyshev's views. A new Commander-in-Chief, Aleksandr Ivanovich Neidhardt,[49] was soon nominated to implement the new policy. He was told by the Tsar 'not to spare money' in order to 'draw to us some of Shamil's brothers in arms', to 'sow discord and contention among the others' and to 'reassure and encourage the pacified and semi-pacified tribe'.[50] To facilitate the new policy and prevent any further disasters, a two-year-long ban was imposed on raids and expeditions. This truce helped Shamil greatly in preparing for his next operation. In September and again in November 1843 he launched two successful surprise attacks and reconquered Avaristan and most of the other territories held by the Russians in northern Daghestan.[51]

Exasperated by the news, Nicholas decided to make 1844 'a year of retaliation for the enemy for the Avar catastrophe'. He ordered Neidhardt 'to deal Shamil a few strong blows' in order to 'satisfy the honour of our arms' and 'undermine his importance and influence in the mountains'.[52] For this purpose the Caucasian Corps was reinforced by the Fifth Infantry Corps. A complicated and coordinated offensive from three sides on Dargo was planned but logistics, never the strong point of the Russian army, collapsed and Neidhardt 'had enough spirit in him' to cancel it.[53]

Disappointed with the meagre results of this campaign, the Tsar replaced Neidhart by Count (later Prince) Mikhail Semenovich Vorontsov.[54] As 'Viceroy of the Caucasus and Commander-in-Chief of all the forces in the Caucasus', Vorontsov was given almost a free hand on condition that he conducted the expedition on Dargo. Vorontsov started the campaign with 21,000 men and forty-two pieces of artillery. He occupied Dargo, but was surrounded there, and only the intervention of Freitag,[55] the commander of the left flank of the Caucasian Line, saved the Viceroy from complete destruction. In this expedition Vorontsov's force lost 3,916 men (including three generals killed), three guns, a great sum of money in coins which had been carried along, and all the luggage and supplies.[56]

The 'Vorontsov System'

The disaster of 1845, although it was never acknowledged as such, convinced Vorontsov, and he in turn convinced the Emperor, that the system had to be changed. A return to the siege system was now adopted. To start with, existing gaps in the defence were closed by the establishment of the two new fortified regimental headquarters in Central Daghestan (in 1846 and 1847) and a third one on the Kumyk plain (1845). The 'Upper Sunja Line' (established 1845–6) closed a gap in the west, and some re-adjustments were carried out at the Lesghin Line in the south-west.

In Chechnia the third parallel was erected by the completion of the 'Advanced Chechen Line'. Centering on Vozdvizhenskoe (the 'Elevated', established in 1844 by Neidhart), Achkhoy (1846) and Urus Martan (1848), it was built near the 'Black Mountains'. The Russians were set to take full control of Chechnia. To do so, expeditions were sent to clear avenues in the primeval forests of Chechnia, wide enough to prevent a passing column from being under artillery fire. Such avenues made it possible for the Russians to control the country and to transfer their troops quickly and safely. 'The system of the axe' was replacing 'the system of the bayonet'.[57] As a rule, these clearing operations were accompanied by the systematic destruction of hamlets, supplies and gardens, the stampeding and burning of fields and the seizure of livestock. In this way the Russians intended to 'force the Chechens to migrate into our territory, where no-one would disturb them any more'.[58] The alternative was for them to migrate into and behind the 'Black Mountains' and live on the verge of starvation.

Starting from Lesser Chechnia the Russians now mounted a series of expeditions — at least once a year and usually from two directions. Operating from fortified camps and in strong columns with powerful artillery support, the Russians were practically impregnable despite the Mountaineers' desperate resistance. By March 1848 the first results could be seen: while the majority of the Chechens preferred to migrate into the 'Black Mountains', 3,000 families submitted to the Russians and were resettled in the vicinity of the new forts.

However, an attack by the Imam in Central Daghestan in 1846 diverted Vorontsov's attention in that direction. He decided to establish a second parallel along the Kara Koisu, and therefore planned to storm the villages of Gergebil, Salty, Sogratl, Chokh and Irib. In 1847 he set out himself with a column of 10,000–12,000 men to conquer Gergebil, but failed. He then moved to Salty where he was successful after a seven-week-long siege. The following year Prince Argutinskii-Dolgorukii, the Commander of Daghestan,[59] tried again to capture Gergebil, and this time the attempt succeeded following a siege lasting twenty-five days. In 1849, Argutinskii besieged Chokh, but was forced to retreat without storming it.

The retreat from Chokh set the seal of failure on Vorontsov's plans for Daghestan. Three years of major effort, 4,340 killed and wounded in the hostilities — many more died from various diseases, including cholera, and from accidents — and a great amount of money, ammunition and supplies, seemed too high a price to pay even if Vorontsov's aims were ultimately achieved. To invest all this only to destroy three villages, which soon after the Russian retreat were rebuilt and refortified, was simply a waste. It was a double waste because all the efforts, and part of these resources and manpower, could have been used much more effectively in Chechnia.

Another diversion hampering speedy progress in Chechnia proved to be raids by local commanders. It was originally Veliaminov who was instrumental in overcoming the ban on such raids in the early 1830s. By the early 1840s many local commanders 'liberated themselves' from their superiors. Each of them 'conducted the war according to his own views', in many cases letting 'his instincts loose' and 'turning the war with the Mountaineers into a special kind of sport, aimless, and with no relevance whatsoever to the overall situation'.[60] Such raids, concluded a Russian general, 'turn in the final account to our disfavour because they exhaust the troops by forced marches . . . and provoke the enemy by the accompanying cruelties and robberies.'[61] By 1848, after several years in which such raids were banned, a new generation of colonels was in command. Young, ambitious, eager for action and glory, they took advantage of any excuse to carry out 'searches in enemy territory', justifying them as 'necessary under the circumstances'.[62]

One of the reasons for Vorontsov's enhanced powers was to control the conduct of his subordinates. However, because of his age — he was sixty-eight — he started to lose control. Such raids intensified in numbers in 1851 when the commander of the Left Flank fell ill and was released from his duties. During the interregnum a race developed between the candidates to take over the command, one of them being Prince Bariatinskii.[63] The result was that the Left Flank 'occupied the first place in the numbers of losses . . . in the [entire] Caucasian Corps'.[64] The raids reached a peak, with disastrous results for the

Russians, in 1852, following the appointment of Prince Bariatinskii as commander of the Left Flank. Only his 'freshness' and youth, wrote a Russian author, could explain 'the military actions he undertook' and his 'pompous reports'.[65]

Despite these obstructions, by October 1850 the lowland of Lesser Chechnia was under full Russian control. In January 1850 the Russians moved their operations to Greater Chechnia. The bitter opposition led by Shamil personally failed to repel their advance, and by March 1853 they had gained control over the lowland of Greater Chechnia, following which the population migrated into the 'Black Mountains'.

Conclusion

At first glance it looks as though Veliaminov's prediction proved correct. However, one should not forget the following points. First, even if the strategy of siege looks effective in retrospect, it was not necessarily so at the time of its conception. There might have been — and were in fact — other approaches which were never given serious consideration. Secondly, it was in a way a self-fulfilling prophecy. It was the attempt to implement this strategy, coupled with the brutal methods and devastating raids of the Ermolov years, which pushed the Mountaineers to present a common front, and thus created the need for this approach. The Caucasus might have been 'a mighty fortress' at the time of Veliaminov's memorandum, but its defenders were far from being united. And thirdly, its implementation did not necessarily shorten the time of the conquest or bring the desired results. On the only occasion when Veliaminov had a free hand to put his strategy into effect, that is as Commander-in-Chief of the Right Flank in 1831–8, his attempts backfired — admittedly after his death — when the Circassians successfully stormed a number of forts.

But all these are hypotheses, as are the attempts to use Veliaminov's words as a yardstick, because the 'strategy of siege' was never fully applied, not even in the days of Ermolov and Veliaminov, yet it was never completely abandoned either. It was this partial implementation of Veliaminov's approach and a mixture of other elements, this use of half-measures, that was so detrimental to the Russians. And to this state of affairs Veliaminov made his contribution by advocating and promoting the 'punitive raid'. On this, as on other subjects, he was in agreement with his former chief, Ermolov.

It seems that Veliaminov himself never thought that the 'siege' of the

Caucasus would be a lengthy process. Russian generals were constantly over-optimistic in their forecasts and over-confident of their own strength, and underestimated the Mountaineers. The Tsar for his part was always impatient. He expected the army which had defeated Napoleon — that was how all Russians regarded the matter —, and which had dispersed Persian and Turkish armies vastly superior in numbers, to 'put a quick end' to a 'few bands of robbers'.

Misunderstanding — or choosing to misunderstand — Paskevich's plan for a 'one blow' approach, Nicholas adopted it wholeheartedly, especially as it seemed to weigh lightly on the treasury. Only a series of increasingly devastating disasters persuaded him finally to abandon this strategy. The Tsar thus showed himself to be 'penny wise and pound foolish', as was proved when the Russians finally conquered Chechnia and Daghestan. A great part of their success was due to the determination to do it at all costs, not sparing money, means or manpower. Of course, the Mountaineers were by then exhausted by a thirty-year-long war and starved by a forty-year-long blockade. In addition one should not forget that their morale had collapsed after the Crimean War and the failure of the Ottomans and the Western Powers to come to their rescue.

NOTES

1. N.A. Volkonskii, F. von Kliman and P. Bublitskii, 'Voina na vostochnom Kavkaze s 1824 po 1834 g. v sviazi s miuridizmom', *Kavkazskii sbornik*, vol. XV, p. 524 (hereafter 'Voina'). Translation based on John F. Baddeley, *The Russian Conquest of the Caucasus*, London, 1908, p. 112 (hereafter Baddeley).
2. For his biography see Sh. (otherwise anonymous), 'General Veliaminov i ego znachenie dlia istorii kavkazskoi voiny', *Kavkazskii Sbornik*, vol. VII, pp. 1–47.
3. The tribes subdued before the arrival of Ermolov were the Georgian Mountain tribes — the T'suhs, P'shavs and Khevsurs — and the partly christianised Ossetians living astride Russia's life-line to the Caucasus, the Georgian Military Highway.
4. M. Whittock, 'Ermolov: Proconsul of the Caucasus', *The Russian Review*, vol. XVIII, no. 1, 1959, pp. 53–60. For Ermolov's biography see Aleksandr Ermolov, *Aleksei Petrovich Ermolov, 1777–1861. Biograficheskii ocherk*, St Petersburg, 1912.
5. Baddeley, pp. 109–10.
6. *ibid.*, p. 123.
7. He was the teacher of the (future) first and third imams, and later became an opponent of the Naqshbandis.

8. Lawrence Lockhart, *Nadir Shah: A Critical Study based mainly upon Contemporary Sources*, London, 1938.
9. Quoted in Baddeley, pp. 137-8.
10. 'Voina', vol. X, p. 19.
11. Quoted by Whittock, p. 58.
12. Quoted by Baddeley, p. 97.
13. *ibid.*
14. This sheds a rather cynical light on the Russian argument that one of their major aims in the 'pacifying' of the Caucasus was to stop the slave trade.
15. Baddeley, p. 145. Ermolov himself fathered a daughter who remained for all her life an object of curiosity and pilgrimage for Russian officers passing near her village. The shocking effect of this licentious behaviour by infidels with Muslim women can be easily imagined.
16. Quoted by Lesley Blanch, *The Sabres of Paradise*, London, 1960, p. 93.
17. V.G. Gadzhiev and Kh.Kh. Ramazanov (eds), *Dvizhenie gortsev severnogo Kavkaza v 20-50 gg. XIX veka. Sbornik dokumentov*, Makhachkala, 1959, pp. 345-7, document no. 192, Ladyzhinskii to Golovin, 16 (28) July 1842, quotation from p. 346 (hereafter *Dvizhenie*).
18. Baddeley, p. 99.
19. Tsitsianov to the Emperor as quoted in Baddeley, p. 65.
20. For his biography see 'Voina', vol. X, pp. 42-4.
21. Baddeley, pp. 147-8.
22. This incident is typical of Russian behaviour in the Caucasus. On 28 July, Grekov and Lisanevich invited 300 men from Aksay to the fort of Gurzul (Gerzel *aul* in Russian sources) with the intention of arresting them. Lisanevich strongly abused and insulted them in their own languages and, threatening to punish them for treachery, ordered them to give up their *kinjals* (daggers). A certain Haji Uchar Yaqub refused to do so. Grekov lost his temper and struck Uchar in the face. Within seconds Uchar killed Grekov and two other officers and dealt mortal wounds to Lisanevich. The Russian general ordered the death of all 300 Mountaineers before dying himself.
23. Baddeley, p. 153.
24. *ibid.*
25. For his biography, see Shcherbatov, *General Feldmarshal Kniaz' Paskevich. Ego zhizn' i deiatel'nost'*, St Petersburg, 1888-1904.
26. Karl Marx, 'The Russian Failure', leader in the *New York Tribune*, 11 July 1854, as republished in *The Oriental Question*, London, 1969 (reprint), p. 397.
27. Paskevich was the military instructor of Nicholas I in his youth, and some elements of a pupil's attitude to his teacher remained in the Tsar's relationship with Paskevich during all his life. The Count (later Prince) was not only the first soldier of the Empire but the Emperor also consulted him on all military matters and ended by accepting his advice.
28. Baddeley (pp. 226-7) misunderstood Paskevich when he attributed to him the intention to conquer the mountains by peaceful means.
29. *Dvizhenie*, pp. 60-2, 68-72, documents nos 35, 39, Paskevich to Nesselrode, 18 February (2 March), Paskevich to the Emperor, 6 (18) May 1830; 'Voina', vol. XI, pp. 150-2; vol. XII, pp. 63-9 (quotation from p. 69, note 14).
30. The Emperor to Neidhardt, as quoted in A. Iurov, '1844-i god na Kavkaze', *Kavkazskii Sbornik*, vol. VII, p. 158.

31. The most comprehensive work on the conquest of Chartalah is I.P. Petrushevskii, *Dzharo-Belakanskie vol'nye obshechestva v pervoi tret'i' XIX stoletiia*. *Vnutrennii stroi i bor'ba s Rossiiskim kolonial'nym nastupleniem*, Tiflis, 1934.

32. For Rosen's biography see A.P. Berzhe (ed.), *Akty sobrannye kavkazskoi arkheograficheskoi kommissiei*, vol. IX, p. xxvii (hereafter *AKAK*).

33. G.E. Griumberg and S.K. Bushnev (eds), *Materialy po istorii Dagestana i Chechni*, vol. III, part I: *1800–1839*, Makhachkala, pp. 263–9, document no. 114, Rosen to Chernyshev, 5 (17) May 1832, no. 16. For hints of change in Paskevich's mind see *ibid.*, pp. 219–24, document no. 97, Paskevich to the Emperor, 8 (20) May 1830.

34. 'Voina', vol. XV, pp. 507–8.

35. See *AKAK*, vol. VIII, pp. 340–1, 674–5, documents nos 252, 574, Rosen to Chernyshev, 12 (24) September 1837, Chernyshev to Rosen, 5 (17) April 1832, nos 137 and 544 respectively; *Dvizhenie*, pp. 103–4, document no. 61, Chernyshev to Rosen, 11 (23) Jan. 1832; 'Voina', vol. XIV, pp. 132–3; vol. XV, pp. 506–48, 561–576.

36. One of the two survivors was Shamil, the third Imam. For the description of this and all the other campaigns mentioned below, see Baddeley whose book is still, more than eighty years after publication, the best on the subject,

37. *AKAK*, vol. VIII, p. 517, document no. 452, Rosen to Chernyshev, 31 Aug. (12 Sept.) 1833, no. 606.

38. For the description of this expedition according to Shamil's propaganda see J. Milton, *Life of Shamyl and Narrative of the Circassian War of Independence against Russia*, Boston, 1856, pp. 202–6.

39. Baddeley, p. 364.

40. For Golovin's biography, see Iuri Tolstoi, 'Ocherk zhizni i sluzhby E.A. Golovina' in Petr Batenev (ed.), *Devetnadtsatyi vek. Istoricheskii sbornik*, vol. I, Moscow, 1872, pp. 1–64.

41. For Grabbe's biography see *AKAK*, vol. IX, pp. xviii-xix.

42. For a military study of this campaign by a Daghestani expatriate see Baha-Eddin Khoursch, *Obrona twierdzy Achulgo przez Imama Szamila*, Warsaw, 1939.

43. *AKAK*, vol. IX, p. 333, document no. 298, Grabbe to Golovin, 24 August (5 September) 1839, no. 456.

44. Baddeley, p. 364.

45. A. Iurov, '1840, 1841 i 1842 gody na Kavkaze', *Kavkazskii Sbornik*, vol. X, p. 76.

46. A.I. Gagarin, 'Zapiski o Kavkaze', *Voennyi Sbornik*, 1906, no. 3, p. 17.

47. For an excellent description of the Caucasian realities of the late 1830 and early 1840s, see E.G. Veidenbaum, 'Prodelki na Kavkaze' in *Kavkazskie Etiudy*, Tiflis, 1901, pp. 312–13.

48. *Dvizhenie*, pp. 352–3, document no. 195, Chernyshev to Golovin, 19 (31) July 1841.

49. For his biography see *AKAK*, vol. IX, p. xxiv.

50. A. Iurov, '1844-i god na Kavkaze', *Kavkazskii Sbornik*, vol. VII, p. 159.

51. For a military study of these offensives by a Daghestani expatriate see (Baha-Eddin) Khoursch, 'Voennaia operatsiia v Dagestane v 1843 godu', *Gortsy Kavkaza*, no. 39, pp. 8–20; no. 40, pp. 10–14; no. 48, pp. 10–14; no. 49, pp. 12–19.

52. A. Iurov, '1844-i god', *op. cit.* p. 157, and note 30 above.

53. Aleksandr Dondukov-Korsakov, 'Moi vospominaniia', *Novizna i Starina*, vol. 5, p. 207.

54. For Vorontsov's biography see M.P. Shcherbinin, *Biografiia general-fel'dmarshala kniazia Mikhaila Semenovicha Vorontsova*, St Petersburg, 1858.
55. For his biography see *AKAK*, vol. IX, p. xxix.
56. For an independent contemporary description of this expedition see M. Gammer, 'Vorontsov's 1845 Expedition against Shamil: A British Report', *Central Asian Survey*, vol. 4, no. 4, 1985, pp. 13–33.
57. A. Zisserman, *Otryvki iz moikh vospominanii*, 1876, vol. 4, p. 424.
58. K., 'Levyi flang kavkazskoi linii v 1848 godu', *Kavkazskii Sbornik*, vol. XI, p. 349.
59. For his biography see 'Kratkii obzor sluzhebnoi deiatel'nosti general-ad'iutanta kniazia Argutinskogo-Dolgorukogo', *Kavkazskii Kalendar'*, 1856, part IV, pp. 565–81.
60. Veidenbaum, *op. cit.*, pp. 312–13.
61. *Dvizhenie*, pp. 360–1, document no. 202, Gurko to C.O. Vladikavkaz, 7 (19) Jan. 1843.
62. K. (otherwise anonymous), 'Levyi flang . . .', vol. XI, p. 433, *op. cit.* Sometimes a visit by a neighbouring unit was deemed a good enough reason for a raid — *ibid.*, pp. 433–9.
63. The future viceroy under whom Chechnia and Daghestan were finally conquered. For his biography see A.L. Zisserman, *Fel'dmarshal kniaz Aleksandr Ivanovich Bariatinski 1815–1879*, Moscow, 1888–91.
64. K., 'Obzor sobytii na Kavkaze v 1852 godu', *Kavkazskii Sbornik*, vol. XXI, p. 21.
65. N.A. Volkonskii, 'Pogrom Chechni v 1852 godu', *Kavkazskii Sbornik*, vol. V, p. 20.

CIRCASSIAN RESISTANCE TO RUSSIA

Paul B. Henze

The long struggle of the North Caucasian Mountaineers against Russia in the mid-nineteenth century attracted broad European sympathy and admiration. Among prominent writers who championed the cause of the Caucasian Muslims we find Karl Marx, whose writings about this and other freedom struggles of subject peoples in the Russian empire, such as the Poles, were a constant source of embarrassment to the Soviets.[1] Marx and even professional historians described the struggle primarily in terms of the leadership and personality of the Imam Shamil. Shamil is unquestionably one of the most colourful and effective anti-colonial resistance leaders of the nineteenth century.[2]

The late-twentieth century resurgence of Islam as a dynamic political force in many parts of the world, including the Soviet empire, has generated new interest in Shamil's religious motivation and techniques of leadership. But Shamil is only part of the history of North Caucasian resistance. His successes were all in the eastern Caucasus. The resistance of the Circassians in the western Caucasus is at least as significant, for it began earlier, lasted longer and ended more disastrously for those who were fighting to defend their freedom. There are similarities and some interconnections between these two sides of the struggle. There are also important differences.

Why has the Circassians' long and stubborn resistance to the Russians attracted so little attention? Two reasons can be advanced. One is that leadership among them was diffuse. They produced brave, intelligent and colourful leaders, but no single personality dominated their struggle. More important, probably, is the fact that when the Circassians were defeated after a half-century of hard fighting, the majority of them emigrated to the Ottoman empire. The lands where they once lived were colonised by Slavs. The small groups of Circassians who remained in their traditional homeland were separated from each other and were less able to maintain their traditions and sense of cohesiveness than the tribes that had supported Shamil. Their dispersal has reduced awareness of them both in the Russian/Soviet empire and in the West.

The majority of the Mountaineers in the central and eastern Caucasus stayed in their ancestral territories after Shamil's capture, accommodated to Russian rule, but never becoming fully reconciled to it. Whenever an opportunity to take their destiny into their own hands presented itself, e.g. at the time of the Bolshevik Revolution and during the German invasion in the Second World War, they revolted. In between, passive resistance persisted. The memory of the long fight which Shamil led remained vividly alive, passed on from one generation to the next.[3] Over and over during seventy years of Soviet rule, intellectuals among these peoples took advantage of opportunities to write, lecture, debate and publish about the heroic events of the mid-nineteenth century. Official Kremlin policy toward Shamil wavered from relative benevolence early in the Soviet period, through extreme hostility in the late Stalin era, to uneasy accommodation from the 1960s onwards.[4]

Circassians who emigrated to the Ottoman empire found it easier to assimilate when they settled in Anatolia among Turks than when they went to Arab lands. Consciousness of Circassian origin is nevertheless widespread among their descendants in modern Turkey, and distinctive customs survive. As interest in roots, historic origins and, therefore, in *Dış Türkler* ('Outside Turks') has grown in recent years, scholars in Turkey have directed their attention to Caucasian history as well as that of Central Asia. In Jordan, Israel, Saudi Arabia and other countries which formed part of the Ottoman empire, substantial compact communities of Circassians have retained their identity. In Jordan they exercise important functions as military officers and businessmen. These Circassians have maintained tenuous, though now expanding, links with kinsmen remaining in the former Soviet Union. Like them, they have preserved their language and their traditions. All share pride in the bitter struggle their ancestors waged in the nineteenth century.

What lay behind the Russian advance into the Caucasus? Several distinguished historians see it as the natural result of the advance of the Princes of Muscovy against the Golden Horde which led to the capture of Kazan in 1552 and Astrakhan in 1554.[5] The need to protect conquests already made and to secure trade routes kept drawing the Russians further on. This movement was only occasionally the result of consciously articulated strategic calculations by the people who participated in it. A major component of it in its early stages was the steady expansion of Cossack power and numbers in regions beyond the frontiers. Peter the Great was attempting to implement an energetic expansionist policy when he captured Derbent in 1723, but his forces were overextended and had to withdraw. Catherine the Great was less audacious and more successful.

Many motivations and interests usually combine to determine both the policies and the actions of expanding empires. It is possible to find evidence of a Russian imperial drive toward warm seas well before the eighteenth century.[6] But the drive was based on more than strategic calculations. By the end of that century Russian rulers and statesmen had become eager to emulate European colonial powers by expanding into new territories in search of land for settlers, raw materials, increased military security for existing frontiers, and greater political influence beyond them.[7] The claim that Russia was carrying out a divinely sanctioned civilising mission was not always pretence, though it was sometimes expressed pompously and arrogantly.[8]

As they advanced southward the Russians faced unavoidable confrontation with two long-powerful empires which had dominated the Middle East since the sixteenth century: the Ottoman and the Persian. Territories under Ottoman suzerainty in the Caucasus were vaguely defined at their outer edges. They represented the northeasternmost extension of imperial holdings extending from Hungary across the Black Sea steppes to the Kuban and beyond, where the Ottomans were heirs of Turkic peoples extending back to the Cumans and the Khazars. Persian holdings in the Caucasus had even more ancient beginnings in ties to Georgians and Armenians that had their roots in pre-Roman times. The Persian-dominated Caucasian territories formed the north-west flank of an empire which extended deep into Central Asia. Although the Turkic element in Persia had been strong from the time of the Seljuks, Ottomans and Persians were more often rivals than allies and fought many wars along their frontiers both in the Caucasus and in the lands extending south to the Persian Gulf. As both empires lost their dynamism in the eighteenth century, this legacy of rivalry served to blind them to the danger threatening them from the north: the expanding power of Russia.

The Russians succeeded in driving the Persians from the Caucasus more rapidly and decisively than they were able to do with the Ottomans. A series of decisive Russian victories leading first to the Treaty of Gulistan in 1813 and culminating in the Treaty of Turkmanchay in 1828 established the border where it has remained ever since, splitting Azerbaijan and leaving the historic Armenian centres, Erevan and Echmiadzin, under Russian control.[9] The Ottoman empire was not only an Asian power, but since the fourteenth century had been deeply involved in the power politics of Europe as well, and the desire of European powers to prevent Russia from overwhelming and obliterating it was an important factor in its survival. Politically, developments in the Balkans often affected the course of events in the Caucasus throughout the nineteenth century. In the end, this interrelationship did not work to the advantage of the inhabitants of the Caucasus. By the early twentieth century all the peoples of the Balkans had managed to exploit great power rivalries to secure independence. Those of the Caucasus all fell under the control of the Russian empire.

The Caucasian peoples with the most highly developed sense of national identity — the Georgians and the Armenians — became allies of the Russians in their southward advance. Their sense of nationality rested on several interconnected factors: language, religion and historic traditions. Of these, their Christianity was arguably the most important for, even when these peoples were politically fragmented, their ancient church organisations provided a durable national symbol and rallying-point for popular sentiment. Although the relationship of these two peoples to the Persian and Ottoman empires was for centuries characterised by at least as many positive as negative features, by the late eighteenth century both found the prospect of closer links with Orthodox Christian Russia increasingly attractive. This was not merely a question of Christians desiring to come closer to fellow-Christians. There were profound tensions between Armenians and Georgians. Both peoples had found ways to cohabit successfully with Islam for a millennium. Russia's attractiveness for them had more to do with the seemingly irreversible decline into which the two great Middle Eastern Islamic empires had fallen. It was increasingly difficult for peoples on their periphery to manage a stable, calculable relationship with them. Georgians saw their monarchy threatened by neighboring Islamic principalities over which distant Islamic capitals exercised little control. Armenians had long since ceased to occupy any extensive consolidated territory in the Caucasus and lived either as peasants among Muslims and Georgians or as craftsmen and traders in towns where they almost never formed a majority. When the prospect of living under the protection of a dynamic Russian empire became a real possibility, both Georgians and Armenians welcomed it.

The dominant Shia Muslim inhabitants of Azerbaijan — who had long lived in khanates whose rulers acknowledged varying degrees of Persian overlordship — were much more equivocal about the Russian advance. The peoples of Daghestan and those who lived in the mountains and foothills to the north of the main Caucasus range were mostly Sunni Muslims, although some had been converted only in the seventeenth and eighteenth centuries. Speaking of themselves as *Dagh* or *Tawlu* — Mountaineers — they included more than a dozen tribal groups speaking languages which were for the most part not mutually intelligible. They had little sense of nationhood, but Islam and opposition to the imperial Russian advance gave them a sense of common purpose, although realisation of interlocking mutual interests was often not strong enough to overcome traditional tribal rivalries and feuds or social strains within these tribes.

The basic Russian tactic everywhere in the Caucasus was to co-opt indigenous élites and turn them into allies in gaining domination over their peoples. The tactic proved particularly effective in Georgia. Among the Mountaineers, however, it was much less successful, for traditional leaders who cooperated with the Russians often lost the confidence of their own people. As Russian pressure increased, more and more Mountaineers were ready to take their defence into their own hands. The situation was ripe for Shamil, whose populist, purist Islam appealed to the majority of tribesmen in the central and eastern Caucasus.

Geography played a role too. Advance into the Caucasus was easiest for the Russians along the Caspian littoral. The only militarily feasible route through the mountains was up the valley of the Terek and over the Daryal pass. In advancing along this route the Russians had a further advantage, for here lived the Ossetians, least Islamicised of the Mountaineers, Iranian rather than Turkic or indigenous in origin, and to some degree already christianised and amenable to cooperation with the Russians. It was through their territory and with their collaboration that the Georgian Military Highway was constructed.

By far the most difficult area to penetrate militarily was the long Black Sea coast. Geographically this region was extremely fragmented, consisting of a succession of lush valleys formed by short, non-navigable rivers leading back into the high mountains with steep sections of coast and only poor natural harbours in between. Rainfall was high, so forests grew luxuriantly. When cleared for agriculture and grazing, these valleys were a dependable source of food and could support a comparatively large population. The Circassian peoples who had inhabited these territories from time immemorial kept livestock, farmed and lived in dispersed settlements linked by trails. No major highways existed. No cities developed. The Circassians were fragmented into many tribes and subgroups who were often at odds with each other, raided each other's cattle, and made a sport of fighting. There was, nevertheless, a deep historical consciousness and sense of cultural unity among them.

Circassian identity

After the Georgians and the Armenians, the Circassians came closest of all the Caucasian peoples to developing the prerequisites for nationhood. They had traditions of roots extending back to the dawn of recorded history.[10] Their ancestors may well have greeted the first Greeks who came to Colchis in search of the Golden Fleece. Archaeological and linguistic evidence supports the hypothesis that people speaking dialects ancestral to Circassian may have extended deep into the present area of the Ukraine in prehistoric times.[11] They appear to have been the dominant inhabitants along the northern and eastern Black Sea littoral from the Crimea to the mouth of the Rioni (the ancient Phasis) in Hellenistic times.

For the next two millennia the Circassians lived on the edge of the Greco-Byzantine world and interacted with it. Greek trading colonies, followed by Byzantine traders and eventually by the Genoese, provided links with the Mediterranean. (In the nineteenth century Circassians still attributed all old fortifications along their coast to the *Ceneviz*, i.e. the Genoese). Nomads whose way of life had been formed in great open spaces showed little inclination to challenge the Circassians for possession of their rugged mountains and heavily forested foothills.[12] Only along the northern edges of their territory were the Circassians gradually pushed back — driven out or assimilated (probably a combination of both) — by the Turkic pastoral groups who came in across the steppes from the east. Circassian princes intermarried with the leading families of these groups and formed alliances. Through centuries of movement of peoples across the hills and plains directly to the north of the mountains, Circassians remained an important component in the population of the regions that came to be known as Greater and Lesser Kabarda.[13]

Christianity came to the Circassian lands from Byzantium. Ties were also maintained through christianised Georgia, but as far as we know Christianity never became more than a veneer over traditional beliefs and customs. If a national church ever formed among the Circassians, it was never strong and disappeared in medieval times. No separate priestly class developed to maintain literacy and preserve written records; the Circassian language remained unwritten and unstandardised. Thus Christianity was of only marginal importance in the survival of Circassian identity, and the same was true, until a very late period, of Islam. Islam appears first to have penetrated Circassian territories from the Crimea, where a strong Turkic dynasty, the Girays, who claimed direct descent from Chingiz Khan, established control over broad steppe territories and had close relations with the northern Circassian tribes, especially those of Kabarda. After the Russian conquest of the Crimea in 1783, many Crimeans took refuge among the Circassians.[14]

A Circassian Muslim dignitary explained to the Englishman James Bell in 1837 that since it was only about sixty years since 'general religious observances' and 'social order' (by which he meant Islam) had been introduced into Circassia, a mixed situation had to be expected. Four books, he said, were recognised by Circassians as important for their system of religion and morality: the Bible (by which he seems to have meant the Pentateuch), the Psalms of David, the four Gospels, and the Quran. His own view was that the revelations which Mohammed had communicated were entitled to greater respect than those of Christ, which he claimed had come through the medium of the Archangel Michael.[15]

The attitude of the majority of the population toward religion was even more eclectic. Ceremonies honoring Tshible (the thunder-god) and Merem (the Virgin Mary) were important annual events and included feasting, prayers and dancing in which both sexes participated together. Ancient crosses in sacred groves were still common in Circassian lands in the early nineteenth century, and burial grounds were usually located nearby. Some of the crosses became the object of controversy, as Bell reported:

> There is a great debate at Sashe about removing some ancient crosses, of which there are three particularly noted — one pendent from a tree and two erect — besides several others of iron, as these are, and some gilt. The people, in general, wish them removed for fear they should fall into the hands of the Russians, who might thereupon found some claim to the country as having been originally Christian; while the chief, Ali Achmet Bey — who drinks wine profusely, has never been known to say Mussulman prayers, and is suspected of a bias to the ancient faith of the country — protests against the profanation — by removal — of these relics of their forefathers; prefers defending them where they are, and claims the right of ordering that they shall be left intact.[16]

There was little differentiation of profession among Circassians. All farmed and most kept livestock. Those who acquired wealth kept large herds of cattle and many horses. Forests were rich in game and supplied more than enough wood for fuel and construction. People did not live in fortified villages with stone towers like the inhabitants of the central and eastern Caucasus, but isolated farmsteads were common, often surrounded by orchards and groves of walnut trees. Circassians seldom built in stone, preferring wood and thatch. For those times, health conditions were good and there was usually surplus population. For hundreds of years, in fact, the main export of the Circassian lands was people; dedicated as they were to their own traditions, Circassian men were always ready to venture into the wider world as soldiers. The Mamluks of Egypt were largely Circassians and Georgians. The tradition of military service in the lands to the south continued into the eighteenth century. Even before their beauty became legendary in Ottoman times, Circassian women were sought after as slaves and concubines throughout the Middle East.[17]

Circassian society was originally hierarchical with four classes: princes (*pshi*), nobles (*warq, uzden*), freemen (*tokav, tlfoqotl*) and serfs (*pshitl*), but there were many regional variations. By the time of the great resistance struggle in the nineteenth century, much differentiation in social structure had developed with and among Circassian tribal groups. There had apparently been decisive changes in the seventeenth century. Bell was told by elders:

> . . . About two centuries ago there was a fierce struggle between the free men and the nobles of Circassia, and . . . the power of the latter, who were then much more numerous . . . was then first effectively broken. Mohammedanism farther reduced it. Its renovation, and the reduction of all below to a servile equality, have been distinctly promised to individuals of that class by the Russians in the event of their success. But although the liberty now enjoyed appears thus to have been wrenched from the hands of the nobles, there remains enough of respect and precedence allowed to those of that class to evince the forbearance and good feeling of the rest; and the expression in common use [for] done genteelly is *vorkhi khabse* (*à la noble*). Nobles boast of Arabian or Crimean ancestry.[18]

Traditional princes remained strongest among the tribes of Kabarda, who were the first to have extensive contact with the Russians. They had lost much of their authority — if indeed they ever had it — in the mountain and coastal tribes.

Islam was most readily accepted initially by the upper classes, and in some cases, despite its theoretical leveling effect, bolstered the authority of princes and nobles. Crimean influence in the north from the fifteenth century onward and the influx of Crimeans after 1783 strengthened the position of Islam. So did deliberate Ottoman efforts to encourage its consolidation and spread. But, like Christianity, Islam too remained a veneer. Circassia differed sharply from the eastern Caucasus. *Muridism* had very limited appeal. Conflict between *adat* (customary law) and *shariat* (Muslim canon law) seldom reached serious dimensions among Circassians. Islamic law tended to be observed only when it did not come into direct conflict with *adat*. The German Moritz Wagner reported a discussion among an assembly of *uzdens* in the 1840s about whether grain should be burned in case of a Russian attack:

> One chieftain remarked: 'Our book forbids this.' 'Oh', rejoined another, 'a good deal of nonsense is written in our book.' A remark of this kind would hardly have been ventured by [Turks]. . . . It would never occur [to them] openly to reject the language of the Qoran, whilst the principal grounds for resistance to Russia among the Circassians are an innate love of freedom and independence together with, perhaps, the hope of plunder and booty.[19]

The factors which made for divisiveness among Circassians were also part of their heritage from the past: rivalries among the tribes and among clan and family groups within the tribes. There were patterns of feuding which had persisted for generations. Tribal groups did not readily submit to centralised leadership or accept unified command in military operations. Successful offensive action was frequently not sustained, and defeats of the enemy were not effectively exploited. Individual warriors preferred to charge the enemy in the open on horseback but were reluctant to take time to fortify defiles, build defence lines, and plan either sustained attacks or defence in depth. There was little coordination between groups in battle, and careful preparation for a continual campaign was a concept Circassians found hard to accept. These shortcomings were not absent among other Caucasians, but Shamil's strong leadership mitigated them.

In a sense, therefore, the Circassians seem to present an anomaly — a people with a common language, common pride in their history, and fierce adherence to traditions, but without a written language or recorded laws, and with an absence of administrative structure and of organisation to provide for their own defence. It was not only their classical education that caused many of the Europeans who visited the Circassians in the nineteenth century to compare them to the ancient Greeks and see among them survivals of classical Greek customs and habits. Classical Greeks were never united politically, even though they had developed urban culture to a much higher degree. Individual city-states fought bitter wars against each other. Still, Greeks were all conscious of belonging to a Greek nation which was sharply differentiated from the barbarians around them. Like the ancient Greeks, Circassian tribes raided each other and took prisoners and hostages and then met in councils on neutral ground to regulate relations between tribes and clans, debate political issues, and then hold games and festivals, but their feeling of common nationality was not institutionalised beyond this level.

The Circassian dialects were all mutually intelligible, especially those grouped under the heading *Adyghe*, which came to be used by almost all Circassians as a common name not only for their language but for themselves as a people and for their country.[20] Circassian is phonetically among the most complex languages in a region notorious for language variety and intricacy. It is extraordinarily rich in consonants, with its basic dialects featuring nearly sixty consonantal phonemes. The grammar permits many unusual forms of expression. The vocabulary is unique to this Caucasian group, though it became infused with many Turkic loanwords.[21] Circassians had a rich tradition of oral poetry. Oratory was a highly developed art. Leaders gained as much renown for their speechmaking ability as for their skill in battle.

Few outsiders learned Circassian, and not many, except occasional Armenian traders, regularly penetrated into Circassian territory until the Russian advance began. The *lingua franca* of the entire Caucasus was Turkish, then termed Tatar. It was widely understood among Circassians on the coast because of regular trade with Turkey and contacts with Ottoman administrators. Men who had been to Turkey or had extensive contact with Ottoman officials spoke Ottoman Turkish well. Of the situation prevailing in Circassia in the 1830s Bell commented: 'The number of persons I have met who can speak Turkish has . . . been considerable; many can also read and write it.'[22] Knowledge of Arabic was much rarer among Circassians than in the eastern Caucasus, where it was maintained by adherence to Quranic traditions and by religious links with Iran and Arab lands. When religious schools began teaching small numbers of children in the nineteenth century, Turkish was more often used than Arabic.

Russia and the Circassians

The first Russians to come into regular contact with Circassians were Cossacks who established themselves in the steppes north of the Kuban

river in the sixteenth and seventeenth centuries and advanced up the
Terek valley. This region, Kabarda, has a complicated history.
Circassians and several other steppe and mountain peoples have interacted and mixed. Some Kabardian princes traced their ancestry back to
an original leader named Inal, believed to have returned from Mamluk
service in Egypt. The country was divided among several local princes.
Cossacks, who included men of very diverse origins, struck up alliances
with these leaders and married and intermingled with both Circassians
and Nogay Tatars, adopting to a large extent their customs and style of
life which was in many respects of a higher quality than the Russians had
attained at the time.[23]

In common with most Ottomans, the Circassian princes of Kabarda
did not originally perceive the expanding power of Moscow as an
immediate threat to them but looked upon the still distant Russians as
potential allies against rivals and enemies nearer at hand. Circassian
envoys from the Besleney tribe who dominated the strategically important region of Beshtau (*Pyatigorie* — the Five Mountains) sent envoys to
Moscow as early as 1552. In 1556 these Circassians aided the Russians in
attacking territories of the Crimean khan. Other Kabardian princes soon
made approaches to Moscow, and the most powerful of them,
Kemirgoko, known to the Russians as Temruk Aydarovich, succeeded
in 1561 in getting Tsar Ivan IV (the Terrible) to accept his daughter
in marriage. Baptised Maria Temrukovna, she died childless in 1569 and
her father's fortunes, which had for a few years prospered because of the
Russian connection, took an abrupt turn for the worse when he was
defeated by the Crimean khan in alliance with the Nogays in 1570.
Other Kabardian princes who allied themselves with the Russians fared
better over time, and became founders of several Cherkasskii noble lines
which eventually played a prominent role in Russian politics in succeeding centuries.[24]

During the seventeenth century, the Russian state was still too preoccupied with consolidating its control over territories nearer to Muscovy
to be interested in gaining direct control of Caucasian territory.
Kabardians began to feel direct Russian state power pressing upon them
only at the beginning of the eighteenth century when Russia first
made serious military efforts to gain full control over the approaches
to the Caucasus. The basic Russian approach was to develop alliance
relationships with as many of the Kabardian aristocracy as possible, gain
their acquiescence in a permanent Russian presence in the region, and
construct chains of fortified settlements. Over time, they achieved

considerable success, but there were repeated rebellions, for, like all Circassians, the Kabardian freemen did not acknowledge the dominance of any single prince, and some princes resented favoritism shown to rivals. The bulk of the people seldom saw much gain for themselves in Russian domination. These episodes were particularly difficult for Soviet historians to deal with and resulted in much controversy and sophistry about the 'voluntary' incorporation of Kabarda into the Russian empire and about which groups among Kabardians actually favored it.[25]

The Ottomans were reluctant to withdraw from steppe territories over which they had long exercised dominant influence, often in conjunction with the Crimean khans. They attempted to rally the Kabardians during the Russo-Turkish war of 1768–74 to block Russian access to the Caucasus, but tsarist forces made further advances. In the Treaty of Kuchuk Kaynardji, which ended this war, the Ottoman empire was forced to surrender claims of sovereignty over both the Crimea and Kabarda. Russia agreed to recognise the independence of local rulers in both regions. The treaty was ambiguous about the status of the Black Sea coast, which included both Circassian and Georgian lands. Meanwhile, in 1769–70, General Todleben had brought the first organised Russian military force through the Daryal Pass, and met the Georgian King Irakli II who ruled the two eastern Georgian kingdoms of Karthli and Kakheti. This expedition marked the beginning of Russia's direct involvement in the affairs of the Transcaucasus. In 1783, by the Treaty of Georgievsk, Irakli accepted Russian protection. In this same year Russia annexed the Crimea, and large numbers of Crimeans began to emigrate to Ottoman territory.

Open war broke out between the Ottoman and Russian empires again in 1787 and lasted until 1791. There was heavy fighting between Russian and Turkish forces over the fortress of Anapa at the northern end of the Circassian coast. The Russians succeeded in capturing it in 1790 after defeating a large Turkish force which had invaded the Kuban. During this same war, Russian advances against Ottoman territories in the Balkans disturbed Britain and Prussia. For the first time Russia was thwarted in the Caucasus by developments elsewhere in her empire and by pressure from the European powers — a pattern that was to recur frequently in the nineteenth century. The Poles had risen to oppose partition, and Empress Catherine was ready to make concessions to secure peace with Turkey in order to be able to concentrate her attention on Europe. The Treaty of Jassy of 1792 returned Anapa to Ottoman control.

In the years that followed, Russia advanced most successfully against
Persian-held Caucasian territories. The European powers were relatively
unconcerned about these. In 1796 Russian forces captured Derbent and
advanced through Baku as far as Karabakh. The death of King Irakli II in
1798 brought about a situation favourable to Russian interests in
Georgia. The new king, Georgi XII, 'slothful, weak and gluttonous,
devout and middle-aged',[26] was unable to rule successfully. He died two
years later, and competing claimants to the throne fought each other.
The Russian took advantage of this confused situation to proclaim
incorporation of the two eastern Georgian kingdoms into the empire in
1801 and advanced against western Georgia, where the kingdom of
Imereti was still oriented toward the Ottoman empire.

Once again developments in the Caucasus were affected by the course
of events in Europe, where Napoleon was ascendant. He succeeded in
maneuvering the Ottoman empire into open war against Russia again in
1807. As a result, after temporary losses on the Caucasian front,
Ottoman control over Anapa, Poti and Akhalkalaki in western Georgia
was confirmed in the Treaty of Bucharest in 1812. The Georgians
revolted during Napoleon's invasion of Russia in the same year, but
Russian control over central and eastern Georgia was eventually
reestablished. The Circassians, as a result of all these events, became
more consciously oriented toward Istanbul.

Turkey and the Circassians

After the Treaty of Kuchuk Kaynardji in 1774, the growing power of
Russia and the threat of further losses convinced the Ottoman government of the need to strengthen its position in the North Caucasus.
Sultan Abdulhamid I decided to establish a formal governmental structure in the Circassian territories and appointed Ferah Ali Pasha *vali* of
Sogucak in 1780. By origin a Georgian slave, he was a good choice, for
he understood Caucasian conditions. He developed a coherent program
involving several complementary actions: (*a*) strengthening Ottoman
positions militarily; (*b*) introducing regular administration in the
Circassian territories; (*c*) encouraging the consolidation of orthodox
Sunni Islam. With great energy he set about renovating and extending
fortified positions along the Black Sea coast, building a major new fort
at Anapa. He facilitated the settlement of refugees from the Crimea
along the coast. He persuaded the major Circassian tribes of the interior
to submit to Ottoman authority and mediation of disputes between

them. He took measures to control piracy and began construction of a port at Gelincik. Although Ferah Ali Pasha died in 1785, his successors continued his program, and the Turkish hold on Circassia was substantially strengthened for the tests of strength that came in the early nineteenth century.[27]

In 1785 a new force appeared on the North Caucasian scene — a dynamic religious leader who rallied all the native peoples against the Russians: Sheikh Mansur. He has since been seen as a precursor of Shamil's *Muridist* movement, for his basic religious message and his methods of mobilising support were very similar to those of Shamil.[28] At the time, however, he was somewhat of a mystery to both Turks and Russians, and until recently his treatment by historians has been erratic.[29] He was neither a renegade Italian Jesuit nor an Orenburg Tatar serving as a Turkish agent, as many Russians maintained at the time and Soviet historians as late as the 1960s still tried to claim. Recent research in Ottoman archives demonstrates that he was regarded with considerable reserve, and at times hostility, by the Ottoman authorities, for Sunni clerics were suspicious of the Naqshbandi Sufi doctrines which motivated him and his followers.

Born about 1748 in the Chechen village of Aldy and originally called Ushurma, he had led the life of a typical North Caucasian farmer. He took the name Mansur — Victor — when he launched his offensive against the Russians at approximately the same age as Shamil. His mission had been revealed to him in a dream in which the Prophet ordered him to lead a holy war — *ghazawat* — against the encroaching unbelievers. Like Shamil, he reached far beyond petty tribal loyalties and preached unity of all North Caucasians. After his first victory over the Russians at his native village, warriors from as far away as Daghestan came to join his forces. During the first period of his *ghazawat* Sheikh Mansur repeatedly defeated Russian contingents sent to hunt him down. He assembled an army reputed to contain more than 20,000 men.[30] He besieged the Russian fortress of Kizliar on the Terek, where it forms a delta and flows into the Caspian Sea, but was unable to reduce it. Eventually his forces were defeated in Kabarda and driven from the Kuban, but he fought on for six years, receiving little Turkish help until the final stages of the war which began in 1787.

If the Turks had been less equivocal about Sheikh Mansur's holy war, they might have gained a good deal by coordinating their military operations against the Russians to take advantage of his capabilities. Until it was too late, they regarded the Sheikh as disruptive of their aim of ending rivalries among competitive Circassian princes and consolidating Sunni Islam among the Circassian rank-and-file.[31] The Sheikh happened to be in Anapa in 1791 when the fortress was besieged by Russian forces and, after sixty-one days, surrendered. Captured, he was sent to St Petersburg and imprisoned in Schlusselburg, where he died in 1794. If it had not been for this accident, he might well have continued his holy war for years, for he had only reached his mid-forties. The fact that the Ottomans regained control of Anapa in the Treaty of Jassy ensured a Turkish presence in this strategically important region for another generation.

Nevertheless, Sheikh Mansur remained alive in legend. Nearly fifty years later a Tatar bard with the distinguished name of Kaplan-Giray was singing a ballad about 'Elijah Mansur' who unified the Caucasus to fight against the Russians:

He was born to tread the Moscoff's pride
Down to the lowly dust;
He fought, he conquered, near and wide,
That northern race accursed . . .[32]

Moving through the defile of Gagra, a party of Circassian warriors halted to pray in a cottage said to have been a favorite stopping-place of Sheikh Mansur:

No situation could have been better adapted as the headquarters of a guerrilla chieftain: the only approach was by a drawbridge over a deep chasm that, once passed, there was an easy communication opened with the whole of the surrounding mountains and glens, capable of serving as a secure retreat to a numerous population, and from whence they could at any time issue and deal destruction on their enemies.[33]

Thus, though neither a Circassian nor a Tatar, Sheikh Mansur became for the Circassians a symbol of their resistance struggle — but with many characteristics of a national as well as a religious leader.[34]

The Russians made no lasting gains in Circassian territory during the first quarter of the nineteenth century, though they pursued a policy of carrot-and-stick with the Circassians: encouraging disaffection and tribal rivalries, tempting the common people to become dependent on overland trade, threatening attack, offering rewards to princes and nobles for collaboration. Ottoman policy remained unchanged — reduce tribal rivalries, spread Islam, ensure order and promote trade by sea — and

Circassian orientation toward Turkey increased during this period, especially in the coastal districts. The Ottomans gave highest priority to preservation of long-held positions in Abkhazia and western Georgia.[35]

The Russo-Turkish war of 1828–9 came about primarily because of developments relating to Egypt and Greece. The Balkans were the main theatre of hostilities, and here, although operations at first went well for the Russians, they soon experienced reverses. Things went better on the Caucasian front, where the Tsar's forces captured Anapa in June 1828 and made important advances on the Georgian front in the south: Akhaltsikhe and Kars were captured by the end of the summer. The next summer Russian forces penetrated deep into Ottoman territory and captured Erzurum.[36] Circassian territories south of Anapa saw no significant action, but in the Treaty of Adrianople (Edirne) in 1829 Turkey agreed to give up all positions and claims on the Circassian coast in return for restoration of Kars and Batum. The implication in this treaty was that Turkey was transferring her suzerainty over Circassia to Russia — but the situation was not spelled out specifically. Lack of clarity caused much legal and diplomatic debate during the next two decades.[37]

Diplomatic niceties were of little concern to the Circassians. They had not submitted to any outside power. The only one to which they felt any affinity was Turkey. The formal withdrawal of Ottoman power from their coast marked the beginning of more than three decades of intense resistance to Russian attempts to establish complete hegemony over their lands. The Ottomans had weakened their claim to suzerainty over Circassia by agreeing to the terms of the Treaty of Adrianople, but Ottoman merchants were still interested in trade and there were many other links between Turks and Circassians which were actually becoming stronger during this period. Turkey had by no means abandoned interest in the Caucasus, and the Circassians were an integral part of the Caucasian scene.

The tactics which the Russians now adopted — to establish strong points on the coast and eventually link them overland to territory firmly under their control north of the mountains — took thirty-five years, and cost tens of thousands of lives on both sides and heavy material investment to produce success. Even then the great bulk of the Circassian population refused to accept Russian rule and emigrated.

Why did the intensity of Circassian resistance mount as the Russians pressed harder and prospects for sustained foreign support waned? How important were expectations of foreign support? Would more coherent Ottoman military and diplomatic policies have made a difference? To what extent did the Circassian resistance and that led by Shamil in the eastern Caucasus reinforce each other? Would the Circassians have been better off following Lermontov's advice, surrendering and accommodating themselves to being 'slaves of the Ruler of the Universe' after 1829?

In the remaining sections of this chapter, while describing the main stages of the thirty-five-year Circassian fight for freedom, some basis will be provided for answering these questions.

Russian tactics in the 1830s and 1840s

For almost two decades Russia pursued a war of attrition in Circassia which appears to have been at least as costly to her as to the Circassians. Until the very end, following the defeat of Shamil, the balance of forces was little changed from what it had been at the beginning. Spencer described the situation at the end of the 1830s:

> . . . along the whole line of coast from Kouban-Tartary to the port of Anakria [Poti] in Mingrelia, the Russian government does not possess a foot of land, with the exception of the forts, or rather mud entrenchments we visited, and these are constantly besieged by the indefatigable mountaineers.[38]

Wagner reported an expedition of 600 Russian regulars accompanied by 2,000 Georgian auxiliaries against the Ubykhs in October 1841. They were transported by sea to the fortress of Ardler from where they attempted to penetrate inland. An aged Circassian prince, Barzek Haji Dokhum-oku,[39] led the Circassian defence. The Russian force succeeded in making its way overland 20 miles to Sochi, but at a cost of 500 men. Little, if anything, was gained from it:

> . . . the only advantage derived from this operation was a more accurate survey of the section of coast between Ardler and [Sochi] . . . Though the loss of the natives was, according to all appearances, greater than that of the Russians, yet the facts of the case prove that the expedition against the Ubiches, which is the last military operation of any importance that has taken place on the coast of the Black Sea, did not terminate favorably to the Russians.[40]

This was the last of the energetic forays that had begun with General Veliaminov's 12,000-man expedition against the Abkhaz and

Circassians in 1835. First threatening scorched-earth tactics and resorting to deliberate brutalities,[41] Veliaminov later tried to persuade the Circassians to submit to 'pacification'. Neither approach worked. A decade of fort-building along the coast did not greatly advance Russian control of it. Nor did the naval blockade which the Russians tried to maintain; Turkish vessels from Samsun and Sinop maintained a brisk trade with Circassian ports.[42] A steady supply of weapons, lead and gunpowder flowed in from Turkey, along with consumer goods such as salt and cloth. Thus a boycott of Russian commerce over the Kuban was feasible.

During the early 1830s the Russians made some inroads into Circassian solidarity by pursuing a policy of peaceful enticement of the northern tribes, gaining the collaboration of some of the princes and nobles as they had done earlier in Kabarda, and enticing the free peasantry by trade. By the end of this decade, however, the efforts of Circassian leaders, encouraged by Turks and Britons, created a greater sense of national solidarity among the Kuban tribes. Wagner observed in 1843 that the Russians had made no real progress but concluded that they were probably not unduly concerned with the failure of their policy, for the Kuban and northern Black Sea region were at least quiet and tsarist generals were thus able to concentrate all their military strength in the eastern Caucasus.[43]

By refraining from sending expeditions into the Circassian heartlands, the Russians were able to achieve some degree of *modus vivendi* with some Circassian leaders — but even Circassian collaborators, while accepting Russian tolerance, gave very little in return for the favors accorded them, as Wagner observed in Tiflis in 1843:

> The Circassian warrior is seldom seen in the streets of Tiflis, and is immediately distinguished in the crowd by his knightly form, the noble profile of his countenance, whose expression bespeaks manly boldness and energy. . . . With firm and haughty step, the Circassian stalks through the crowd, and all, including the drunken Cossack, make way for him. . . . The majority of Circassians whom I saw at Tiflis consisted of chieftains, or of influential Usdens, of confederate or subdued tribes, who had come down to pay their respects to, and obtain, perhaps, some presents from the commander-in-chief of the Russian army.[44]

An American, George Leighton Ditson, one of the first of his nationality to visit the region,[45] came to the Caucasus in 1848. He was unreservedly sympathetic to the Russians and dedicated the published account of his travels to Prince Michael Vorontsov, then in his fourth year as Viceroy of the Caucasus. Although he had no contact with independent Circassians, and most of his book deals with the Crimea, Georgia and reports of Shamil's struggle, Ditson's choice of title[46] demonstrates the extent to which the Circassians as a people had come to symbolise Caucasian resistance to the Russians. Ditson's book confirms the existence of a stalemate in the western Caucasus at this time. Approvingly he cited Prince Kochubey:

> These Circassians are just like your American Indians — as untamable and uncivilized . . . and, owing to their natural energy of character, extermination only would keep them quiet, or . . . if they came under Russian rule, the only safe policy would be to employ their wild and warlike tastes against others.[47]

By this time Prince Vorontsov had made his mark on Russian strategy in the Caucasus.[48] His great expedition against Shamil in 1845 had been disastrous, but it had been undertaken against his better judgment in response to pressure from Tsar Nicholas I. Elated at having humiliated the Russians, Shamil moved into Kabarda in the spring of 1846, hoping to establish a permanent link with the Circassians. The Kabardians failed to rise, and the Circassians farther west were not responsive to his appeal. At least two factors appear to have contributed to this lukewarm response: first, parochialism — since they were not under heavy pressure from the Russians, the Circassians felt little need to mobilise to join Shamil — and, secondly, lack of enthusiasm for *Muridism*, the austere militant Sufi religious faith that inspired Shamil's followers in Chechnia and Daghestan. Subsequently, Vorontsov was able to take strategy into his own hands, and deliberately eased pressure on the Circassians to be able to concentrate on Shamil.

Britain and the Circassians

There is much still to be learned about foreign interest in, and involvement with, the Circassian (and entire Caucasian) resistance struggle. Ottoman archives should eventually broaden our understanding.[49] What we already know permits tentative conclusions: both British and Turkish efforts to encourage and support resistance in the Caucasus were almost entirely outside the margin of conventional diplomacy. In late twentienth-century terminology they would be called covert action operations or low-intensity warfare. They were intended to keep hopes of resistance alive, harass a potential enemy, and preserve options for more vigorous future action if international developments made it desirable and circumstances favoured it. If Lord Palmerston had not in some degree approved of the activities of the Englishmen who went to Circassia in the 1830s, they would not have persisted for so long. Among Ottoman officialdom there were many who abetted what their countrymen were doing to help the Circassians. But neither Palmerston nor the Ottoman government was willing to risk the overt consequences of their sympathies or their ultimate hopes. Views which Palmerston expressed in a letter to Lord John Russell during the Crimean War are probably not far from those he held in the 1830s:

> [To expel the Russians from the Danubian principalities and leave them in full strength] would only be like turning a burglar out of your house, to break in again at a more fitting opportunity. The best and most effectual security for the future peace of Europe would be the severance from Russia of some of the frontier territories acquired by her in later times, Georgia, Circassia, the Crimea, Bessarabia, Poland and Finland. . . . She could still remain an enormous Power, but far less advantageously posted for aggression on her neighbours.[50]

Bell recounted how in 1837 a Circassian prince

> . . . . pointed out the sacred spot (as they justly esteem it) where Daud Bey [David Urquhart] had held (just three years ago [in 1834]) his meeting with the chieftains of this neighbourhood, and first inspired them with the idea of combining themselves with the other inhabitants of the mountain provinces as a nation, under one government and standard.[51]

The Englishmen who were active among the Circassians in the 1830s urged closer coordination with Shamil's movement, and tried to develop a sense of common purpose among all the North Caucasians resisting the imposition of Russian rule. Some even convinced themselves that this latter effort had succeeded, but Circassian particularism was difficult to overcome. These men and the Turks who played the same role (we know much less about them, for their memoirs, if written, have not come to light) were more successful in inspiring the Circassians to a stronger sense of national unity and cooperation. A great program of 'oathing' was carried out with good results. The leaders of each tribe gathered their men together and had all swear to keep faith with the cause of resistance to the Russians, to avoid cooperation with Russian officialdom or trade with Russian merchants, and to come to the assistance of neighbouring tribesmen under attack. Shirkers or collaborators were ostracised or driven out; some were killed. The populace were alerted to spies. Circassian groups along the Kuban who had accepted Russian protection were raided and their cattle carried off. Joint expeditions against the Russian forts on the coast were mounted and word of successes spread into the interior. Britons and Turks, working together in Constantinople, helped Circassians draw up a declaration of independence which served both to encourage resistance and to publicise their cause abroad. On arrival in Circassia, Edmund Spencer reported:

> I was shown . . . several copies of the *Portfolio* containing their declaration of independence, translated into Turkish, one of which every prince and noble carries about with him, whether he can read it or not, and regards with the same veneration as the Turks do the Qoran. Whenever they sally forth on a warlike excursion, the national banner is carried at the head of the party, and at every general assembly it is exhibited in some conspicuous place. . . . This circumstance, alone, has given an accession of moral strength, and a confidence in the justness of their cause, with the certainty of ultimately triumphing, that the Russians will find extremely difficult to overcome, and renders the final issue of the contest more than doubtful, even should the mountaineers be left to their own limited resources.[52]

Portfolio, a private journal alleged to enjoy the favour of the British Foreign Office, was the creation of a remarkable Scot, the first Briton to become a Circassian enthusiast, David Urquhart. Born in 1805, he had first gone to Greece to help that country consolidate its independence. He arrived in Turkey from Greece in 1831 and was employed by the British ambassador Stratford Canning as a confidential aide. He had been transformed into an ardent Turcophile by the time he returned to England, where in 1833 he published a book entitled *Turkey and its Resources*. This book so pleased King William IV that he sent it to all his ministers and urged his Foreign Minister, Palmerston, to make further use of the young activist author. A plan was developed to send him on an 18-month reconnaissance of the East, as far, perhaps, as Central Asia and Afghanistan. This scheme never materialised, for he found plenty to do on the Caucasian fringes of Europe. Urquhart arrived back in Turkey at the end of 1833. He visited Circassia in July and August 1834, ostensibly to investigate the possibilities for British trade, but his interests extended far beyond the commercial field. Meanwhile, Canning had been replaced as British ambassador at the Porte by John Ponsonby who, like his predecessor, seems to have taken a considerable liking to the energetic young Scot.[53]

The international situation was in ferment at this period with many of the same ingredients as in the 1980s, 150 years later. The Poles had revolted in 1830 against Russian oppression. The European powers were still distressed by their inability to do much for them and eager to find ways of easing both their consciences and the Poles' lot. Palmerston had a strong personal interest in Poland.[54] The Middle East, a region in which several of the European powers had interests, was unstable. The Ottoman empire, in the wake of the loss of Greece and defeat by Russia a few years before, was now beset by internal strains. The Ottoman Sultan's Egyptian vassal Mehmet Ali had invaded Anatolia itself, and the Russians had opportunistically exploited the crisis to send their forces to protect Constantinople. Britain was determined to preserve the integrity of Turkey against Russian encroachment and was also becoming concerned over Russian designs on Central Asia which could threaten India.

Students of the diplomatic interplay of the era and of the ideas that motivated the main actors — Palmerston in London and Ponsonby in Constantinople — assess their motives and intentions differently.[55] Further investigation of the subject could well focus on Urquhart himself. When, having been officially appointed secretary to the British ambassador, he arrived again in Constantinople early in 1836, he made little effort to behave as a conventional diplomat. While in England he had created a sensation by publishing in *Portfolio* a collection of Russian documents brought from Warsaw by Polish exiles who fled following the suppression of the rebellion of 1830. The documents exposed tsarist expansionist ambitions and lack of intention to abide by the normal rules of great-power diplomacy.

It is possible that Palmerston had personally encouraged Urquhart's enthusiasm for the Circassian cause. Whatever his confidential instructions may have been, Urquhart quickly became a focal point for the Circassian exile community in the Ottoman capital. His fortunes took a bad turn when a small British vessel, the *Vixen*, was captured late in 1836 by the Russians when it was trying to run their blockade of the Circassian coast with a cargo of salt. The diplomatic incident was embarrassing to all the powers involved. Urquhart had persuaded another Briton, James Stanislaus Bell, who had chartered the vessel as a merchant, to dispatch it contrary to the advice of Ponsonby, the ambassador — or so at least it was said. In the ensuing *contretemps*, Urquhart was expelled from the embassy and then recalled to London in 1837.

Bell, ostensibly a merchant but with interests that extended far beyond commerce, remained active in the Circassian cause until 1840. He stayed in Circassia for long periods during 1837-9, accompanying the Circassians on raids behind the Russian lines and publishing in 1840 the most comprehensive first-hand account of their resistance struggle available. At least four other Englishmen spent long periods in Circassia in the late 1830s. *The Times* correspondent J.A. Longworth stayed a year together with Bell and published an informative two-volume work describing his experiences, as did Edmund Spencer.

The most prominent Circassian with whom Urquhart and all these other Englishmen came into contact in Constantinople was a prince of distinguished lineage, Zann-oku Sefir Bey, who had gone to Turkey as representative of the Confederated Circassian Princes to organise support for Circassian resistance.[56] Much about his background and status remains unclear and should eventually be learned from Ottoman archives or memoirs. He appeared to have been promised, and given, support from the Ottoman government, and for a time he enjoyed the *de facto* rank of ambassador at the Sultan's court and participated in the diplomatic life of Constantinople. For example, he was rewarded by Sultan Mahmut for his skill in archery at a competition in the Okmeydanı. The Russian ambassador, who was present, provoked a diplomatic incident and declared that the Tsar had been insulted by such honour shown to a renegade. He threatened to leave his post if the Circassian 'ambassador' was not banished from Constantinople. The Ottoman authorities acquiesced and moved Sefir Bey to a small town near Edirne where, during the late 1830s, he received emissaries from Circassia and from time to time sent messages of encouragement to his countrymen.

The unoffical British representatives in Circassia regarded Zann-oku Sefir Bey as a potential leader around whom the highly individualistic Circassian princes and nobles could rally, but their effort to cast him in this role was abortive. How well he was actually suited to it is difficult to judge, for in the historial record he remains a somewhat hazy personality. After Urquhart's departure, the British embassy in Constantinople kept the Englishmen who were dealing directly with the Circassians at arm's length. This may have made Sefir Bey more sceptical than most of his countrymen about the likelihood that substantial British support — either diplomatic or military — would ever materialise.[57]

Men such as Spencer, Bell and Longworth became great enthusiasts of the Circassian cause but were more realistic than Urquhart in seeing the Circassians' shortcomings as well as their virtues:

> The congress was held on a green. . . . The first message was . . . that union and the appointment of some species of government were certainly most requisite, and that if the people could have accomplished these things themselves, there would have been no need of their seeking external aid; but that in the present position of affairs, it was beyond their power to attempt any change and that there was reason, moreover, to believe that any chief elected from among themselves would not obtain sufficient respect and authority. 'One must be sent us', they said, 'either from England or Turkey, and then everything he orders will be cheerfully performed'.[58]

These unoffical British representatives were eager to persuade both the British public and Her Majesty's Government that support for Circassian independence would be in the interest of both British commercial endeavour and British political ideals. They saw Russia's actions in the Caucasus as unworthy of a nation that aspired to be considered one of the civilised powers of Europe; they argued that there was a relationship between the entire Caucasian resistance struggle and the larger political scene in the East:

> The present unequal contest [is] carried on against the pastoral tribes of the Caucasus not so much for the value of the territory as [for its significance as] a *pied à terre* to prepare for future conquests. Can we, therefore, wonder at the suppressed murmur of universal hatred which is heard throughout the East at the very name of Russia? Every advantage gained by the Circassians over their oppressors is hailed by the Oriental, whether Mahometan, Christian or Jew, with the most enthusiastic delight. Of the sacrifices and generosity of the Turks in behalf of the poor mountaineers, I could relate many instances, alike honourable to them as individuals and as a nation; but, in so doing, I should only expose these noble-minded men to the attacks of Russian malignity.[59]

There was considerable oversimplification in this argumentation, but in retrospect it is clear that there was a core of validity to it that remains pertinent in the late twentieth century. The Circassians themselves were not ignorant of the larger strategic context in which they were waging their struggle. Bell, for example, reported:

Old Ali Achmet, the prince of Sutscha . . . said England and the
other powers of Europe had interfered on behalf of Greece, although
that country had not fought for its liberty a quarter of the time that
Circassia had.[60]

But the Englishmen and Circassian leaders both sensed the thinness of
the hopes on which the Circassians based their expectations for the
future. Longworth recorded a Circassian dignitary's farewell to him:

> So then you are leaving us, Bey, forever. You have been so long
> amongst us, that we had begun to consider you as one of ourselves;
> but, happily for you, you have a country to go to where you may live
> in peace and where there is yet no dread of the Moscovite. We, alas!
> have no other home to fly to; nor if we had, would we leave that of
> our forefathers, in which we were born, which Allah has given us,
> and for which it is our duty to die.[61]

Longworth consoled himself with thoughts of the impermanence of
tyranny as he departed:

> Tyranny can never long prevail, or freedom be forever suppressed in
> the Caucasus; the tide of conquest may for a while submerge its
> valleys, but the time will come when, in spite of all the forts that
> Russia can erect there, it must recede even from them.[62]

Soviet historians with their fondness for conspiracy theories of history
have tried to paint the Circassians' resistance struggle as the creation of
Urquhart and the Englishmen who followed him, backed by resentful
Turkish pashas unwilling to acknowledge the historical inevitability of
Russia's civilising mission in the Caucasus. The fact that Circassian
resolve did not decline after the last Englishman departed, but grew, is
the best evidence we have of the wrongness of Soviet argumentation.

The German, Moritz Wagner, was not impressed by Russian performance, but was sceptical that the Mountaineers could long delay the
Russian advance into Asia:

> A mountain war against an inflexible, fanatical and freedom-loving
> people is attended with difficulties which baffle the most learned com-
> binations of European tacticians, and the Russians with all their
> immense hordes, their inexhaustible resources, their firmness and
> bravery, are not much nearer the subjugation of the Caucasus than the
> Tatars, the Turks and the Persians were before them. We do not
> imply by this that the [Chechens], by means of Shamyl or his successors,

will be ever destined, or will ever be able to preserve Asia from a Russian invasion.[63]

In spite of its small scope and unofficial nature, British and Turkish support for the Circassians in the 1830s was valuable to them. It helped them overcome their internal divisions and deterred weak men, and exposed tribes, who were inclined to compromise with the Russians. Russian frustrations over their inability to subdue any of the Mountaineers led them to resort repeatedly to scorched-earth tactics — which backfired.[64]

Russian manpower was not inexhaustible, so Caucasian Christian auxiliaries were recruited and trained to fight against the Mountaineers. They seldom fought well and many deserted. Russia's Caucasian armies also had a large number of Poles who had been drafted to reduce the rebelliousness of their homeland; many of them cast in their lot with the Mountaineers. Spencer reported that 'hundreds of Poles' were fighting with the Circassians and had become so popular that some of their national songs had been translated into Circassian and were sung with enthusiasm.[65]

The vigorous resistance which the Circassians demonstrated against the Russians enabled them to survive with no significant territorial losses into the 1840s. When Tsar Nicholas I appointed Prince Vorontsov as Viceroy of the Caucasus in 1845, he hoped for a quick suppression of Caucasian resistance to Russian expansion. The wise and experienced Vorontsov knew that such hopes were unrealistic but he acceded to his sovereign's wishes and mounted a great offensive against Shamil. It was a disaster. Only through this heavy defeat was Vorontsov able to return to the Caucasian strategy which had the best chance of success: to ease the pressure against the Circassians while Russian forces proceeded systematically against Shamil in the east. Thus the Circassians were able to maintain a strong position into the 1850s when international circumstances suddenly combined to create what for a time appeared to be an unexpectedly positive situation both for them and for Shamil.

The Caucasus in the Crimean war

From the late 1820s onward it became a basic tenet of policy among all the European powers that Russia must not be permitted to finish off the Ottoman empire and annex its once-Byzantine heartlands, including Constantinople. The Russians had recognised this determination and acceded to it in the Treaty of Adrianople, but this treaty was in part negated by the Treaty of Hünkâr Iskelesi in 1833 — the outgrowth of Ottoman weakness and Russian assertiveness. The notion that it was Russia's manifest destiny to gain control of Constantinople remained an article of faith among a broad segment of tsarist statesmen and military leaders. Wagner reported the enthusiasm which greeted the appointment of Vorontsov in the mid-1840s, where many Russians in Tiflis felt that the Caucasus was too small a theatre for his talents:

> They were of the opinion that the proper post and suitable sphere for such a man would be that of governor-general of Turkey after the conquest of Constantinople. They affirmed that no person was so well adapted as Michael Worontsoff . . . to impose on the Orientals and to conciliate their affections, to reconcile the Turks to the Russian yoke, the contradictions between Christendom and Islam, and between the West and the East . . .[66]

But Wagner was sceptical of Russia's ability to realise her aims in the foreseeable future:

> But it is not probable that the undertaking of governing Constantinople will fall to the lot of any Russian now living. Russia has still to digest the conquests of Catherine and, until Poland and the Caucasus are more effectively Russianized, a Russian Emperor will scarcely stretch forth his hand in earnest for a booty whose maintenance might easily cost him more blood than all the previous conquests of Russia put together.[67]

By the early 1850s the Russians, however, were no longer disinclined to remain cautious about advancing toward Constantinople. 'We have on our hands a very sick man,' Nicholas I said of Turkey. He aspired to work out a deal with Britain whereby, in return for a free hand in Egypt, Russia would be given more freedom of movement in the Balkans and Asia Minor. Many other factors were involved in the mounting tensions which culminated in the Crimean war. These included complex church politics, Greek and Italian issues, trade, and various groups' claims and rights in Jerusalem — but the step which precipitated the war was the occupation of the principalities of Moldavia and Wallachia by Russia in 1853.

The British and French fleets moved eastward. There was a flurry of European diplomatic activity, culminating in a meeting between Nicholas I and the Austrian Emperor Franz Josef at Olmutz at the end of

September, but it was to no avail. On 8 October 1853 Turkey declared war as the British fleet was ordered to pass the Dardanelles. At the end of November 1853 the Russian Admiral Nakhimov surprised the Turkish fleet in the harbour of Sinop and destroyed it. This action sent a shock-wave through the British and French governments, and the attack was condemned in the British press as a massacre. All of Europe was preoccupied with these events. Rising tension was chronicled and commented upon at length in the *New York Tribune* by its 'most trustworthy source in London', Karl Marx,[68] who was a consistent champion of strong action to put 'Russia, true to the old Asiatic system of cheating and petty tricks',[69] in her place:

> The great end of Russia has been to crush the spirit of religious and political independence which has manifested itself of late among the Christian subjects of the Porte.[70]

Marx did not regard Russia's advance into the Balkans as in the ultimate interest of the people who lived there, especially the non-Slavs. In early January 1854 the British and French fleets passed the Bosphorus and entered the Black Sea. At the end of February Britain and France gave the Tsar an ultimatum: to evacuate Moldavia and Wallachia within two months or face war. It was made clear by Russian actions that the demand was to be ignored, and the two powers declared war on Russia at the end of March. Marx, critical of the long delay and suspicious of secret compromises, was relieved.

The causes of wars such as this are always difficult to sum up briefly — for there are many. It is difficult to disagree with the judgement of Hugh Seton-Watson when attempting to sort them all out:

> It can be argued that the Western Powers entered the war to protect [Louis] Napoleon's prestige, to protect Turkey, to fight tyranny, or to restore the balance of power. Of these four reasons, the last was the most important.[71]

The war was not called Crimean at the beginning, and the Crimea did not figure in the early actions; these were concentrated in the Balkans where the Russian army laid siege to the Turkish stronghold of Silistria, which the Turks defended with determination. The first hostile contact between Russia and the Western Powers came in the Baltic at the end of the spring of 1854. At the end of the summer the British attacked the Kola Peninsula, and on the other side of the globe an Anglo-French squadron unsuccessfully attacked Kamchatka in early September. It looked like a worldwide conflict.

The Turks had concentrated sizeable forces on their Caucasian frontier during the summer of 1853, but the Russians had to keep their forces in the Caucasus thin in order to concentrate on the Danube. Prince Vorontsov had only two regular divisions supported by ten Cossack regiments and irregular formations of Georgian and even some local Muslim militia to deploy in Circassia, Chechnia and Daghestan — about 23,000 men in all. Shamil moved quickly to take advantage of their weakness and mounted an attack into eastern Georgia in August 1853. It caused great alarm but was neutralised by a Russian counter-attack. This raid encouraged the Turks — and many Europeans, including Marx — to develop high hopes of the Mountaineers' effectiveness. The Turkish commander at Batum attacked along the coast and captured the Russian post at Fort St Nicholas. In subsequent fighting, the Russian garrison at Redutkale was withdrawn, and sea communications from the Crimea to Poti were broken. All this happened during the weeks before the annihilation of the Turkish fleet at Sinop.

When Britain and France entered the war, the Russians evacuated the rest of their coastal forts in Circassia. Shamil envisioned a general offensive coordinated with the Circassians, but his emissary Mohammed Emin had difficulty persuading the Circassians to cooperate systematically. Sefir Bey took a mission from Constantinople to Sukhumi and then to Tuapse to try to mobilise Circassian efforts. The Shapsugs in the south were equivocal, although the northern tribes in the vicinity of Anapa were eager for action. The Abkhaz, who had both Christian and Russian princes, were divided, with the Christians favouring the Russians. As a price for cooperation the Abkhaz Muslim Prince Iskender asked for assurance that he would be recognised as independent and allocated additional Georgian territory. This territory happened to belong to the Dadianis, a Georgian noble family that had kept its distance from the Russians. The Turks did not want to alienate them. While parleying proceeded, the Turks developed plans for a general Caucasian offensive which would include Allied landings on the coast and a three-pronged offensive from Batum, Ardahan and Kars. They argued that the Muslim population along the entire coast and in western Georgia could be depended upon to rise. The ultimate objective would be to occupy Tiflis. Their British and French allies were lukewarm to such thinking. They were more concerned about destroying Russian naval power in the

Black Sea. Karl Marx had a more comprehensive view of the potential- ities of the situation and favoured Turkish plans. He wrote in November 1854:

> The chances for the Turks are, indeed, far more encouraging in Asia than in Europe. In Asia they have but one important post to guard: Batum; and an advance, be it from Batum or from Erzurum, towards the Caucasus, opens to them, in case of success, a direct communi- cation with their allies, the mountaineers, and may at once cut off the communication, at least by land, of the Russian army south of the Caucasus with Russia; a result which may lead to the entire destruc- tion of that army.[72]

There is no way of knowing whether the Turks' expectation that a general Allied offensive against the Caucasus, backed by the substantial naval power the British and French had at their disposal, would have generated full cooperation among the Circassians, Abkhaz and Muslims in Georgia. Shamil's cooperation was assured. However, this was a period when anti-Russian sentiment in Georgia as a whole had receded to insignificance, and Shamil's raid aroused Georgian fears. Neverthe- less, Russian border defences were in poor condition. The old Turkish fortress at Akhaltsikhe and others in this region were as they had been in 1829; no improvements had been made to them. New fortifications in the Alexandropol (Gumru/Leninakan) region had been planned but not completed. During the winter of 1853–4 the Turks did not capitalise on their initial advances, although they had brought Akhaltsikhe under siege in mid-November.

Local victories and the destruction of the Turkish fleet at Sinop notwithstanding, Prince Vorontsov was depressed by the presence of the British and French fleets in the Black Sea. He feared a surge of activity among the Circassians as well as in Daghestan and even among the pacified Muslim population of Azerbaijan. Although the threat of Turkish invasion aroused both Georgians and Armenians to rally to the support of Russia, Vorontsov felt the need for substantial troop reinforcements. Few could be sent. In March 1854, even before the British and French had formally entered the war, he asked for sick leave and left Tiflis for Moscow, never to return.

General Read,[73] who replaced him, made a highly pessimistic initial assessment of the situation and recommended to Nicholas I that all the eastern Muslim territories be evacuated and that Russia also reconcile herself, if further pressed by the Turks, to sacrificing all the Georgian

territories and withdrawing north of the main Caucasus chain. The
Tsar, appalled, replaced Read by Prince Bariatinskii — who was to
accept the surrender of Shamil five years later. Nicholas I's stubborn
refusal to give ground in the Caucasus was in the end to prove correct,
but he did not live long enough to have the satisfaction of realising it.
The year 1854 turned out to be a bad one for the Turks. They were
forced back to Batum, and their hopes for Allied landings on the
Circassian coast were in vain. At the eastern end of the Turco-Russian
frontier, Russian forces advancing from Erevan captured Bayazit at the
end of July. In early August, General Bebutov defeated the main Turkish
army at Kurudere, between Alexandropol and Kars. Turkish casualties
and prisoners totalled 10,000, against losses of 3,000 on the Russian side.
This Russian victory influenced Persia, which up till then had been on
the alert for an opportunity to regain lost ground in the Caucasus, to
remain neutral. It also confirmed a decision which had been made by the
British and French governments at the end of June to make a direct
attack on Russian territory in the Crimea and destroy the basis of
Russian naval power in the Black Sea.

Thus the war became Crimean on 14 September 1854 when an Allied
(British-French-Turkish) army began landing near Eupatoria. With this
landing the possibility that the North Caucasian freedom struggle might
receive substantial Allied help — turning Vorontsov's fears and General
Read's defeatist vision into reality — became remote.

During the very time when the decision to attack in the Crimea was
being reached between London and Paris, Shamil sent a delegation to
confer with British and French commanders at Varna. They were more
interested in Circassia, where Shamil's influence was tenuous, than in
the areas he controlled in Daghestan and Chechnia. The discussions were
inconclusive. Allied agents who visited Circassia did not share the opti-
mism of some of their Turkish colleagues about the situation there.
Allied officers attached to the Turkish armies on the Caucasian front
were sceptical of both the Mountaineers' potential and, in the light of
continuing setbacks, of Turkish offensive capabilities in the Caucasus.[74]
Shamil decided to lie low and restrain his forces from major offensive
action against Russian positions.

Like Shamil, Karl Marx in London was depressed at the lack of audacity and strategic concept on the part of the Allies, and their lack of will
to engage Russia decisively in the face of the 'scornful boldness and self-
reliance of the Czarian policy'.[75] There were many reasons, including a heightened degree of public awareness and debate over tactics and

strategy by journalists and politicians. A case has been made for characterising many nineteenth-century wars as 'the first modern war', but for media attention and emotional public preoccupation stemming from it, a good claim can be made for the Crimean war:

> War correspondents, observers and even wives, were able to wander freely around the battlefield and record the astonishing fact that when wars came men died, were killed, were wounded and suffered. These points were more easily seen than the gains of a campaign and therefore were faithfully and dramatically recorded. It would seem from [journalists'] accounts that the Crimean War was the most mismanaged, brutal and futile campaign that has ever been fought.[76]

But as we have seen in recent decades, journalistic perceptions can skew and obscure reality. Public preoccupation with the melodrama of a conflict can produce pressures which divert statesmen from devising strategy and force military commanders to give priority to matters that distort the conduct of the war.

Seen from St Petersburg and Moscow, the Allied invasion of the Crimea — Russian territory that had not been contested for almost a century — and the fact that Russian forces had difficulty defending themselves there, while they were already fighting hard in the Balkans and in the Caucasus, was a disaster and humiliation of major proportions. During the winter of 1854–5 the Russians reluctantly agreed to negotiations, and a conference in Vienna was agreed to. Meanwhile, Nicholas I died:

> All that he had thought he had achieved in 30 years seemed on the point of collapse. It has been suggested that he committed suicide. Perhaps it would be more correct to say that he had lost the will to live.[77]

The Vienna conference dragged on for nearly three months. The Allies wanted Russian naval power in the Black Sea eliminated, but as long as Sevastopol held out, this was a condition the Russians could not accept. There had been some Caucasian action in the spring of 1855, when Allied naval forces had assisted a Circassian prince coming from Constantinople to capture Novorossiisk and gain control of part of the Taman' peninsula, but this venture was more part of the Crimean campaign than of the Caucasian. There was hard, bloody fighting in the Crimea all summer but no inclination on the part of the British and French seriously to consider offensive action against the Caucasus itself.

Sevastopol finally fell on 10 September; the final assault had cost the Allies nearly 11,000 casualties against almost 13,000 on the Russian side. Meanwhile, the Russians found themselves threatened with serious defeat in the Caucasus as well. Ömer Pasha, who commanded the Turkish contingent in the Crimea, had revived the plan for offensive action in the western Caucasus. It envisaged an undertaking which would have confronted the Russians with

. . . an advance on Kutaisi, and subsequently on Tiflis which might threaten a union with the Murids descending into Kakheti [eastern Georgia] and the isolation of all Russian forces on the Turkish frontier.[78]

The British would at first hear nothing of this scheme, but the Turks were eager to seize the initiative in the east and found new troops to send to the Caucasian front. Ömer Pasha was recalled to Constantinople in mid-July to begin implementing his plan. The British withdrew their objections to it in August 1855.

Muraviev, the Russian commander on the Caucasian front, had made good progress in the border region during the summer of 1855; he had laid siege to Kars and threatened Erzurum, but hesitated to press his advantage out of fear of Turkish counterattack from the direction of Trabzon with Allied naval support behind it. In late September he learned that Ömer Pasha had arrived not in Trabzon but in Batum, with 8,000 reinforcements, and had pushed on to Sukhumi and Redutkale where further landings were expected. The Turkish plan was now clear. News of the fall of Sevastopol arrived and heartened the defenders of Kars. Muraviev decided to storm Kars. The attack failed, with Russian losses of 8,000 against Turkish casualties of 1,500, but the Russians were still able to maintain the siege.

By the end of September the Turks had concentrated 35,000 troops on the Caucasian coast, but they were far from meeting the requirements for full execution of Ömer Pasha's plan. The plan also depended heavily on help from the Abkhaz and Circassians of the coastal region. With the approach of winter, their leaders preferred to wait. So did Shamil, with whom coordination was poor. Nevertheless, when Ömer Pasha received news of the repulse of the Russians at Kars in early October, he decided to begin the push inland along the valley of the Ingur. But like Vorontsov in Chechnia in 1845, he found himself entangled in forests with few roads and frequent stream crossings. He covered only 50 miles in twenty days even though there was little organised Russian resistance.

In fact, the Russians were poorly organised for defence, and the Turks won an easy victory at the first real engagement near Zugdidi. Ömer Pasha was slow to follow up on this good fortune, and the region was soon deluged with heavy rains, as always happens at this time of year along the Black Sea. Even with the Turks marooned in mud, the Russian commander Prince Bagration panicked, prepared further withdrawals, and burned large quantities of stores.

Muraviev, whose perseverance had led to the capitulation of Kars on 6 November 1855, dismissed Bagration. Although their offensive had been remarkably successful up to this point, the Turks were unnerved by the fact that the Mountaineers had not exerted themselves. Ömer Pasha established his headquarters in Zugdidi, but returned to Constantinople during the winter. His troops remained until spring and were then evacuated to Batum.[79]

Theoretically the Caucasian offensive could have been resumed, and the Turks could have gone on the offensive against Muraviev's forces who were planning a march on Erzurum. It might even have been possible in the summer of 1856 to forge effective links with the Mountaineers, certainly in Circassia and probably with Shamil, whose forces retained some offensive capability which might well have been augmented. The Turks had transferred 30,000 men from the Crimea after Sevastopol, but a British expeditionary force would also have been desirable. With the British public regarding the war as won with the fall of Sevastopol, this would have been an extremely controversial action, probably insupportable politically. The issue never had to be faced, for peace negotiations intervened. The new tsar, Alexander II, saw this as the best course after attempting to deal separately with the Austrians over arrangements in the Balkans. Muraviev's victory at Kars, where 24,000 prisoners had been taken, including British officers, saved Russian pride, but it also had a more practical effect. It commanded respect from the Western Allies, who had no particular interest in advancing Turkey's frontiers in the Caucasus. Thus Russia's bargaining position was improved.

The Treaty of Paris was worked out in a conference in that city which extended from late February until mid-April 1856. Russia accepted terms which severely curtailed the ambitions with which she had moved into the Romanian principalities in 1853 and gone on the offensive against Turkey in the Caucasus, but otherwise she did not pay a heavy price for defeat. The Crimea, scene of so much dramatic fighting on both sides, was returned intact. The Black Sea was demilitarised, thus excluding Russia from a military presence in the Mediterranean, this was an important gain for Turkey, especially since in the Caucasus the frontier was reconfirmed where it had been since the Treaty of Adrianople. Russian and Turkish gains and losses in nearly three years of fighting there had simply balanced each other out.

The Crimean war, in the course of being fought, became a limited war. In the heady period when Britain and France first joined in Turkey's war against Russia, they had attacked in the Baltic, in the Arctic, and in distant Kamchatka. It was a general war. None of this early initiative had anything to do with the Russo-Turkish rivalry which had originally set the war going. The first phase of the conflict did not last long. By the time the offensive against the Crimea had been decided upon, the war had been transformed from a worldwide conflict to one which was narrower than the basic Russo-Turkish war itself. The primary British-French objective became simply the elimination of Russian naval power in the Black Sea.

The fact that in the treaty which concluded the war the situation on the Caucasian front was returned to the *status quo ante bellum* underscores the absence of agreed objectives in the Caucasus throughout the conflict. From the viewpoint of grand strategy, actions in the Caucasus were undertaken to affect the course of the war elsewhere — at least where Britain and France were concerned. They opposed Ömer Pasha's offensive along the Caucasian coast in 1855. Turkish attitudes were different, but never coherently formulated and not pressed consistently upon Turkey's European allies. In the end the defeat of Russian naval power seemed as important to the Turks as any other objective.

It can be argued that the Caucasian peoples were as much entitled as those of the Balkans to having the European powers ensure arrangements whereby they could achieve their national aspirations. But in European eyes the Caucasus was part of the Middle East, utterly foreign and barely civilised; it may have been exotic and exciting but had little direct relationship to the affairs of Europe. Many Europeans may have had the same feelings about the Balkans, but this region was too close to home to be ignored, and too many European powers had a direct interest in it. Russia could not be allowed a free hand in the Balkans; Austria would not tolerate it. There was no counterbalancing power in the Caucasus comparable to Austria.

Had the Ottoman empire possessed more internal dynamism and more far-sighted leadership, it could perhaps have prevailed upon the British to support a Caucasian strategy either for direct reassertion of territorial claims or for some degree of recognition of the local peoples' status. Such ambitions were articulated in Turkey, but public opinion did not impact on foreign policy the way it did in Britain and elsewhere in Europe. There were other intrinsic problems too.

The Georgians were the keystone of the Russian position in the Caucasus. If they had been determinedly anti-Russian, Vorontsov's and Read's pessimism would have been proved justified, for they were probably also the largest numerically of the Caucasian peoples. Armenian attitudes toward the Russians were similar to those of the Georgians (in spite of rivalry between the two peoples), but the Armenians were in a much weaker position and therefore more dependent on Russia, even though there were still more Armenians living in the Ottoman empire than in the Russian empire. Even among Ottoman Armenians, however, there was a growing tendency of orientation toward Russia. Had the North Caucasian Mountaineers possessed a direct territorial link with Turkey, their fate could have been very different. Had Persia been more assertive, the political calculus in the Caucasus might also have been altered. But Persia was weak although it still had substantial residual influence in Azerbaijan which caused the Russians apprehension.

With his characteristic strategic long view Sir Henry Rawlinson, British official and oreintalist, had written in 1849 of the significance of the Caucasian independence struggle for containing Russia and preserving the balance of power in Europe:

> . . . Moderate support of Shamil might still, perhaps, save the Danubian principalities, and as long as his banner floats from the summits of the Caucasus, so long is Persia safe from the hostile invasion of a Russian army.[80]

Looking back in 1873 on what he had written a quarter-century earlier, Rawlinson concluded that the failure of the British to take advantage of the opportunity the Crimean war offered to check and/or reverse Russia's absorption of the Caucasus had even more far-reaching consequences than he had anticipated. The first impact was not on Persia, as he expected, but on Central Asia:

> . . . It was not until after the submission of Shamil in 1859 and the consequent pacification of Circassia, that Russia began to push her way up the Jaxartes [Syr-Darya]. [My] forecast only failed in anticipating that the first development of the power of Russia, when freed from the Caucasian entanglement, would take place in the

direction of Persia; whereas in reality . . . the Persian question is
deferred to a later period.[81]

Defeat

The recurrent Russian and, until recently at least, even more frequent
Soviet allegation that the freedom struggle of the Caucasian Mountaineers owed its intensity to propaganda, arms shipments and money supplied by Turkish and British agents is negated by the events that followed the Treaty of Paris.[82] Neither Shamil's *murids* nor the Circassians
and Abkhaz laid down their arms. Shamil and the Circassians had never
achieved effective coordination of their operations, although they had
almost never operated at cross-purposes. Failures and frustrations caused
strain on both sides. Shamil had lost popularity among some of the
peoples of Chechnia and Daghestan because of the severity of his religious prescriptions. After a quarter of a century of unbroken warfare,
there had been heavy loss of manpower. The total population had
undoubtedly declined in some regions; agriculture, trade and handicrafts
had been disrupted. But Shamil could not have continued fighting by
himself. The forces which the Russians had to bring to bear to defeat
him are the best measure of the extent and intensity of the support which
he still enjoyed. And the fact that it required another five years after
Shamil's surrender for the Circassians to be subdued demonstrates how
deep-rooted was their antipathy to Russian domination.

Prince Vorontsov would in all likelihood have endorsed the plan
Prince Bariatinskii developed to subdue Shamil. Only half the Russian
military forces in the Caucasus could be committed to the struggle
against the Mountaineers during the Crimean war. With the war over,
all available soldiery could be brought against the Mountaineers, and
reinforcements could be brought in from other parts of the country.
Three armies were assigned to the task. They moved systematically to
surround *murid* strongholds. General Evdokimov, for example, spent
two years bringing Chechnia to heel. During the winter of 1858-9 he
advanced through the thickly forested region of Ichkeria to the borders
of Daghestan. Shamil took refuge in the *aul* of Gunib, deep in the heart
of Daghestan, above the gorge of the Kara Koisu — a formidable position that brings to mind Magdala, where the Emperor Tewodros made
his final stand against the British incursion into Ethiopia a decade later.
To cut Gunib off from the rest of the Caucasus, Bariatinskii deployed
40,000 men and forty-eight guns around it. He moved forward slowly

and deliberately, in keeping with the classical Russian military tradition. On Tsar Alexander II's birthday, 25 August 1859, he stormed Gunib. Shamil surrendered personally to Bariatinskii at four o'clock in the afternoon.[83]

Although word of it must have spread rapidly, Shamil's surrender had only limited effect on the will to resist of the majority of the Circassians. Several thousand northern Circassians, it is true, assembled their families and movable possessions and sailed for Turkey in 1860. But the largest Circassian tribes — the Abadzekhs, Shapsugs and the related Ubykhs — formed an alliance and convened a national assembly at Sochi. They appealed to Turkey and Britain for support. None came, not even promises. Tsar Alexander II came to Ekaterinodar (now Krasnodar) in 1861 and met Circassian leaders as part of an effort to work out a truce. The Abadzekhs agreed to be evacuated to a territory offered to them south of the Kuban. Their descendants continue to live there today in the Adyghe Autonomous Region of the RSFSR.[84] The other Circassians, by far the majority, saw no basis for compromise.

So the fighting continued, but Circassian resources were limited. Russian military operations in Circassia were resumed in earnest in 1862. Bariatinskii's tactics were the same as those applied against Shamil. It took two years to complete formal 'pacification'; a Russian column finally forced its way through to Tuapse in early 1864. In the following months, the great majority of Circassians submitted to, or fell under, Russian control, but many did not surrender officially, and some groups in inaccessible areas continued resistance until the end of the decade. Passive resistance never ceased.

Aftermath

The contrast between the respect shown to Shamil by the tsarist regime during the final years of his life and the treatment of those who were captured or surrendered after armed — or unarmed — opposition to the Soviet reincarnation of the Russian empire is a striking measure of the degree of retrogression in observance of humanitarian principles that occurred under twentieth-century 'scientific socialism'. Shamil was subjected to no physical discomfort, treated honourably, taken to Moscow and St Petersburg, and received by many prominent figures. He was a prominent guest at the wedding of the Tsar's son in 1866. He was never permitted to return to the Caucasus, but spent a decade in Kaluga enjoying the comforts of a Russian country gentleman. He was given

General Aleksei Petrovich Ermolov

Imam Shamil

permission to go to Mecca in 1870, embarking at the old Circassian fortress of Anapa and stopping in Constantinople to be received by Sultan Abdulaziz *en route*. He died in Medina in February 1871. The Mountaineers whom Shamil had had to abandon were less fortunate, except for the few who became open collaborators of the Russians. Local situations varied, but mostly the populations of the central and eastern Caucasus were simply left to fend for themselves. They were not subjected to calculated scorched-earth treatment designed to force them to emigrate. Russian settlers did not rush in to claim their lands. By continuing resistance, the Circassians brought Russian wrath upon themselves, but there was more to it than vengeance. The fertile Black Sea valleys were more attractive than the high mountains of Daghestan. The Russians were eager to repopulate them with settlers they considered reliable. They did nothing to discourage the mass emigration of Circassians to the Ottoman empire, and there is plentiful evidence that Russian military forces who occupied the Circassian lands pursued a policy calculated to force as many of the Circassians as possible to emigrate. The reports of British diplomats during this period strongly indicate Russian vindictiveness and even atrocities. A few examples:

The Russians in order to compel the natives of Netauchee and Shapsik to abandon the country and emigrate to Turkey have lately destroyed the whole of that part of Circassia, burning down the houses and crops of the people and thus obliging them to fly.[85]

A Russian detachment having captured the village of Toobah on the Soobashi river inhabited by about a hundred Abadzekh. . . . After they had surrendered . . . they were all massacred by the Russian troops. Among the victims were two women in an advanced state of pregnancy and five children. The detachment in question belongs to Count Evdokimoff's army and is said to have advanced from the Pshesh valley. As the Russian[s] gain ground on the coast, the natives are not allowed to remain there on any terms, but are compelled either to transfer themselves to the plains of the Kouban or emigrate to Turkey.[86]

The Ubikh and Fighett tribes are . . . fast embarking for Trebizond. In fact, after their land had been laid waste by fire and sword, emigration to Turkey is the only alternative allowed to these mountaineers who refuse to transfer themselves to the Kouban steppes and contribute periodically to the militia.[87]

Most of [the Abkhaz] have been plundered of everything by the Russians before embarking and have barely been allowed to bring with them the strict necessities of life for a short period. In many villages, and especially in the district of Zibeldah, their houses have been wantonly burnt by the Cossack soldiery and their cattle and other property forcibly taken away or sold under compulsion to Russian traders at a nominal price.[88]

The Russian government has now acquired the territory of that brave and devoted race who have only prized one thing more than country — liberty, or at least the life that is free from the domination of a foreign foe. They are flying the shores immortalized by their defense and seeking an asylum in a neighboring empire. In short, Circassia is gone; what yet remains is to save the Circassians. The Ottoman Government is willing to afford the refuge they desire. But its means for doing this are . . . scanty; what it has already done — and this, comparatively speaking, is little — has been at a cost of 200,000 pounds.[89]

How many people left? The subject has only recently attracted the consistent attention of historians who have begun combing through Turkish archives, British Foreign Office files, contemporary reports of eye-witnesses and, insofar as they are available, Russian materials on the great exodus. The Ottoman government set up a migration commission as early as 1860, but it was prepared to deal only with the 40–50,000 refugees expected at that time.[90] It was eventually almost overwhelmed by the influx. During the winter and spring of 1864 alone, 257,068 individuals were listed as departing for Turkey from seven Black Sea ports under Russian control. Many also reached Turkey overland. Some sources estimate that Circassian migration had already reached a million by the end of 1866. Emigration, which included other Caucasians in smaller numbers, continued on a large scale to the end of the 1860s and did not cease during the following decade. There was a further upsurge during and after the Russo-Turkish war of 1876–8.[91]

Mortality among Caucasians *en route* was high, and large numbers died of illness after reaching Ottoman territory. Excerpts from another British diplomatic dispatch provides some impression of the appalling results of this vast mass movement of defeated people to new homes:

According to the report of the [Ottoman governmental] Commission, the number of Circassian emigrants which sailed from Samsoon [in one particular group] was 2,718. Died between Samsoon and Constantinople . . . 202. Transshipped at Constantinople . . . 528. Died between Constantinople and Cyprus . . . 637. Landed at Cyprus . . . 1,351. The suffering and mortality of the Circassian emigrants continue unabated. A report received by the Board of Health from the quarantine physicians of the Dardanelles . . . announces the arrival of the tug *Maria Despina* in tow of two other vessels laden with 1,130 Circassians from Samsoon. The original number shipped was 1,800 and during the voyage, which lasted 35 days, 670 died from disease, exhaustion, hunger and, above all, from horrible crowding.[92]

The most comprehensive study of the Caucasian exodus to date sums up a review of a wide range of data on numbers emigrating with the following observations:

There is much debate over the numbers of Circassians and others evicted from their lands in the Caucasus. No accurate counts were made . . . so one cannot say how many set out. Upon analysis of various estimates, it seems reasonable to state that approximately 1.2 million Caucasians emigrated from Russian-conquered territories. 800,000 of them lived to settle in the Ottoman dominions.

The Russian[s] . . . saw to it that the conquered Muslim lands were settled with what they considered to be more reliable populations. Just as Russians and Ukrainians had become the main population of the Crimea, Russians and Cossacks took most of the old Circassian lands. Armenians, Georgians and Russians were settled in the coastal lands of the Abkhaz. The first . . . reliable Russian census, taken in 1897, recorded the transformation of the Muslim lands of the Caucasus. The lands of the Circassians and the Abkhaz, once overwhelmingly Muslim, had become overwhelmingly Christian.[93]

Circassians who came to the Ottoman empire did not forget their homeland or lose their resentment at the manner in which they had been expelled from it by the Russians. Some among them were always ready to attempt to return. In early 1877 war broke out again between the Ottoman and Russian empires and, although the attention of Europe was focussed on the fighting in the Balkans, the Caucasian front was equally important to the Turks. They found thousands of Circassians, Abkhaz and other Caucasians ready to take up arms. Muslim Georgians, known as Ajars, inhabiting the coastal region north of Batumi (which up till this time had remained in Turkish possession), revolted and joined the Turks in April 1877. It took major Russian exertions to gain control of the area. The Turks launched an amphibious operation farther north. The force included perhaps 3,000 Circassians and Abkhaz. They carried 30,000 rifles to arm compatriots still living in the Caucasus. When the Turkish fleet bombarded Sukhumi, the Russian commander withdrew his forces, and the Turks occupied the town and surrounding region. The Russians' situation continued to deteriorate through June as the Turks landed more Caucasian exiles farther north along the coast.

Fear of risings in the eastern Caucasus made Russian commanders reluctant to move immediately against the Turkish/Caucasian exile incursions. Revolt did break out in both Chechnia and Daghestan, where it was not suppressed until October 1877. There was much indecisive fighting in Abkhazia during the summer, and more Turkish landings were made, but by August Russian counter-attacks forced the Turks to withdraw from Sukhumi. The Russians, meanwhile, mounted massive flanking operations against the Turks, crossing the border, capturing Ardahan, and laying siege to Kars. Kars fell in November and the Turks pulled their forces back to Erzurum, but the Russians, in spite of repeated attempts, had been unable to capture Batumi. Once again the Caucasian situation was adversely affected by developments in Europe, where Turkish forces suffered serious defeats. Eager to limit Russian gains in the Balkans, the European Powers pressed the Turks to cede Kars, Ardahan and Batumi in the Treaty of Berlin signed in the summer of 1878.[94]

So, like Ömer Pasha's invasion of the Circassian coast during the final year of the Crimean War, Turkish operations in the eastern Black Sea in 1877 had little bearing on the course of the war and, despite the hopes of all involved in them, did not advance the interests of the Muslims of the Caucasus. Nevertheless, traditions of resistance and revolt against the Russian colossus remained a live memory among the North Caucasians. Each of three succeeding generations took advantage of Russian defeats to attempt to regain freedom. The ferment generated by the Japanese defeat of Russia at the beginning of the twentieth century led to the 1905 Revolution with widespread reverberations in the Caucasus. The upheaval of the 1917 Revolution and Civil War brought new upsurges of resistance which extended into the period of collectivisation and the Great Purges. Many North Caucasians attempted to free themselves of the Soviet Russian yoke again during the German invasion of 1941–3. Stalin's subsequent deportation of several of these peoples *en masse* in 1944 was the most brutal action the Russians had taken against Caucasians in more than a century and a half of effort to subdue them.[95]

NOTES

1. See Paul B. Henze, 'Marx on Muslims and Russians', *Central Asian Survey*, VI/4, 1987, pp. 33–45.
2. Paul B. Henze, 'Fire and Sword in the Caucasus: The 19th Century Resistance of the North Caucasian Mountaineers', *Central Asian Survey* II/1 (1983), pp. 5–44.
3. See, e.g., Dmitri I. Trunov, *V gorakh Dagestana*, Moscow: Molodaya Gvardia, 1958, pp. 126–36.
4. See Paul B. Henze, 'The Shamil Problem' in Walter Z. Laqueur, *The Middle East in Transition*, London/New York, 1958, pp. 415–43.
5. W.E.D. Allen, *Problems of Turkish Power in the 16th Century*, London: Central Asian Research Centre, 1963.
6. Alexandre Bennigsen and Chantal Lemercier-Quelequejay, 'La Poussée vers les Mers Chaudes et la Barrière du Caucase' in 'Raiyyet Rusumu: Essays presented to Halil Inalcık . . .', *Journal of Turkish Studies*, vol. 10, 1986, pp. 15–46.
7. 'There was an attitude toward expansion that affected the overall climate in which . . . decisions were made. . . . This had nothing to do with some legendary Russian drive to obtain warm-water ports or some grand design for the conquest of Asia. Instead, Russia, after a century of westernization, developed a colonialist outlook that was consciously imitative of Western overseas expansion. Exotic alien lands made attractive targets for colonization because it was believed that they could make their colonial master rich, and because the colonial master could in return benefit the subject peoples by introducing them to civilization. Furthermore, all of this would prove that Russia, too, was as great and civilized an empire as those of western Europe.' Muriel Atkin, *Russia and Iran, 1780–1828*, Minneapolis: University of Minnesota Press, 1980, p. 163.
8. E.g. by the poet Lermontov who predicted to the Circassians that they would one day say proudly: 'We may truly be slaves, but at least we are slaves of the Ruler of the Universe!' — cited by Walter Kolarz, *Russia and her Colonies*, London: George Philip, 1952, p. 181.
9. Muriel Atkin's detailed study of these developments concludes: 'The Iranian government was left defeated, humiliated and less capable than ever to deal with the great challenges of a rapidly changing world. A long process of decline had begun, and its aftermath is with us still.' *Op. cit.*, p. 164. Russian ambitions to expand further into Persia did not, of course, end here.
10. For an example of the scope and tenacity of Circassian traditions see Shauket Mufti Habjoka, *Heroes and Emperors in Circassian History*, Beirut: Librairie du Liban, 1972. Although this book makes little distinction between myth and history and is chaotic in its organisation, it is significant for the evidence it provides of the tenacity of traditions and national spirit prevailing, after five and more generations of exile, among Circassians living in the Arab Middle East.
11. See W.E.D. Allen, *Russian Embassies to the Georgian Kings (1589–1605)*, Cambridge: Hakluyt Society, 1970, vol. I, p. 24 (hereafter cited as *Embassies*).
12. *Ellis's Memoir of a map of the countries comprehended between the Black Sea and the Caspian; with an account of the Caucasian nations and Vocabularies of their languages*, London: J.Edwards, 1788.
13. Allen, *Embassies*, vol. I, pp. 270–85.

14. For background on the Crimea see Alan W. Fisher, *The Russian Annexation of the Crimea, 1771–1783*, Cambridge University Press, 1970 and Fisher, *The Crimean Tatars*, Stanford, CA: Hoover Institution, 1978.
15. James Stanislaus Bell, *Journal of a Residence in Circassia*, London: Edward Moxon, 1840, vol. I, p. 178. See also Friedrich Bodenstedt, *Die Völker des Kaukasus und ihre Freiheitskaempfe gegen die Russen*, Frankfurt/Main: Verlag Lizius, 1849, p. 125.
16. J.S. Bell, *Journal*, vol. II, p. 24.
17. See the introduction to Allen, *Embassies*, vol. I, pp. 23–9.
18. J.S. Bell, *Journal*, vol. II, p. 219.
19. Moritz Wagner, *Travels in Persia, Georgia and Koordistan with Sketches of the Cossacks and the Caucasus*, London: Hurst and Blackett, 1856, vol. I, pp. 259–60.
20. The subject is treated in the introductory chapters of a classic Circassian historical work originally composed in the 1840s: Shora Bekmurza Nogmov, *Istoriya adygeiskovo naroda*, reissued by the Kabardino-Balkarskoe Knizhnoe Izdatel'stvo, Nal'chik, 1958.
21. Dr L. Loewe, *Dictionary of the Circassian Language*, London: George Bell, 1854.
22. J.S. Bell, *Journal*, vol. I, p. 87.
23. 'Commentary 12, The Princely Families of Kabarda' in Allen, *Embassies*, vol. I, pp. 270–85.
24. Allen, *Embassies*, vol. I, pp. 282–3.
25. N.A. Smirnov, *Politika Rossii na Kavkaze v XVI–XIX vv.*, Moscow: Sotsekgiz, 1958; E.N. Kusheva, *Narody Severnogo Kavkaza i ikh sviazi s Rossiei*, Moscow: Akademia Nauk, 1963.
26. W.E.D. Allen, *A History of the Georgian People from the Beginning down to the Russian Conquest in the 19th Century*, London: Routledge & Kegan Paul, 1932, p. 214.
27. Cemal Gökçe, *Kafkasya ve Osmanlı İmparatorluğu'nun Kafkasya Siyaseti*, Istanbul: Şamil Vakfı, 1979.
28. Aytek Kundukh, *Kafkasya Muridizmi (Gazavat Tarihi)*, Istanbul: Gözde Kitapları Yayınevi, 1987.
29. E.g. by W.E.D. Allen and Paul Muratoff in *Caucasian Battlefields*, Cambridge University Press: 1953, p. 47 Alexandre Bennigsen, on the basis of both Russian and Ottoman archival sources, put this movement in historical perspective in an important article, 'Un mouvement populaire au Caucase au XVIIIe siècle' in *Cahiers du monde russe et soviétique*, V/2 (1964), pp. 159–97.
30. Tarık Cemal Kutlu, whose recent study *Kuzey Kafkasya'nın İlk Milli Mucahidi ve Önderi, İmam Mansur*, Istanbul: Bayrak Yayimcilik, 1987, is based on careful review of all available primary and secondary sources, concludes that his army probably numbered 6,000.
31. Gökçe, *op. cit.*, pp. 247–53; Kutlu, *op. cit.*, pp. 42–5.
32. Edmund Spencer, *Travels in Circassia, Krim-Tartary, etc.*, London: Henry Colburn, 1839, vol. II, p. 290. For an appraisal of his influence in the 1840s and another example of a ballad celebrating Sheikh Mansur see Bodenstedt, *Die Völker . . .*, pp. 199–200.
33. Spencer, *Travels*, vol. II, p. 294.
34. For a measure of the extent to which Sheikh Mansur's memory remains alive among Circassians, though with a great many distortions and accretions, see Shauket Mufti Habjoka, *op. cit.*, pp. 117–19. For a contemporary comparison of

the importance of Islam in the western and eastern Caucasus see Bodenstedt, *op. cit.*, pp. 522–3.

35. Ali Arslan, *'Rusya'nın Kırım ve Gürcistan'ı Ilhakkindan sonra Osmanlı Devleti'nin Çerkes Kabileleri ile Münasebetleri (1784–1829)'*, in *Kafkas Araştırmaları*, Istanbul: Acar Yayınları, 1988, pp. 46–51.
36. See 'The Russo-Turkish Campaign of 1828–29' in W.E.D. Allen and Paul Muratoff, *Caucasian Battlefields: A History of the Wars on the Turco-Caucasian Border, 1828–1921*, Cambridge University Press, 1953, pp. 23–45.
37. See, e.g., the appendix in J.S. Bell, *Journal*, vol. II, 'Abstract of treaties between Russia and Turkey relating to Circassia', pp. 460–81. Bodenstedt argued in the 1840s that whatever interpretation might be given to various treaties between the Ottoman and Russian empires, the Turkish Sultan had no right to surrender Circassian sovereignty to anyone, since it had never been conceded to any outside power: *op. cit.*, p. 290.
38. Spencer, *Travels*, vol. I, p. 336.
39. Bell called Barzek Haji 'a Circassian Washington' and judged him one of the most capable of all leaders he encountered in Circassia: *Journal*, vol. II, pp. 344–6.
40. Wagner, *Travels*, vol. I, pp. 33–4. J.S. Bell reported that Georgian and Abkhaz auxiliaries used by the Russians often sympathised with and sometimes deserted to the Circassians: *Journal*, vol. I, pp. 168, 286.
41. E.g. decapitation; see J.S. Bell, *Journal*, vol. II, pp. 158–60. For a discussion of the futility of scorched-earth tactics, still being used in the 1840s, see Bodenstedt, *Die Völker . . .*, p. 543.
42. J.S. Bell estimated that 150 vessels were continually involved in this trade: *Journal*, vol. II, p. 72.
43. Wagner, *Travels*, vol. II, pp. 102–3.
44. *ibid.*, vol. II, pp. 146–7.
45. The first Americans in the Caucasus appear to have been the young missionaries Eli Smith and H.G.O. Dwight who made their way across Anatolia to Tbilisi in the summer of 1830. See James A. Field, *America in the Mediterranean World, 1776–1882*, Princeton University Press, 1969, pp. 155–65.
46. *Circassia, or a Tour of the Caucasus*, New York: Stringer-Townshend (London: T.C. Newby), 1850.
47. *ibid.*, p. 31.
48. L.H. Rhinelander, 'Viceroy Vorontsov's Administration of the Caucasus' in Ronald G. Suny (ed.), *Transcaucasia, Nationalism and Social Change*, Ann Arbor: Univ. of Michigan Press, 1983, pp. 87–104.
49. A good beginning has been made with the publication of 61 documents in the original and Latin transcription as an appendix to Mehmet Saray (ed.), *Kafkas Araştırmaları I*, Istanbul: Acar Yayinlari, 1988.
50. Palmerston to Russell, 26 May 1854, as cited in Herbert C.F. Bell, *Lord Palmerston*, London: Longmans Green, 1936, vol. II, p. 105.
51. J.S. Bell, *Journal*, vol. I, p. 166.
52. Spencer, *Travels*, vol. II, p. 265.
53. G.H. Bolsover, 'David Urquhart and the Eastern Question, 1833–37: A Study in Publicity and Diplomacy', *J. of Modern History*, 1936, pp. 444–67.
54. H.C.F. Bell, *Lord Palmerston*, vol. I, pp. 165–86, 256–71.

55. Compare, e.g., H.C.F. Bell, *op. cit.*, pp. 280–4, and Edward Ingram, *The Beginning of the Great Game in Asia, 1828–1834*, Oxford: Clarendon Press, 1979, pp. 272–6, 279 ff.

56. According to J.S. Bell (*Journal*, vol I., pp. 269–71; vol. II, pp. 232–4), Sefir Bey's father was said to have given Ferah Ali Pasha the property on which the new fort at Anapa was built. Numbering among his relatives the famous Prince Jambolet, he is said nevertheless to have suffered discrimination because his mother was of lesser ancestry. After his father's death, he was sold into serfdom, eventually escaped, and made his way to Egypt. On returning to Circassia, he married a Nogay princess and served under the Pasha of Anapa until it was surrendered to the Russians. His Nogay wife was still living near Anapa in the 1830s.

57. J.A. Longworth, *A Year Among the Circassians*, London: Henry Colburn, 1840, vol. I, p. 129.

58. J.S. Bell, *Journal*, vol. I, p. 450.

59. Spencer, *Travels*, vol. II, pp. 161–2.

60. J.S. Bell, *Journal*, vol. I, pp. 54–5.

61. Longworth, *A Year . . .* , vol II, p. 336.

62. *ibid.*, vol. II, pp. 338–9.

63. Wagner, *Travels*, vol. I, pp. 203–4.

64. Bodenstedt, *Die Völker . . .* , p. 543.

65. Spencer, *op. cit.*, vol. II, p. 370. Bodenstedt met a Polish engineer officer at Ardler who had spent twelve years in Circassia, *op. cit.*, p. 195. We see here a remarkable parallel to the identification of Afghans and Poles in their resistance to Soviet domination in the 1980s. See also numerous references in Thadée Gasztowtt, *La Pologne et l'Islam. Notes historiques*, Paris: Société Française d'Imprimerie et de Librairie, 1907.

66. Wagner, *Travels*, vol. II, pp. 95–6.

67. *ibid.* A century and a half later, at the end of the 1980s, as both Poland and the Caucasus confronted Gorbachev with severe and seemingly intractable dilemmas, the same judgment might well have applied to Russian prospects for expanding its influence southward into Iran and Turkey.

68. *New York Tribune*, 9 March 1854.

69. Karl Marx, *The Eastern Question: Letters written 1853–1856 dealing with the Events of the Crimean War*, Eleanor Marx Aveling and Edward Aveling (eds), New York: Augustus M. Kelley, 1969 (reissue of 1897 London edn), p. 146.

70. *ibid.*, p. 108.

71. Hugh Seton-Watson, *The Russian Empire, 1801–1917*, Oxford: Clarendon Press, 1967, p. 321.

72. Marx, *Eastern Question*, p. 167.

73. See footnote in Allen and Muratoff, *Caucasian Battlefields*, p. 66, on his probable Scottish ancestry.

74. E.g., see Charles Duncan, *A Campaign with the Turks in Asia*, London, 1855, vol. I, pp. 216–17.

75. Marx, *Eastern Question*, p. 413.

76. Philip Warner, *The Crimean War: A Reappraisal*, London, 1972, p. 3.

77. Seton-Watson, *Russian Empire*, p. 327.

78. Allen and Muratoff, *Caucasian Battlefields*; p. 86.

79. *ibid.*, pp. 81–102.

80. Maj.-Gen. Sir Henry Rawlinson, *England and Russia in the East*, London: John Murray, 1875, pp. 68–69.

81. *ibid.*, p. 69fn.

82. See, e.g., Khadzhi Murat Ibragimbeili, *Kavkaz v Krymskoi Voine 1853–1856 gg. i Mezhdunarodnye Otnosheniia*, Moscow: Nauka, 1971.

83. Gunib and all the other sites in Daghestan associated with Shamil were protected by the Mountaineers and remained shrines to his memory through the vicissitudes of the Soviet era. On the site of Shamil's actual surrender a gazebo has been erected with a plaque inscribed 'On this stone General Field-Marshall Prince Bariatinskii sat when receiving the captive Shamil on 25 August 1859', but the local people call the gazebo 'Shamil's summer house'. An old man who guided a sympathetic Russian writer around Gunib in the 1950s said he believed that Gunib had fallen to tsarist troops only because of treachery, and insisted that the monument had been erected in honor of Shamil, not Bariatinskii. 'Then why did the Mountaineers tear it down during an uprising at the end of the last century?' the Russian writer asked. 'I don't know', the old man answered. Dmitri I. Trunov, *V gorakh Dagestana*, Moscow: Molodaya Gvardia, 1958, p. 126.

84. Compared to most other Muslim groups in the former Soviet Union in the latter half of the 20th century, they have had a rather low rate of increase. The population of the Adyghe Autonomous Region totalled 404,000 in the 1979 census of which less than 25% was Adyghe. However, these census figures do not give an accurate representation of their number as most of them live outside their nominal territory. See Alexandre Bennigsen and S. Enders Wimbush, *Muslims of the Soviet Empire*, London: Hurst, 1985, pp. 190–1.

85. F.O. 97–424, #29, Stevens to Russell, Trebizond, 10 Oct. 1863, as cited in Justin McCarthy, *The Fate of the Muslims*, forthcoming. Citations which follow are from the text and footnotes of the author's typescript, chapter 2, 'Eastern Anatolia and the Caucasus'.

86. F.O. 97–424, #2, Dickson to Russell, Soukoum-Kale, 17 March 1864, cited McCarthy.

87. F.O. 881–1259, Dickson to Russell, Soukoum-Kale, 13 April 1864, cited McCarthy.

88. F.O. 97–424, #13, Palgrave to Stanley, Trebizond, 16 May 1867, cited McCarthy.

89. F.O. 881–1259, Bulwer to Russell, Constantinople, 3 May 1864, cited McCarthy.

90. An unpublished Istanbul University doctoral dissertation based on extensive exploitation of Turkish archival sources provides the most comprehensive available survey of the Ottoman experience in receiving and resettling Caucasian refugees: Bedri Habicoğlu, 'Kafkasya'dan Osmanlı Imparatorluğu'na Göcler ve Iskanları', History Department, Faculty of Literature, University of Istanbul, 1983. A Turkish work has been published to commemorate the 125th anniversary of the expulsion of the Circassians: I. Aydemir, *Kuzey Kafkasyalilarin Goc Tarihi, Muhaceretin 125. Yılı Anısına*, Ankara, 1988.

91. As cited in Kemal H. Karpat, *Ottoman Population, 1830–1914: Demographic and Social Characteristics*, Madison: Univ. of Wisconsin Press, 1985, pp. 65–70.

92. F.O. 97–424, Dickson to Stuart, Pera, 5 Dec. 1864, as cited in McCarthy, *op. cit.*

93. McCarthy, ms., *op. cit.*, ch. 2, p. 41. McCarthy's careful scholarly work fills a serious gap in modern historiography, which has largely ignored the Circassian freedom struggle and given even less attention to the mass migration which came in

the wake of Russian occupation of Circassian lands. This great exodus was the first of the violent mass transfers of population which this part of the world has suffered in modern times. Two generations later, tragedy began to overwhelm the Armenians of Eastern Anatolia. Millions of Armenians, Greeks, Turks, Kurds, and Nestorians were uprooted and hundreds of thousands died, at least during the commotion of the First World War and its aftermath. None of these ethnic disasters is entirely unrelated to the others.

94. Allen & Muratoff, *Caucasian Battlefields*, pp. 115–31.
95. The most authoritative account of this experience is a book which, originally circulated in the Soviet Union as *samizdat*, was smuggled abroad and published in English translation: Aleksandr M. Nekrich, *The Punished Peoples*, New York: W.W. Norton, 1978.

THE LAST *GHAZAWAT*

THE 1920–1921 UPRISING

Marie Bennigsen Broxup

Nowhere in the Russian empire was the Civil War as confused and ferocious as in the North Caucasus. Between 1917 and 1920 it was fought by four main adversaries: the Bolsheviks (Russians and natives), the Caucasian nationalists, the White Army of Denikin together with Kuban and Terek Cossacks, and the Muslim religious conservatives. Several outsiders also took a direct or indirect part in the conflict: Bicherakhov's army — helped by the British, the Turks, the Azerbaijani Mussavatists, the Georgians and Armenians. In the spring of 1920, when the 11th Red Army coming from the north occupied the lowlands of Daghestan, the Soviets had defeated the White Army in European Russia and conquered Azerbaijan almost without firing a single shot. In the North Caucasus only two adversaries remained to fight the final round of the tragedy: the conservative Muslims led by the Naqshbandiya Sufi *tariqat* and a purely Russian Red Army led by Russian commanders and Russian political cadres. Nadjmuddin Efendiev Samurskii, First Secretary of the Communist Party of Daghestan, acknowledged at the time that 'several mistakes were committed, such as plundering raids, brutalities, atrocities and attacks on religion, that are usually committed by a victorious army in a civil war.' Three months later the whole of Upper Daghestan and Upper Chechnia was ablaze.

In contrast to what happened in Turkestan during the Basmachi war, there were few native Muslims left in 1920 on the Soviet side, although between 1917 and 1920 the leadership of the revolutionary movement in the North Caucasus belonged to the Muslim radicals who had joined the Bolshevik Party. Many of these native Bolsheviks represented the upper levels of Muslim society, and their ancestors had fought the Russians under Shamil. One of them was Makhach Dakhadaev, first president of the Communist organisation in Daghestan, who was married to Shamil's grand-daughter. In spite of siding with Russian communists during the Civil War they remained convinced nationalists and were accepted and trusted by the local populations. Unfortunately for Daghestan, nearly all these native communists had died during the Civil War before the outbreak of the 1920 revolt. The 'comrades from

112

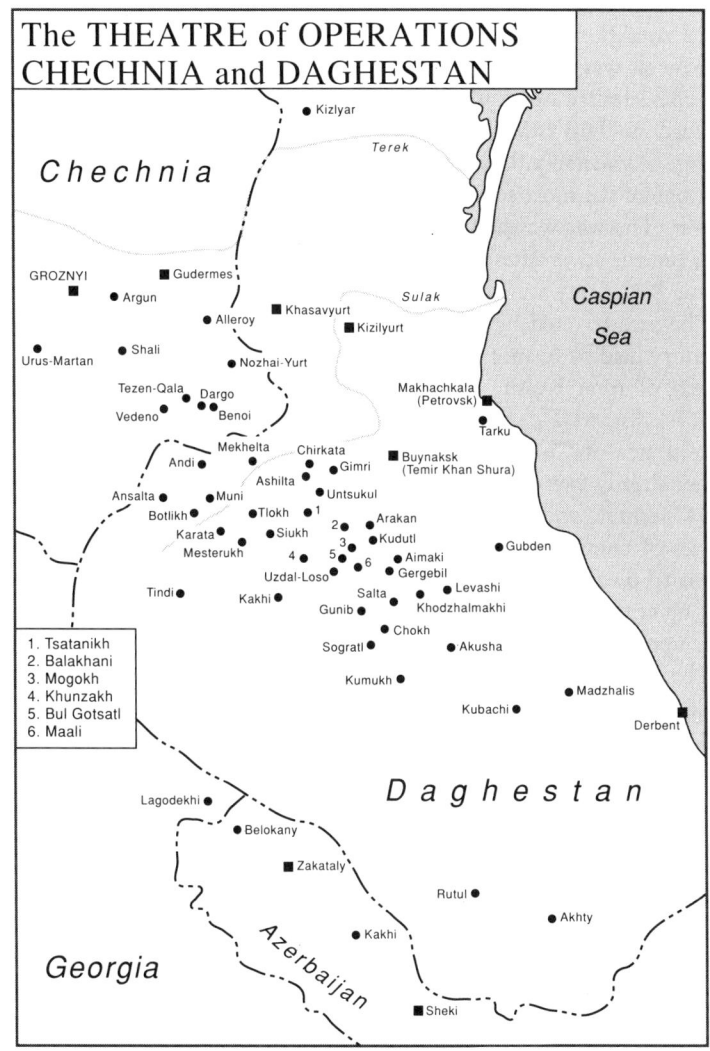

The THEATRE of OPERATIONS
CHECHNIA and DAGHESTAN

Kizlyar

Chechnia

Terek

GROZNYI ■   ■ Gudermes
   ● Argun   *Sulak*
          ● Alleroy   ■ Khasavyurt
●   ■ Kizilyurt
Urus-Martan   ● Shali
              ● Nozhai-Yurt
   Tezen-Qala ● Dargo   Makhachkala
      ● Vedeno ● Benoi   (Petrovsk) ■
                                  ● Tarku
         Mekhelta ● Chirkata
      Andi ●   ● Gimri   ■ Buynaksk
                Ashilta ●   (Temir Khan Shura)
   Ansalta ●   ● Muni ● Untsukul
      Botlikh ● ● Tlokh ● 1
                         2 ● Arakan
      Karata ● ● Siukh 3 ● Kudutl
         Mesterukh ● 4 ● 5 ● ● 6 ● Aimaki   ● Gubden
               Uzdal-Loso ●   ● Gergebil
      Tindi ●   Salta ● ● Levashi
         Kakhi ● Gunib ● Khodzhalmakhi
                         ● Chokh
                  Sogratl ●   ● Akusha
                  Kumukh ●   ● Madzhalis
                       Kubachi ●
                                   Derbent ■

1. Tsatanikh
2. Balakhani
3. Mogokh
4. Khunzakh
5. Bul Gotsatl
6. Maali

Caspian
Sea

D a g h e s t a n

Lagodekhi ●
   ● Belokany
      ■ Zakataly
                Rutul ●
                        ● Akhty
         ● Kakhi
Georgia   *Azerbaijan*
                ■ Sheki

abroad', the Russian communists, who arrived in force with the 11th Red Army, were — according to Samurskii — entirely ignorant of the social conditions of Daghestan and the character of the Mountaineers. The revolt was embraced by the whole Muslim population and it had all the characteristics of a *jihad*, something the Soviet leadership had just avoided in Turkestan by a last-minute clever political *volte-face* and change of leadership. In spite of the small area affected by the rebellion, it was one of the most serious internal military challenges faced by Soviet power. The war was particularly fierce. No compromises were possible between the adversaries; no prisoners were taken and the losses suffered by the Red Army were high.

The area covered by the revolt corresponded almost exactly to the territory held by Shamil at the end of the imamate (1834–59): the upper valleys of Avar Koisu, Andi Koisu, Kara Koisu and their tributaries Ori-Tskalis and Tleiserukh in Daghestan, and the mountainous south-eastern area of Chechnia. At the beginning of the hostilities the Red Army already exercised solid control over the major part of Daghestan and Chechnia, and had garrisons in the most important mountain fortresses of Gunib, Gimri and Vedeno. This made it impossible for the rebels to break through Christian Ossetia into Muslim Kabarda, or to link up with the Ingush (who were to provide the main fighting force in later uprisings in Chechnia-Ingushetia in 1926, 1936 and 1941–3).

The rebels came from the same mountain Chechen, Avar, Andi and Dido clans that had fought the Tsarist armies three generations before, and they were led by the same Naqshbandi Sufi brotherhood that had provided the political and spiritual leadership to Shamil's *murids*. The nominal leader of the revolt was the young Said Bek, great-grandson of Shamil, who came to Daghestan from Turkey to lend the prestige of his family to the cause and to fight with his countrymen. The political and spiritual leader of the revolt was an Avar, Sheikh Najmuddin of Hotso ('Gotsinskii') who had been elected imam of Daghestan and Chechnia in August 1917. The *maître à penser* and the main spiritual authority of the rebellion was his former deputy and fellow Naqshbandi, the Chechen sheikh Uzun Haji of Salty. Uzun Haji never accepted tsarist rule, and in the struggle for the liberation of his homeland spent the fifteen years before February 1917 in a Siberian labour camp. He hated all Russians indiscriminately, and treated them as enemies whatever their politics. During the Civil War he fought the White forces of Denikin (whom he considered worse than the Bolsheviks), Bicherakhov and the Terek Cossacks. He understood the Revolution as meaning the end of Russian power and thus for a time fought alongside Bolshevik detachments against the Whites.

In 1919 he founded a theocratic state in Upper Chechnia, the emirate of the North Caucasus, modelled on Shamil's Imamate. It was placed under the nominal suzerainty of the Ottoman Sultan Khalif, and exercised control over most of Upper Daghestan's Avar and Andi territories. Although Uzun Haji promised 'to weave a rope to hang students, engineers, intellectuals and more generally all those who wrote from left to right', he was enthusiastically admired by his opponents, the very people he was prepared to hang, the Daghestani Bolsheviks. Extremely brave, of iron will, totally honest in politics and fair in war, 'consumed by a fanatical fire' and with a sense of duty to restore the Imamate, a dedicated pan-Islamist, highly intelligent — thus was he assessed by the leading communists in Daghestan. Samurskii described his role and that of other Sufi leaders of the rebellion in these words:

> These men . . . were among the most famous scholars of the entire Muslim world . . . Thousands of disciples from all Muslim lands, from Russia, Turkey, Persia, used to visit them . . . They were hallowed by the glamour of deep learning, and their words were as sacred as the law itself . . . but at the same time they belonged to the people . . . they were armed with the same sword and rifle and in battle they were the leaders fighting in the forefront; they were the bearers of a certain democracy, based on the support of the poorest and of the weakest, which was the very essence of Shamil's rule; they were the defenders of national independence . . . [1]

Uzun Haji died in March 1920 at the age of ninety a few months before the outbreak of the revolt which he had inspired. The leadership and military command of the uprising was divided between Naqshbandis sheikhs true to Uzun Haji's ideals and a group of former tsarist army officers headed by Colonel Kaitmas Alikhanov, an Avar nobleman. The principal religious leaders were the sheikhs Mohammad of Balakhany (the chief military commander), Dervish Mohammad of Andi, Ibragim Haji of Kuchri, Sirajuddin Haji of Avaristan and Seyid Amin of Ansalta. It was the Sufi leadership which gave the Daghestani-Chechen uprising its unique character; only a mystical order could force the fiercely independent Mountaineers to submit to iron discipline in a hopelessly uneven struggle against the Soviets whose grip was becoming total.

The rebels were not numerous given the comparatively small

population of the area affected by the revolt. The commander of the 11th Red Army estimated the number of fighters at 9,690, poorly armed with antique rifles and swords and forty machine-guns which they had captured in battle. However, they enjoyed the complete support and loyalty of the population among whom they were like 'fish in water', and had the advantage of operating in a high mountain terrain with which, unlike the Red Army, they were totally familiar. They were *uzdens*, free clansmen tied by a double loyalty to their Sufi *tariqat* and to their clan. Their commitment to the *ghazawat*, the holy war, and their discipline were absolute. For courage, gallantry and fighting spirit they were acknowledged to be unrivalled. Takho-Godi gave a vivid description of Imam Gotsinskii's troops' first occupation of the capital Temir Khan Shura under the command of Uzun Haji in January 1918:

. . . At 3 o'clock in the afternoon the city suddenly resounded with terrifying cries: it was the 'army' of the Imam entering Shura chanting religious hymns. It would be difficult to imagine such a vision for those who did not witness it, an endless formation stretching on the road from Kazanishch to Shura slowly marching, the advance column having already reached the city. They were dressed in rags with white bandages on their heads, horsemen, infantrymen, old and young, armed with rifles, flintlock guns or simply sticks; some fired by fanaticism, other with indifferent and tired eyes; they felt victorious. After barely an hour they seized all the government buildings. All the city, all the squares and streets were occupied by wildly picturesque turbaned groups. There was one remarkable aspect to these events: over 10,000 people had invested the city, yet there was not a single occurrence of pillage or thieving. The only casualties were a few wooden fences — it was winter, and people spending the night in the squares reluctantly had to use the fences for warmth . . . From the point of view of discipline they could be a model for any professional army units . . . [2]

The Soviets heavily outnumbered the rebels. They had two Red Armies at their disposal, the 11th from Astrakhan (the 'Terek-Daghestan Army') and the 9th (the 'Kuban Army'). These were all-Russian units, commanders and soldiers, hardened veterans of the Civil War, well armed, with very high fighting spirit, but they had never fought in the mountains and had no experience of guerrilla warfare. Together there were twenty-seven rifle regiments, six cavalry regiments, six artillery groups, and two special battalions of Inner Security, plus many special formations such as aviation, armoured cars, technical units, and detachments of Moscow and local *Cheka* — a total of 35,000 to 40,000 fighters.[3]

In this chapter we try to unravel the chronology of events of this little-known but most remarkable page of history. The war went unnoticed in the West and in the rest of the Muslim world, and always remained a forbidden subject in the Soviet Union, despite laudable attempts to rewrite history once *glasnost* had begun. There are two reasons for this: first, the rebels fought to the last — there were no survivors to write their memoirs — and secondly, after 1927, the year marking the beginning of the anti-Islamic campaign in the Soviet Union and the outbreak of a new wave of unrest in the North Caucasus, Soviet censorship forbade all mention of this tragedy — it simply had not happened. Fortunately, four detailed and relatively objective works were published before 1927 by actors in the drama. These were Najmuddin Samurskii-Efendiev, *Dagestan* (Moscow and Leningrad, 1925) and *Grazhdanskaia voina v Dagestane* (Civil War in Daghestan, Makhachkala, 1925); Ali Akbar Takho-Godi, *Revoliutsiia i kontrrevoliutsiia v Dagestane* (Revolution and Counter-Revolution in Daghestan, Makhachkala, 1927); A. Todorskii, *Krasnaia armiia v gorakh — destviia v Dagestane* (The Red Army in the Mountains — The Action in Daghestan, Moscow, 1924). Written by opponents of the rebels, these are the only documented sources at our disposal. Samurskii (a Lezghin) and Takho-Godi (an Avar) were the leading communists in Daghestan at the time of the uprising, and Todorskii, a Russian, was the commander of the 11th Red Army. All three authors were later purged by Stalin. Samurskii was executed in 1937, and Takho-Godi and Todorskii were deported to labour camps.

Pre-Revolutionary Daghestan and Chechnia

After the defeat of Shamil in 1859, the North Caucasus and particularly the mountainous areas of Chechnia and Daghestan lay in ruins, and the human losses were appalling. The Russians with a half-million-strong army in the North Caucasus appeared invincible. The Naqshbandiya *tariqat*, which had provided the ideological driving force behind the holy war and the struggle for independence, was considerably weakened, its activity at a standstill. The main religious authority, Jemaleddin of Kazi-Kumukh, had left Daghestan for Turkey after Shamil's surrender. His nominated successors, the Naqshbandi *murshids* Haqalu Mohammad of Kazi-Kumukh and Haji Ali Asker of Tsakhul, had also left for Mecca, while Haji Nasrullah (from Kabir in the Khanate of Kurin) was killed in 1859 in the battle for Gunib, Shamil's last stronghold. Discouraged by defeat and the ruthless repression imposed by the Russian army of occupation, the North Caucasian Mountaineers were ready to accept a new ideology. The vacuum was filled with the appearance of another religious order, the Qadiriya, brought to the Caucasus by a Kumyk shepherd Kunta Kishiev, a native of northern Daghestan living in the Chechen village of Eliskhan-Yurt.

According to Chechen legend, Kunta 'Haji' visited the tomb of the twelfth-century founder of the *tariqat*, Abd Al-Qadir Al-Ghilani, in Baghdad, on his return from pilgrimage to Mecca in 1848 or 1849, and was initiated by the saint himself. Back in Chechnia, Kunta Haji started his missionary activity, but was obliged to leave the Caucasus because of the hostility of the Naqshbandiya towards his pacifist sermons. He returned in 1861 after the defeat of the *ghazawat*, and this time his preaching of mystical asceticism, detachment from worldly affairs, non-violence and 'non-resistance to evil' was gladly accepted by the war-weary Mountaineers. The new *tariqat* enjoyed immediate success in Chechnia, Avaristan and northern Daghestan, where the war effort had been most wearying and the Russian oppression particularly severe. However, very rapidly the *tariqat* was faced with the dilemma which had confronted the Naqshbandiya in the 1820s: should a Sufi mystical order avoid confrontation with evil or should it join *jihad* against the infidels who dominated their Muslim land? The very reality of Russian rule, oppressive and often unbearable, called for a positive reaction.

In 1862 and 1863 a wave of unrest swept over Chechnia, and in early January 1864 the Russian administration, frightened by the growing number of Qadiri adepts and fearing a new uprising, arrested Kunta Haji and several dozen of his followers. He was not tried but simply declared insane and banished to a prison hospital in Russia, where he died in 1867. His companions were accused of planning a rebellion against Russian rule and deported to hard labour camps in Siberia. Later, on 18 January 1864, some 4,000 *murids* who had assembled in the Chechen *aul* of Shali were attacked by Russian troops and dispersed with gunfire; 200 were killed, 1,000 wounded and several hundred arrested and deported to Siberia. The Qadiriya was not outlawed, but some of its practices such as the loud *zikr* were strictly forbidden, and the Russian authorities encouraged the massive emigration of Chechens and Ingush to the Ottoman empire. As a result some 5,000 families left in 1865.

Despite the repressive measures and the harassment of the Qadiris, the expansion of the order was not impeded, and it continued to make converts to Islam among the still pagan Ingush. But heavy-handed oppression in this fiercely independent land could only have one outcome, and in 1877 both the Naqshbandiya and the Qadiriya joined forces for another great uprising which spread to Daghestan and Chechnia. In Daghestan the leader of the insurgents was Sheikh Haji Mohammad, the son of Abdurrahman of Sogratl, the last remaining Naqshbandi religious authority following the departure of Jemaleddin of Kazi-Kumukh. Abdurahman himself took an active part in the revolt (until his arrest and later death in Siberia), which lasted until 1878. Those leaders who were not killed in battle were almost all hanged, and thousands of *murids* were deported to Siberia. This defeat marked a turning-point in the 'tactics' of the Sufi brotherhoods. Until 1917, they discarded the idea of *ghazawat* and open resistance, and acquired an underground, semi-clandestine character, a fact which in no way tarnished their prestige in the North Caucasus. On the contrary, 'between 1877 and the Revolution of 1917, almost all the adult population of Chechnia and Ingushetia belonged either to the Naqshbandiya or the Qadiriya *tariqat*.'[4] The same was true of Daghestan.

Between 1860 and 1867 Daghestan was kept under a special administrative status within the Russian empire. There was no conscription of the natives, and the *Shariat* courts remained active. In 1867 it became an *oblast* (province), administered by a military governor with judicial power over the natives and supported by large garrisons stationed in twelve fortresses. There was no attempt to colonise the country, which was simply too poor and inhospitable to attract settlers. Nor was any attempt made by the tsarist administration to develop the region, which was kept strictly as a potential military springboard against Turkey and Iran and as a route to the wealth of Azerbaijan. Before the conquest, Daghestan was able to export some fruit and raw materials, and to sustain an abundance of livestock. The new administration, however, presided over the gradual destruction of the local economy; herds destroyed during the war were not replenished, geological surveys for minerals were forbidden for fear of spies, and what little trade there was came to be limited to the cities. The majority of the population, out of a total of approximately one million, lived in the high mountains at heights of between 1,000 and 3,000 metres and suffered chronic food shortages, since the local produce was only sufficient to feed the population for three months of the year.

One could be forgiven for assuming that a century of warfare and economic hardship in a country of inaccessible mountain villages, inhabited by a population having preserved a clanic structure, would have remained culturally primitive. This was not so and Daghestan probably represents a unique case in the history of Muslim civilisation. The religious revival which took place at the end of the eighteenth century as a reaction to the threat from the Christian north was paralleled by a remarkable flourishing of Arabic culture. In the nineteenth century the high mountains of Daghestan became the haven of religious schools and of theologians famed throughout the Muslim world for their pristine command of the Arabic language, literature and theology. Before the Revolution there were some 2,000 Quranic schools with over 40,000 students, a ratio per head of population higher than in many developed countries and certainly higher than in Russia. These schools provided the best teachers of classical Arabic for the rest of the Muslim world, including the Arab world.

The tsarist administration was at first outwardly tolerant towards the national schools and Islam, and generally cautious about interfering with the local traditions and customary laws — the Orthodox Church, for example, was forbidden to proselytise in Daghestan and Chechnia. However, the existence of a highly developed educational network spreading an alien faith and language could not remain unchallenged for long. Several attempts were made to counter Arabism and impose Russian influence, most of them ineffectual or inept, such as the effort to create a Russian village in Gunib, the place of Shamil's surrender, shortly before the First World War.[5] An original but short-lived solution was to establish schools using the native languages transliterated into Cyrillic script. Unfortunately this positive endeavour was soon discarded, the native language schools being replaced by Russian language schools designed to impress the natives with the grandeur of tsarist power. These schools did not give students even elementary notions about their own country. Predictably they were despised and distrusted by the local population and only served to enhance the prestige of the Quranic schools, which were increasingly seen as a protection against Russification.

Unrest and localised uprisings took place in 1905 in the south of Daghestan, following the government efforts to introduce Russian landlords and administrators in the rural areas, and in 1908 when it was proposed to change the language of administration from Arabic to Russian. The disturbances were threatening enough to force the government to abandon the projected reforms. On the eve of the Revolution, after sixty years of Russian administration, there were only ninety-three government schools, barely able to educate a few clerks and minor officials. Russian influence on the life and customs of the Daghestanis and Chechens remained negligible even in the cities, and the Russian rulers made no effort to understand the traditions of the people whom they governed other than through the short-sighted attention of the military police. Tragically for the North Caucasians, the Soviets were to follow in the steps of their tsarist predecessors.

The war of 1920–21

The war which erupted in August 1920 lasted almost a year, but the rebellion was only finally quelled in 1925 when the Bolsheviks succeeded in capturing and executing Najmuddin Gotsinskiii and the surviving Naqshbandi sheikhs Seyid Amin of Ansalta and Wahhab Astemirov. The ideology of the rebels was that of *ghazawat* or *jihad* (a notion which in recent history has been much misused). Most wars fought by Muslims against infidel opponents, and sometimes even among themselves, used the strong compulsive slogans of *jihad*. But in the highly legalistic tradition of Islam, *jihad* in the past could only be called by the khalif or the highest religious authority in the land under certain very precise conditions. To answer the call for *jihad* became an obligation only if a Muslim country was invaded by unbelievers and if the survival of Islam as a religion was threatened. Only for the Sufi orders such as the Naqshbandiya was the fight against 'evil', and *jihad* considered a 'fundamental duty'. *Jihad* is a double fight, against sin (or 'greater *jihad*'), which for Sufis is the most important task, and military *jihad* (or 'lesser *jihad*') against an external enemy endangering the faith or the bad Muslims who serve it. There could be no compromise with 'evil', no solution other than victory or martyrdom. Added to this ideal was the passionate desire for national liberation nurtured among the Caucasian Mountaineers for more than a century and a half, since the days of Sheikh Mansur.

In the spring of 1920, the Civil War was coming to an end. For three years it had brought into conflict the Mountaineers, Red partisans and *murids*, the Whites, the Cossacks, the Turks, the Georgian Mensheviks and the Azeri nationalists, in ever-changing alliances on the battlefields of the North Caucasus. All the outside players had left Daghestan, and only the White Army of Denikin still remained in control of the coastal lowland towns.

In the beginning of March, through the joint efforts of all Daghestani factions — Red partisans supported by the *murids* of Sheikh Ali of Akusha and the followers of Uzun Haji from Upper Daghestan and Chechnia — the towns were regained by them from the Whites. Temir Khan Shura was stormed by a 'cavalry raid' and Derbent was liberated after a nineteen-day street-to-street battle. The White Fleet sailed from Petrovsk surrounded by the Mountaineers. Thus when the 11th Red Army coming from the north reached Daghestan and was marching towards Baku, it was greeted by red flags in all the towns and *auls* of Daghestan already freed from the Whites. As a result of Denikin's intransigence, the Red Army was welcomed and even, according to Samurskii, compared with tolerance to a column of pilgrims on their way to Mecca.

For three years the North Caucasians had fought, giving support and shelter to Bolshevik units. The Red Army behaved with the arrogance and lawlessness of a foreign occupying power in conquered territory, whereas it was greeted as an ally by a people who had waged war for their freedom against a common enemy — the Whites. What happened to bring about four months later the most violent conflict yet to have wracked the Caucasus since the Revolution? Samurskii noted that the Communist Party cells in Temir Khan Shura, Petrovsk and Derbent were gripped by an 'organisational fever' after the arrival of the Red Army and that sovietisation was conducted in 'obviously unsuitable ways in the majority of cases'.[6] This meant an influx of Russians, most Daghestanis being considered unworthy of Party membership, and a centralisation of decision-making by chauvinistic Russian cadres of the Narkomnats from Rostov who applied the tactics of War Communism. Specific 'mistakes', bound to antagonise the Mountaineers, were above all stupid attacks on patriarchal traditions and Islam, as well as various indignities such as punitive raids, police denunciations, blackmail, settling of private feuds, plunders, confiscation of food supplies and fodder, forced conscription into Red regiments, requisitions and destruction of small trade.

Military operations during the first phase of the uprising till December 1920

In August 1920 the rebels began to gather their forces. An assembly was called by Najmuddin Gotsinskii and Colonel Kaitmas Alikhanov in Gidatl, during which Alikhanov was nominated war minister of the '*Shariat* Army of the Mountain Peoples' and an appeal was made to Said

Bek, Shamil's great-grandson, to join the uprising. According to both Takho-Godi and Samurskii, representatives of the Georgian nationalist leaders Zhordania and Ramishvili were present, as well as some of the Daghestani nationalists who had taken refuge in Georgia. The uprising under the slogans of 'National Liberation and *Shariat* State' began in the southern districts of Dido, Antsukho and Kapuchi bordering with Georgia, while Bolshevik forces were concentrated in central and northern Daghestan. The uprising quickly became a mass movement and spread to Gunib, Avar and Andi territories, the most remote and inaccessible areas of Daghestan, obliging the Red Army, militia and partisan units to take refuge in Khunzakh, Botlikh and Gunib fortresses. However, some Andi territories under the leadership of the sheikhs Hassan and Habibullah Haji remained faithful to the Soviet side, a determining factor in the later development of the military operations, since it allowed the Caucasian partisans freedom of movement and shelter.

Soon after the assembly, some 600 nationalist officers crossed the mountain passes of the Andi and Avar ranges from Georgia and joined the rebels in the Andi *auls*. The few existing local soviets in Upper Daghestan disintegrated, and power automatically fell into the hands of the Sufi *tariqat*. The officers provided the initial military cadres but were soon overtaken by local leadership from the *auls*. Every district *raion* provided its own detachment of several hundred fighters divided into 'centuries'. Coordination was good since each centurion reported directly to the high command or to a liaison representative nominated by the high command. As well as Gotsinskii, Said Bek, Colonel Alikhanov, the sheikhs Mohammad of Balakhany, Seyid Amin, Sirajuddin Haji and Wahhab Astemirov, the high command included Dervish Mohammad, Colonel Omar Piralov, Colonel Shamilev, Militia Captain Imam Ali and his brother Gudatlo, Lieutenant Mohammad Sultan Girey, Lieutenant Hassan Abakarov, Sheikh Ibragim Haji of Kuchri, Jemal Aidimirov and Murtaza Ali Chupanov. Colonel Jafarov, a former cavalry officer under the Tsar, an able and talented officer according to Todorskii, was the commander-in-chief.

Food and fodder were supplied by the local population, but each fighter provided his own weapons. The army was mainly infantry but each 'century' had approximately ten horsemen. The rebels had a few canons captured early during the hostilities, but seldom used them due to lack of ammunition. The infantry were armed with Russian rifles, but many fighters only had flintlock guns dating from the days of Shamil or hunting rifles. The only cartridges available were those captured from the Red Army. The cavalry used rifles with shortened barrels of the traditional cavalry model with ammunition left over from the old tsarist garrisons and the Turks. All rebels had daggers and sometimes revolvers. All men were obliged to take part in war on whatever side as a matter of honour. Todorskii described the Daghestani fighters as warlike, with an inborn sense of military discipline acquired from living in difficult climatic conditions, brave, obstinate, excessively proud and arrogant, in love with freedom, good observers, cunning and revengeful — qualities which he ascribed to their tradition of continuous warfare against tsarism. A distinctive trait of the rebel army, according to Todorskii, was its constant combat-readiness and adaptation to mountain warfare.

The initiative in the military operations was taken by the rebels, and they had some spectacular successes. On receiving reports of the rebellion, reinforcements of some 1,000 men were immediately dispatched at the beginning of September from Temir Khan Shura to Botlikh, Gunib and Khunzakh — the 'Mountain War Sector' — under the orders of Osipovskii, commander of the Daghestani brigade. Local militias were also dispatched for intelligence work and to act as scouts and runners because all telegraph lines had been destroyed by the rebels. On reaching the War Sector the first operations mounted by Osipovski were foolhardy: three expeditions were thrown simultaneously against the high mountain *auls*, leaving the fortress garrisons unprotected. The Botlikh detachment was stopped in a snowstorm along the Bogos mountain ridge by a force of some 300 rebels; a reconnaissance party sent to investigate the enemy's position disappeared, probably lost or frozen to death. Not having protected their rear, the Red troops were surrounded and abandoned by their partisan scouts who defected to the rebels. At night, under cover of artillery fire, forty-four men out of an original force of some 350 managed to break through, only to surrender the next day, throwing their weapons into a ravine, as their retreat was cut off by the rebels who had meanwhile captured Botlikh.

The expeditionary detachment from Khunzakh suffered roughly the same fate — first stopped by rebels positioned on the high ground, and then surrounded, forced to break through the encirclement with heavy casualties, and retreat to the point of departure in Khunzakh fortress where a fresh battalion from Petrovsk was sent as a reinforcement. In the first week of October the rebels threatened Khunzakh, which they had cut off from Temir Khan Shura by capturing Salty bridge on the Kara Koisu river and the *aul* of Arakan which controlled the main supply-route from the capital. Thus in their first encounters with the Red

Army, in less than six weeks, the rebels had managed to control most of Upper Daghestan, the Andi, Avar and Gunib districts, destroying or isolating the Soviet headquarters of the Mountain War Sector. The number of fighters at that time, according to Todorskii's estimation, was no more than 3,000.

The Arakan disaster

In the first two weeks of October, reinforcements began to reach the Daghestani capital from the headquarters of the 11th Army stationed in Azerbaijan: the 95th Rifle Brigade comprising the 283rd and 284th Rifle Regiments, the 3rd Light Artillery Division, the 176th Regiment with two battalions and ten guns, and several unit of cadets. Two battalions — the 38th Rifle Battalion of Vokhra and a reserve battalion of the district militia equipped with light artillery — left Temir Khan Shura, marching along the banks of the Kara Koisu with the order to occupy Arakan and join with the 176th Regiment from Azerbaijan which had been dispatched to relieve the Gunib garrison and guard the bridges over Avar Koisu. The 283rd Rifle Regiment, the first to reach Daghestan, was ordered to overrun Arakan and march on to liberate Khunzakh. On 13 October it left Temir Khan Shura under the command of Ganiushkin and Safar Dudarov, head of the Daghestan *Cheka* and one of the few Daghestani communists to have survived the Civil War, and was followed by a light artillery division of two batteries.

The accounts given by Samurskii and Todorskii of the Arakan disaster do not tally exactly, that of Todorskii being perhaps deliberately imprecise. Indeed it must have been hard for a professional soldier like him to relate the sheer stupidity and lack of strategic thinking which led to the disaster. After ten days of artillery fire from the Arakan 'gates' at the entrance of the narrow valley leading to the *aul*, the Reds, a total of 700 men, allowed themselves to be enticed with all their artillery into the gorge, where they had to spread their lines. On 30 October, the troops of Sheikh Mohammad of Balakhany surrounded the detachment by closing the escape routes at both ends of the gorge and destroyed it to the last man, capturing all the military hardware, including twenty-four guns. Dudarov was taken prisoner and beheaded on the spot. Arakan was later called the 'Valley of Death' by Red Army troops. According to Samurskii, it was a typical example of the mistakes and blunders committed by Russian commanders who had no knowledge of the geography, customs and military traditions of the Caucasian Mountaineers.

The battle of Arakan repeated almost exactly the pattern of two famous earlier battles fought in the same area under almost similar conditions: the battle of the Sunja river in May 1785, in which Imam Mansur destroyed a Russian brigade, and the disastrous expedition against Vedeno by Vorontsov in 1845.

Following the Arakan disaster the high command of the 11th Red Army gave priority to the war in Daghestan. On 2 November the order was issued to increase the offensive against the rebels, and Todorskii, then commander of the 32nd Rifle Division in Baku, was given overall responsibility for the operations. From then on, too, the conduct of the war was to be entrusted to the professional soldiers and no longer to the political commissars. The contingent was increased by two rifle regiments (the 282nd and 285th) and a cavalry brigade.

Partisans

It is difficult to assess accurately the impact of the Red partisans, described by Samurskii as the élite of Daghestan, in the conduct of the war. During the Civil War there were, according to him, at least 10,000 Red partisans at any given time fighting against Denikin, but this estimate must surely have included the troops of Uzun Haji who also fought against him. However, at the beginning of the uprising their numbers must have been badly depleted as many died fighting the Whites or defected later to the rebels. Conservatively one could estimate that during the uprising there were no more than a few thousand Red partisans left. Todorskii only gave them grudging credit, while Samurskii and Takho-Godi probably overestimated their role by claiming that they played a decisive part in the final victory. However, there is no doubt that they performed in a way that was truly in the best Caucasian tradition and that their military exploits and gallantry matched those of the rebels. Also their role was essential in action behind enemy lines and in supplying besieged Red Army garrisons which, without their help, would probably have died of starvation. Most of these partisan leaders were later liquidated in the Stalinist purges.

While the battle for Arakan was raging, two partisan units of Daghestanis set up by Samurskii and Sheboldaev left Temir Khan Shura to break the siege of Khunzakh and Gunib fortresses. They numbered some 500 people and were met along the way by partisan groups of Karaev and Bogatyrov. However, despite the personal prestige of the partisan commanders, the cause they defended seems to have attracted little support; with disarming honesty Samurskii boasted that the number of partisans who joined his group was only eight. They marched through Djengutay attacking the rebels from the rear and only with great difficulty managed on 28 October to capture the *aul* of Golotl which controlled the road to Khunzakh, thus relieving the garrison which had been under siege for six weeks. No Red Army units would have been able to achieve this feat in the given time along precipitous mountain tracks and passes at a temperature of 30 degrees below zero.

On 6 November, through the combined efforts of the partisans of Karaev, Bogatyrov and Samurskii and the 176th and 284th Regiments backed up by fresh reserve troops, Khunzakh fortress was finally liberated, and the rebels besieging it — some 400–500, according to Todorskii — were repulsed.

Positions at the beginning of November 1920

Todorskii estimated the number of rebels at that time to be 3,400 (2,800 infantrymen and 600 horsemen). They occupied Gimri and advance posts guarding the approaches to Gimri from the north-east and east. The fighters guarding the posts were not involved in direct military action. Sheikh Mohammad of Balakhany had 600 men and 100 horsemen in Arakan, and another 500 men and 100 horsemen held Chalda and Mogokh. 1,000 men commanded by Imam Gotsinskii and Colonel Alikhanov were facing Khunzakh. Colonel Piralov led a detachment of 400 men and 300 horsemen in the vicinity of the Avar-Kakheti road. 200 fighters of Sheikh Ibragim Haji of Kuchri were positioned in the area of Tlokh-Gonok, and other smaller groups were spread south-west of the Khunzakh line and in Butsra and Shahada area.

New reinforcements were sent from Baku: a cavalry brigade led by Rybakov dispatched towards Arakan, and the 285th Rifle Regiment. The Red Army had at its disposal the 95th Brigade, commanded by Ilia Semenovich Kovalev, which included the 176th, 282nd, 284th and 285th Rifle Regiments together with partisan detachments of Lapin, Omarov, Bogatyrov, Karaev and Samurskii in the Botlikh Sector. The Brigade also had light artillery. As a precaution following the Arakan disaster, the 283rd Rifle Regiment with a new commanding officer, Polazhechnikov, was kept as a reserve in Temir Khan Shura, together with cadets of the 95th Brigade and Daghestani light artillery and cavalry detachments. The order of the day at the beginning of November to all Red units in Daghestan was fairly ambitious: to hold the rebels under observation in Gimri; to immobilise them in Arakan; to advance on Botlikh and join with the 1st Model Revolutionary Discipline Rifle Regiment which was dispatched from Chechnia; to liquidate the uprising in the Avar region and free the Avar-Kakheti road (leading to Georgia) from enemy bands; to destroy the rebels south of the Rugzha-Sogratl line; and to guard the communication lines on the main Temir Khan Shura-Khunzakh road.

In compliance with this order, the Reds intensified their reconnaissance forays along all the resistance fronts, but their initiatives continued to be unsuccessful: a company of forty-eight men led by Chernishev was surrounded and entirely destroyed in Erkachi; the 282nd Regiment held in Temir Khan Shura as a reserve was attacked in the vicinity of Getso and obliged to retreat after all the senior officers and commissars were wounded; Bogatyrov's partisan detachment of 100 men was wiped out in Mochok. Altogether during the incidents in the first days of November, the Reds lost 389 men, forcing Todorskii to issue the order to concentrate the Red Army's efforts only on holding and strengthening Khunzakh and Gunib. Todorskii explained the decision by the inadequate number of his troops and the fact that they were unsuitably dressed and equipped and near to exhaustion.

The 1st Model Revolutionary Discipline Rifle Regiment

On 30 November the Terek High Command announced the loss of the 1st Model Revolutionary Discipline Rifle Regiment, with some 700 men, nine machine-guns and large reserves of ammunitions.

The Regiment had left Groznyi on 9 November and reached Vedeno where it left some 100 soldiers. South of the *aul* of Khorochoi the Regiment met a group of 150 rebels which it dispersed without difficulty, and reached Botlikh on 16 November without further encounters, having left a company in reserve in the *aul* of Khoi. From Botlikh the commissar of the Regiment stormed the surrounding *auls* with two companies and artillery units. On 18 November they captured Muni, the rebels retreating to the higher *aul* Orta-Qala with their guns. The population of Muni was disarmed and, wrote Todorskii, 'antagonised', hostages were taken, food and fodder were confiscated, and the *aul* was looted of all supplies and whatever luxury goods it possessed. After the looting a detachment of 250 men (with three machine-guns) pursued the rebels and occupied Orta-Qala where they immediately began to search for weapons without bothering first to protect or guard their position.

Predictably the rebels, helped by the enraged population of Muni, attacked them from the rear, cut them off without possibility of retreat, and killed them to the last man. Playing on the demoralisation of the rest of the Regiment, the rebels encircled Botlikh. The command of the Regiment decided to parley with the enemy, asking safe passage to Chechnia in exchange for their weapons, although according to Todorskii some were fearful of treachery. Finally and unwisely they surrendered their weapons. The officers and political commissars were massacred and the soldiers ignominiously left naked to freeze to death. A few survivors managed to reach the fortifications of Vedeno, without clothes and with frozen limbs, to report on the 'savage' executions. Being a 'model revolutionary discipline' body we may well imagine that the Regiment had enjoyed applying 'discipline' with particular gusto, hence the indignity of the reprisal.

Second siege of Khunzakh and Gunib

The destruction of the Arakan detachment and the Discipline Regiment gave the rebels considerable confidence and much-needed weapons and ammunition at a time when their supplies were running short, and allowed them to form new units. They intensified their attacks on all strategic points and roads, even those leading to Temir Khan Shura. Furthermore the strategic advantage gained by reconquering Khunzakh and Gunib was nullified by the Red Army itself. As a result of cavalry raids and indiscriminate cruelty to the civilian population, whether enemy, neutral or allied, the Soviets found themselves rapidly isolated again, without supplies of food and armament, and besieged once more in their garrison fortresses.

On 3 December at dawn, the rebels attacked Gotsatl held by the 282nd Rifle Regiment, which retreated in disorder. The 176th Regiment (due to leave for Azerbaijan) was called to the rescue, but only one battalion managed to reach the battle-front in time to back up the scattered units of the 282nd Regiment and cover the retreat. Four days later, on 7 December, all Red Army units of the Botlikh Sector unable to resist, converged on Khunzakh fortress for protection. The besieged troops included units of the 176th, 280th, 282nd and 284th Regiments — altogether some 2,000 men, led by Najmuddin Samurskii. This time the siege of Gunib and Khunzakh fortresses lasted nearly two months. Gunib was completely surrounded; the Red troops, suffering from a typhoid epidemic, lacked food and ammunition and were obliged to eat their horses. The situation in Khunzakh was somewhat better thanks to the political leadership of Samurskii and the activity of Ataev and Shamkhala Salikhov's partisans, who operated and crossed behind enemy lines in the Andi region. Ataev's unit was particularly mobile and maintained a link with the Red Army in Temir Khan Shura, while Salikhov controlled the main road from Andi to Antsukho and Georgia at the rear of the rebels' positions.[7] The garrison kept its hold on the Khunzakh plateau and was able to make forays outside the fortress for skirmishes with the rebels and to capture food provisions from the neighbouring *auls*. The raiding parties usually consisted of 250 men backed up by cavalry and machine-guns. Todorskii claimed that these raids brought heavy casualties and disarray into the ranks of the rebels, but this seems a disingenuous statement since the siege would not have lasted so long if it had been true. The more likely reason was probably that the rebels, greatly outnumbered throughout the course of the war, were not able to spare the manpower to guard the Khunzakh plateau and fortress.

The siege of Gunib provided a remarkable example of the Mountaineers' code of honour and gallantry. When the small besieged garrison was threatened with starvation, Samurskii appealed to the rebels in the following words, reminding them that it was easy for those who are well fed to defeat the hungry: 'If you have honour, if you are indeed the sons of Shamil as you claim, if you want to show yourselves to be eagles of the mountain, send us some food and then we will see who will win.'[8] The following night, under gunfire from the garrison, the rebels approached the fort and left bags of flour and food.

From Gunib the rebels, originally with only 400 men, followed up their advantage by occupying Gergebil and Aimaki. On 20 December a special task force, hurriedly set up under comrade Krivonosov, left Levashi to attempt to break through to relieve Gunib and Khunzakh by way of Khodzhal-Makhi. The task force had two batteries of light artillery and two armoured cars. The Mountaineers allowed Krivonosov to approach Khodzhal-Makhi unopposed along the bottom of a ravine, only to greet him near the *aul* with a salvo of fire from the heights above. Sallying forth and counter-attacking, they drove the detachment back to Levashi, which Krivonosov only managed to hold thanks to his armoured vehicles.

Action during the second phase of the war

The end of the year marked a turning-point in the war, with the Bolsheviks throwing another Red Army division, the 14th 'Stepin' Rifle

Division (with three brigades, the 40th, 41st and 42nd), into the mountains of Daghestan. Furthermore on orders from the high command of the 11th Army, the 2nd Moscow Cadet Brigade (with two rifle and one cavalry regiments), together with the 52nd rifle brigade from Azerbaijan, were also attached to the 32nd Division commanded by Todorskii. The south coastal areas of Daghestan — Kaytak, Tabassaran, Kurin and Samurski districts — were occupied, and to the north the Terek Army stood guard over the Chechen lowlands, the bread-basket of Upper Chechnia and Daghestan during the uprising. From Groznyi the 97th Artillery Brigade was ordered to Vedeno to scout in the direction of Botlikh in an attempt to catch the enemy in a pincer movement. From January 1921 tactics modelled on the experience of the tsarist conquest were applied, but more ruthlessly: one valley after another was occupied, and its population slaughtered or deported. The rebels, heavily outnumbered and hemmed in from north and south, were steadily pushed into the remotest mountains of Upper Daghestan where they were isolated from the rest of the population and deprived of the possibility of further retreat. However, in the short term this strategy of deliberate terror was counter-productive, since it fuelled the resistance with the ardour of despair and greatly slowed the advance of the Red Army.

The plan of campaign issued on 28 December ordered an offensive in three directions: Khodzhal-Makhi, Aimaki-Gergebil which controlled the way to Khunzakh, and Gimri. On 1 January four regiments, including one of cavalry,[9] converged on Khodzhal-Makhi, and after fighting all day managed to take up a position on the high ground facing the *aul*. The battle continued through the night, and at dawn the next day, with the help of armoured vehicles and artillery fire, Khodzhal-Makhi was overrun. It is difficult to estimate the exact numbers on both sides, but it seems that the advantage was three-to-one in favour of the Red Army. According to Todorskii, the rebels lost 100 men killed and 140 were taken prisoner, while the Reds' casualties were twenty-four killed and seventy-one wounded. This was incidentally the only mention of prisoners taken throughout the war. Todorskii spoke with pride about this battle, probably because it was the only rapid and successful engagement of which the Red Army could boast during the war. Also, it was the only time when the Russians were able to surprise the enemy in a sudden round-about attack during the night, taking full advantage of the mountain terrain.[10] The Rebels, an unknown number, retreated to Gergebil where their main force, of an estimated 1,000 fighters, was gathered. Despite their heavy losses, they were able to capture four guns in the process.

The battle of Gergebil

The offensive against Gergebil began on 7 January in a three-pronged movement, to Aimaki, east of Gergebil, and along the Kara Koisu. The *aul* rose from a cliff at the foot of Aimaki defile, and was impregnable from the north-west where it overlooked a precipice. Some places are fated to be at the centre of human conflict, and such was Gergebil. The thunder of war and cannon fire was not unknown there; it was stormed many times during the Russian conquest, destroyed and rebuilt. In 1847 and 1848 Shamil himself, his most famous *naibs* (lieutenants), Haji Murat, and the élite of the Tsar's army fought and died in the surrounding mountains, canyons and torrents. Vorontsov failed to conquer it, but Argutinskii-Dolgorukii, flanked by his most famous generals Wrangel, Orbeliani and Bariatinskii, succeeded. There Todtleben, the defender of Sevastopol and victor of Plevna, received his baptism of fire. It was necessary to fire 10,000 shells and rifle shots to destroy this mountain village.[11]

The narrow path leading up to the *aul* was hard to ascend even for the infantry, and the guns had to be carried. Initially, the Red forces thrown into the attack comprised six battalions and three full regiments of the 41st Brigade. For ten days the battle raged around Gergebil, Red units trying unsuccessfully to secure the mountain positions around the *aul* and capture the strategic Salty bridge. The rebels, highly mobile and elusive in their familiar territory, struck the approaching troops from all sides. The Russian advance was clumsy and painful with 558 casualties in the first week. In one encounter alone on the banks of the Kazi-Kumukh Koisu, in an already classical pattern, several battalions of the 123rd Regiment were lured into the ravine and immediately attacked 'with hurricane-like fire' from the cliffs above, with the consequent loss of 292 men, including twenty-one officers. Reading Todorskii's deliberately dry and unemotional account of these days, one is struck nevertheless by his irritation with the pedestrian spirit, lack of talent and imagination if not sheer stupidity behind the Red officers' thinking. One is far from the revolutionary brilliance of Budenny's command of his cavalry corps.

On 17 January fresh reserves — three rifle regiments of the 42nd Brigade — were brought in from Temir Khan Shura, and a new assault on Gergebil was planned for the next day. It failed, and in spite of receiving reinforcements, Red units continued to fight without success against well defended innaccessible mountain bastions for another four days. Morale among them was deteriorating. They managed, however, to grind their way slowly to positions within half a mile of the *aul*. In desperation, on 21 January, the 11th Army headquarters issued a new set of confused and contradictory directives which showed their total ignorance of the geography of the region:

(1) to regroup all units immediately for a breakthrough towards Karadakh across Salty bridge; to liquidate the rebels there, then turn on Gergebil before advancing to Khunzakh;

(2) this to be achieved by advancing in a strong compact column without wasting time, effort and strength on isolated enemy units;

(3) to increase intelligence and reconnaissance work;

(4) to avoid as far as possible any frontal attacks which are seldom successful in mountain warfare;

(5) to manoeuvre with more flexibility and intelligence, avoid predictability, change routes, and use detours to ambush the enemy;

(6) to increase coordination between all units of the front, and keep communication lines open;

(7) to make full use of artillery; and to

(8) raise the morale of the troops by all possible means.

This order caused a violent clash with Todorskii, who accused the military headquarters of inability to read maps properly — the way to Karadakh through Salty bridge followed a narrow path with a precipice on one side and a rock face on the other. He argued for the need to proceed slowly with full knowledge of the terrain and the opponent's vulnerable points. He also insisted that each attack on a rebel stronghold, even when unsuccessful, weakened the adversaries' defences because it would force them every time to evacuate their civilians and valuable supplies. That same day the Army headquarters accepted Todorskii's recommendation but stressed the urgency of relieving the siege of Khunzakh, and for the first time in the war authorised the use of aeroplanes.

The following day, 18 January, the attack on Gergebil was once again delayed when Red units caught in a mountain storm abandoned their weapons and retreated in disorder having lost 103 men, some frozen in the snow. On 23 January, from their stand on the mountain ridge, the 125th and 126th Regiments were able to fight their way down the mountain slopes and position themselves directly east of Gergebil while the *aul* was bombarded from below. The rebels under the command of Sheikhs Mohammad of Balakhany and Jemal of Gotsatl still defended the direct approaches and summits protecting the access to Gergebil, and attempted several counter-attacks by swiftly moving across the passes. In an unconscious tribute to the courage of the Mountaineers caught in this unequal David and Goliath struggle, Todorskii noted that they even managed to raid the built-up fortifications of the Red troops with hand-grenades.[12]

On 25 January at dawn the Reds attacked from the east, south and south-west. After a battle lasting five hours they were able to approach to within 200 metres of Gergebil, but because of the high casualties and the accurate fire of the rebels they delayed the assault until dark.

The final onslaught was launched at 2 a.m. on 26 January. The rebels were driven towards the *aul*. They divided their forces, some retreating to *aul* Kodutl, while others chose to defend Gergebil. They took cover in the houses and the mosque. Todorskii wrote that Red troops had to throw hand-grenades through the chimneys as the Mountaineers fought for each house. At 10 a.m. the rebels were still holding out in the mosque and the surrounding buildings after several failed attempts to storm it. The decision was then taken to burn the mosque. Some hundred rebels were killed or burned alive. Nonetheless, it was only at 6 p.m. that 'the enemy was finally liquidated', to use Todorskii's words. The Red Army captured nine guns in Gergebil. No prisoners were taken: the women and children had been evacuated to the left bank of the Avar Koisu before the battle, and the men died fighting. In the last two days the Soviets lost 142 men, making a total of 877 killed since the beginning of the campaign. We do not know the Mountaineers' casualties apart from those burned in the mosque. Todorskii simply mentioned that they were several times those of his troops.

The battle for Gergebil had lasted nearly three weeks in a haunting replay, almost day for day, of the combats which it witnessed in the nineteenth century, down to the fighting on the rooftops of the *aul*. The difference? Only the milder season; the Tsar's generals fought in the summer. Haji Murat lost a thousand *murids* who died among alpine flowers defending the orchards of Gergebil. Their descendants lay buried beneath the snow.

The nearby bastions of Kikuni and Kharta fell the same day, and Aimaki the next day at 2 p.m., followed by the *auls* of Darada, Maali, Uzdal-Loso, Kakhi, Takhada and Gotsatl in the evening. On 28

January, the Red Army occupied the fortifications of Karadakh and lifted the siege of Khunzakh. The rebels withdrew to Arakan.

Balance of power at the end of January 1921

At the end of January 1921, Todorskii estimated the resistance to have 9,690 fighters under arms divided as follows: in Andi region 4,400 men including 1,000 horsemen with twenty-three guns; in Avar region 3,630 men including 830 horsemen with fifteen guns; in Gunib region 660 men including 260 horsemen commanded by Colonel Omar Piralov with headquarters in Sogratl; and in Kazi-Kumukh 1,000 men, including 400 horsemen, under the leadership of Sheikh Ibragim Haji of Kuchri. To increase coordination, all Red Army units engaged in the conflict in Daghestan and Chechnia were united under the single command of the 'Terek-Daghestan Group of Armies' on 25 January. They comprised the 14th and 32nd Divisions, the 2nd Moscow Cadet Brigade, the 27th and 49th Armoured Vehicle Detachments, the 18th Air Reconnaissance Detachment, and the 176th Artillery Regiment of the 20th Division which remained, however, under the command of Levandovskii.[13]

Action in Chechnia

The military operations of the resistance in Chechnia could never acquire as wide a range as those in Daghestan because of the tight control exercised by the Red Army on Lower Chechnia. Underground guerrilla activities, however, had some impact. On 19 January, Daghestanis from Andi region, together with Chechens from *aul* Benoi, suddenly attacked a battalion of the 292nd Rifle Regiment stationed in Dargo and Belgatoi, helped by 'underground' elements present there. The Regiment suffered heavy losses and was forced to withdraw to join the units of the 291st Regiment garrisoned in Tezen-Qala. Further pressed, the Red units were obliged to abandon Tezen-Qala from where they were driven into an ambush by their Chechen guides, again sustaining severe casualties.

On 21 January the élite Cavalry Regiment of the Moscow Cadet Brigade was surrounded near Alleroy in Upper Chechnia. The commanding officer of the regiment was the first to be killed when attempting to lead a party to break out of the encirclement. The regiment lost ten officers and eighty-three cadets.[14]

The fall of Arakan

After the victory over Gergebil and the rescue of Khunzakh, the objectives of the Red Army were Arakan and Gimri. So long as Arakan held, Gimri could only be approached by descending a 5,000-foot precipice on the eastern bank of the Sulak river (formed by the four torrents Avar Koisu, Kara Koisu, Kazi-Kumukh Koisu and Andi Koisu).[15] Arakan had been subjected to continuous artillery fire since the disaster of 30 October 1920, and its defence depended on the control of Chalda *aul*, which had changed hands five times between the end of December 1920 and the beginning of February 1921. The best Red Army troops of the 14th Division, nicknamed 'strike force' after their capture of Gergebil, converged on Arakan.

On 8 February, Chalda and Kuiada,[16] another *aul* defending access to Arakan, were finally seized and the Red Army turned its attention to the heights surrounding Arakan itself, securing *aul* Kodutl on 10 February. The final assault took place on 13 February, and on the 14th, after fierce hand-to-hand fighting, Arakan fell. With the defeat of Arakan the Soviets were in control of most of north-east Daghestan with the exception of Gimri.

The surrender of Gimri

More than any other place, Gimri, the birthplace of Shamil and Ghazi Mohammad, is sacred in Daghestani memory. Ghazi Mohammad, the first imam of Daghestan, was killed on its walls in October 1832 during one of the most tragic episodes of the Russian conquest.

The campaign against Gimri, an eagle's nest, began on 25 December 1920 and ended with its surrender on 18 February 1921. Gimri was protected by guard posts situated roughly 8 kilometres ahead of the village. In November 1920, the Red Army had sent a message to Gimri to the effect that it did not consider the *aul* 'guilty', and suggested disbanding the guard posts and establishing a *revkom*. Gimri replied that it did not wish to take sides in the war, hence the need for its own protection. Because of its natural defences, there was no possibility to storm the *aul*, and the action had to be led by artillery units. Todorskii judged the operation to be technically the most difficult of the war. As in 1832, the invading Russians chose the Karanai path, the easier of the only two routes leading to Gimri, to move their artillery. It took a month, until 24 January 1921, to transport by hand or on donkeys four batteries of two light artillery guns, three field guns, four howitzers and two heavy artillery guns. It is interesting here to compare the achievement of the Red Army to that of its tsarist predecessors. During the first campaign against Gimri, Klugenau and Rosen, marching from Temir Khan Shura, needed only one week, from 10 to 18 October, to build their fortifications, set up their artillery for the assault, and storm the bastion. Furthermore, some of Klugenau's squadrons worked their way down the 5,000-foot ravine, an alpinist feat which the Soviets did not even envisage. Winter had set in early in 1832 and the mountains were already covered in snow in October, thus the weather and the terrain alone could not explain the difference in performance.[17]

Heavy bombardment of Gimri began in the last week of December. Grenades used against the *aul* before the artillery batteries had been positioned caused some damage to the houses, but until then the Mountaineers were able to repair them at night. However, the heavy batteries and howitzers placed at approximately 4 miles from their targets inflicted such devastation that the rebels did not bother with any repairs — 90 per cent of the buildings were destroyed before the end of December. The Red Army also used chemical weapons which were meant to 'demoralise' their adversaries, although Todorskii admitted that only a few cows were affected.[18] The *aul* was bombarded day and night. Todorskii, who knew the history of the nineteenth-century Caucasian war well, for once departed from his usual objectivity to find weak explanations for the delays of the campaign, such as fog and low clouds over the mountains. He also claimed that the rebels 'panicked' during the nightly shelling — a statement inconsistent with his own description of their resistance. What the Daghestanis did was to take cover in the mountains during the cannonades, then ambush and attack artillery units with rifle-fire, and raid the Reds' fortifications at night to push the guns into the canyons, so much so that Todorskii complained that his troops had to move the guns every night to protect them from destruction. On one occasion they even managed to capture a gun from the Moscow cadets.

On 16 February, Red Caucasian partisans and Moscow cadets invested Untsukhul, a large and revolutionary *aul* frequently hostile in the past to its celebrated neighbour Gimri. A Red militia of 400 riflemen was immediately formed under Hassan. On 17 February a delegation was sent to Gimri to offer a cease-fire, and on the 18th, at 5 p.m., battered and ravaged, it was occupied without a fight by Hassan and three battalions of the Cadet Regiment, followed two hours later by the general staff. Only two machine-guns and a box of ammunitions were left in the *aul*. Todorskii gave no details of the casualties among the rebels. We may therefore assume that the majority of the defenders of Gimri had either retreated higher in the mountains or were killed. Given the state of destruction during the artillery siege, and the rebels' concern for their non-combatants, it is likely that the civilian population had been evacuated earlier. A grim episode, however, gives an indication of the mood prevailing among the Mountaineers: a neighbouring *aul*, Ashilta, had been occupied without resistance by a 125-man unit of the Cadet Regiment on the day of Gimri's surrender, and stockpiled with weapons. During the night rebels surrounded Ashilta, and with the help of the villagers destroyed the detachment to the last man. When the situation was restored the next day, the mutilated bodies of fifty-two cadets were found.[19] This is the only such occurrence during the war reported by Todorskii and one wonders what provoked this unusual behaviour.

Towards the endgame

With Gimri vanquished, the Red Army controlled most of north-east Daghestan. The rebels began to retreat from Avaristan towards the remote high mountain Andi territory. Gunib fortress had been liberated by the partisans of Karaev on 3 January and the recalcitrant *auls* of Rigzha and Sogratl captured after fierce resistance on 9 and 14 February respectively. The rebels were still in possession of all western Daghestan and the region north-west of Khunzakh, with advance posts in Mochok, Matlasy and Siukh.[20]

The Reconquest, March 1921

Throughout March the major resistance citadels fell one after the other: Misterukh and Karada, 4 March; Botlikh, 5 March; Ansalta, 7 March; *auls* Tsiditl, Siukh, Mekhelta, Shavdukh, Tsundi, Inachali and many others, 8 March. On 9 March, Ataev linked up with the Terek Army in Chechnia. In a hopeless position after continuous fighting for control of the left bank of the Andi Koisu, Chirkat, an *aul* situated some 9 miles from Gimri, declared submission on 11 March, offering eighteen hostages. Chirkat had rejected all offers to surrender since the end of February. When it was finally overrun by Hassan's partisans, only two guns and 100 rifles were found. On 13 March, with the capture of

Artlukh, Danukh, Argani and Garadi, Avaristan was cleared of rebels up to the Salatau range, and following on the footsteps of Ataev's partisans, the 123rd and 295th linked up with the Terek Army. The offensive was then turned towards the southern sector, the *auls* were occupied and the population disarmed. Some rebels began to disappear and melt into the population. Simultaneously most strongholds in Upper Chechnia — Dargo, Alleroy, Benoi, Datakh and Tezen-Qala — were subdued between 7 and 14 March.

On 18 March the 14th Division was ordered to join with the Terek Army. On the 25th Todorskii requested the Red Army stationed in Tiflis since the fall of the Georgian Republic on 25 February 1921 to help liquidate the uprising by attacking the rebels in west Daghestan from Georgia. From then on the rebels were doomed. In the last week of March they gathered their last remaining forces, some 800 fighters, to launch a ferocious counter-attack, but obviously to little avail against such overwhelming odds. Three factors stood out during the March events. First, from a military viewpoint, there was the predominant role played by the Caucasian Red partisans; almost everywhere they led the way with audacity for the Red Army to toil behind. Secondly, the tenacity of the rebels, who continued to attempt counter-attacks as they retreated, was also remarkable. And finally, there were the numerous 'uprisings' in the defeated *auls* and assassinations of Red Army occupation forces.[21]

Declaration of the 'Revolutionary Military Soviet'

On 15 March the Military Soviet in Petrovsk issued the following statement:

> Thanks to the heroic efforts of the valiant units of the Terek-Daghestan Army, the counter-revolutionary uprising in Chechnia and Daghestan was crushed and liquidated. The bloody initiators, ideological leaders and organisers of the uprising, unbidden by the Daghestani and Chechen poor, have hidden in the wilds of Salatau and Daghestan. Thus they have escaped the well-deserved punishment for the innumerable crimes and misfortunes which the deceived poor of Daghestan and Chechnia had to bear.
>
> At the price of innumerable victims from the Red Army, abundant bloodshed from modest unknown Red Army heroes, the backward Daghestani and Chechen masses were freed from the cabal of the

White guard officer class, and the lies and deceptions of parasitic sheikhs and mullahs.

The heroic units of the Red Army have endured heavy privations during the liquidation of the Terek-Daghestan uprising, fighting without interruption and bearing inhuman hardships.

Hungry, cut off from the home front, overcoming all obstacles, they marched on towards their goal, breaking on the way the bitter resistance of the deceived Chechens and Daghestanis.

The valiant units of the Red Army have shown to all counter-revolutionary elements of Chechnia and Daghestan the futility of their plots to overthrow Soviet power and destroy the Red Army.

The Revolutionary Military Soviet greatly appreciated the heroism shown by all the Terek-Daghestan Army units, and in the name of the Revolution thanked all the Red Army and commissars' leading personnel.

However, with a view to strengthening the achievements of the Red Army, the Revolutionary Military Soviet ordered its units stationed in the occupied *raions* of Chechnia and Daghestan strictly to amend their behaviour by taking into account the historical, customary and political aspects of the Mountaineers' way of life, in order to convince the mountain poor of the peaceful intentions of the Red Army — the friend and mighty defender of the poor.

The Military Soviet further ordered that political work be started — the utmost priority being the establishment of friendly relations between the army and the population. The Revolutionary Military Soviet was convinced that the commanders and commissars would show their personal initiative and would earn the love and respect of the mountain poor.[22]

The rebels' last stand

In April the rebels withdrew to set up their defences for their last stand. The chosen place, Gidatl, was situated in the Dido-Avar region in the western corner of Daghestan on the border with Georgia, half a mile south of the confluence of the Avar Koisu and Tomsadin rivers. The last rebel detachment, led by Colonel Jafarov, was 250–300 men strong and included the few surviving leaders of the uprising, Colonel Alikhanov and his three sons, Lieutenant Hassan Abakarov, and the population of Bezhita and Gidatl *auls*. They had four machine-guns. Their stronghold was well defended while the mountains were still covered in snow with only one approach through a narrow winding path. After one attempt to climb the path, during which Osmanov's partisans lost five men and twelve horses, it was decided to wait until the snow melted. A few rebel groups were also still holding out in the Andi territory.

Red Army forces gathered for the last onslaught. They comprised six rifle regiments from the 14th and 32nd Divisions and four cavalry squadrons of the 18th Division of the 11th Army based in Georgia,[23] as well as Ataev's partisan detachment held in reserve.

On 6 and 7 May the Red cavalry crossed into Daghestan through the Kodor, Gavazi, Lagodekhi and Belakany passes. On 20 May the two armies joined to launch the attack on Gidatl. Typically, the assault was led by the partisan Ataev, with the Red Army regiments following behind. Resistance was no more possible for the rebels than it had been for Shamil and his fifty remaining faithful *murids* in their last refuge of Gunib in August 1859, when Bariatinskii had deployed 40,000 men to overpower them.

Gidatl fell. On 21 May the remaining *auls*, Megitl and Shidi, were captured. Colonel Kaitmas Alikhanov with his three sons were captured and killed during the battle; Colonel Jafarov escaped but later gave himself up to the Soviets in Temir Khan Shura — his fate after that is unknown; Colonel Omar Piralov was killed later; Lieutenant Abakarov was caught alive but killed himself by jumping off Gidatl bridge into the Avar Koisu; Said Bek escaped to Turkey; Gotsinskii went into hiding and was only captured and killed in 1925. Thus ended the last Caucasian *Ghazawat*. Total Red Army casualties in Daghestan numbered some 5,000 men.[24] According to Todorskii, there could not have been a successful outcome to the war in Daghestan against such a 'determined' and militarily well trained adversary had the Red Army not been able to use artillery.[25]

Some character outlines

We have little information on the religious and military leaders of the uprising. While it was safe for his adversaries to praise Uzun Haji, who died before the beginning of the uprising, the same did not apply to Imam Najmuddin Gotsinskii. Samurskii and Todorskii disliked him intensely; Takho-Godi, more objective, conceding that he was a captivating and charismatic personality. Certainly he seemed to have been a more complex and ambiguous figure than Uzun Haji. Takho-

Godi and Todorskii reported that he was the son of a *naib* of Shamil, Dono Magoma, who surrendered to the Russians and later sided with them during the 1877 uprising. It was added that his father received rich lands and 10,000 sheep for his betrayal, an unverified claim aimed at discrediting Gotsinskii in the eyes of the North Caucasians. Takho-Godi further wrote that Najmuddin was a distinguished Arabist and a talented poet. Having finished his schooling he joined the horse guards of the tsarist governor, was nominated a judge of the Daghestani National Tribunal, and later became 'chief *naib*' of Koisubul region. In 1903, he spent three months in Istanbul, after which he was regarded by the Russian administration as an emissary of the Ottomans. It was rumoured that he had participated in the disturbances of 1905, secretly favouring the socialists. In 1913, he was suspected by Volskii, the military governor, of having instigated the *Pisar* movement (which demanded the replacement of all Russian clerks). At the time of the 1920 uprising he was sixty years old. Takho-Godi described him as resembling an old eagle, with a sombre expression, seldom smiling, proud and domineering. He was said to have hypnotic gifts and to be able to interpret dreams. He liked to indulge in religious and philosophical debates with his *murids*.[26] His major political mistake was to have compromised with Denikin during the Civil War.

Todorskii gave a few brief details of the other insurgent leaders. Colonel Kaitmas Alikhanov, born in Khunzakh, was sixty-two years old when he was killed. He was the brother of the Tsarist General Alikhan Avarskii, and had begun his military service in 1887 in the cavalry. He fought in the Russian-Japanese war and on the side of the Whites during the Civil War. Colonel Jafarov, aged thirty-seven at the time of the uprising, was born in *aul* Kudali of Gunib district. He served in the Daghestani Horse Regiment before the Revolution, and during the Civil War led a regiment of Mountaineers against the Red Army in Kachalin and Tsaritsyn under the command of Wrangel. Lieutenant Hassan Abakarov joined the Daghestani Horse Regiment and was promoted to officer grade during the First World War for military distinction. Todorskii described Abakarov as outstandingly courageous and energetic, and Shamil's great-grandson as exceptionally brave. Sheikh Mohammad of Balakhany, probably the most important military commander of the uprising, had great influence on the population thanks to his strong religious idealism and sincerity. Sirajuddin Haji, sixty years old, another distinguished Arabist, was renowned for his uncompromising opposition to the Bolsheviks ever since 1917. Dervish Mohammad

Haji, an Arabist scholar from the Andi region, was decisive and cruel but enjoyed a large following. Ibragim Haji of Kuchri, a native of *aul* Kuchri, had fought against the Whites. According to Todorskii, he was deceitful and a coward but not without authority in his home territory.[27]

Immediate aftermath of the uprising

The country lay completely in ruins, with ninety major centres having been obliterated. Khasavyurt was completely destroyed, and ancient Derbent devastated. Bridges and telegraph lines were down, and the roads had became unusable. Agriculture was completely disrupted, grapes had gone wild, and only 25 per cent of the pre-war population of cattle — the main resource of Daghestan — had survived. Immediately after the end of the military operations, famine struck. Other calamities followed: an epidemic of cattle disease in 1922; the beginning of the forced resettlement of the Mountaineers into the lowlands in 1923 (they numbered approximately 10,000, according to Samurskii); and a failed harvest in 1924. In the mountain *auls*, wrote Samurskii, people wore animal skins, and at certain times of the day the men were forbidden to leave the houses, so that the women, half-naked, could go unobserved to the water springs.[28]

In the 1920s domestic troubles in the Muslim territories of Soviet Russia weighed heavily on Soviet strategy in the Muslim world abroad. As an immediate consequence, the uprising in Daghestan and Chechnia made any military or political intervention in Turkey and Iran impossible. Indeed it was difficult to preach a holy war against the British imperialists in Ghilan, as Zinoviev proposed in September 1920 in Baku, while resisting an authentic *jihad* in Daghestan. In the long run, the war left a long-lasting heritage of anti-Russian xenophobia. From 1922 to 1943, the history of Chechnia and Daghestan was an almost uninterrupted succession of rebellions, counter-expeditions and 'political banditism' — uprisings took place in 1924, 1928, 1936 — culminating in the attempted but unsuccessful genocide by Stalin of four North Caucasian Muslim nations (the Chechens, Ingush, Karachays and Balkars) in February 1944.

Far from slowing down the development of militant Sufism, the defeat of the resistance gave it a new impetus.[29] The *ghazis* of 1920, together with Shamil's *murids*, remain for their descendants today the models of perfect heroism and symbols of national liberation.

NOTES

1. N. Samurskii (Efendiev), *Dagestan*, Moscow and Leningrad: Gosudarstvennoe Izdatel'stvo, 1925, p. 128.
2. A. Takho-Godi, *Revoliutsiia i kontr-revoliutsiia v Dagestane*, Makhachkala: Dagestanskii Nauch-Issl. Institut, 1927, pp. 39–40.
3. See Alexandre Bennigsen, 'Muslim Guerilla Warfare in the Caucasus (1918–1928)', *Central Asian Survey*, July 1983, vol. 2, no 1.
4. Chantal Lemercier-Quelquejay, 'Sufi Brotherhoods in the USSR', *Central Asian Survey*, 1983, vol. 2, no. 4, pp. 1–35, quoting A.A. Salamov, 'Pravda o sviatykh mestakh v Checheno Ingushetii', *Trudy Checheno Ingushskogo Nauchnogo-Issledovatel'skogo Instituta pri Sovete Ministrov Checheno Ingushskoi ASSR*, Groznyi, 1964, vol. IX, p. 162.
5. N. Samurskii, *op. cit.* p. 55.
6. *Ibid.*, p. 107.
7. During the siege, Salikhov was able to repel two attacks by Said Bek on the Akhvakh area of the Andi *okrug*, and to destroy a rebel unit of fifty men.
8. N. Samurskii, *op. cit.*, p. 87.
9. The 118th, 119th and 120th Rifle Regiments and the Cavalry Regiment of the 32nd Division.
10. A. Todorskii, *Krasnaia armiia v gorakh. Deistviia v Dagestane*, Moscow, Voennyi Vestnik, 1924. Todorskii's estimates of the number of rebels are not accurate and vary substantially from one paragraph to another. For information on this battle, see Todorskii, p. 106.
11. John F. Baddeley, *The Russian Conquest of the Caucasus*, London: Longmans, Green, 1908, pp. 428–36.
12. A. Todorskii, *op. cit.*, p. 118.
13. Mikhail Karlovich Levandovskii (1890–1937), born in Tiflis, was at the time commander-in-chief of the 9th Red Army. He was later engaged in 1924–5 in the war against the Basmachi in Central Asia.
14. A. Todorskii, *op. cit.*, p. 134.
15. W.E.D. Allen and P. Muratoff, *Caucasian Battlefields: A History of the Wars on the Turco-Caucasian Border, 1828–1921*, Cambridge University Press, 1953, p. 525.
16. Kuiada was captured by the partisans of Osmanov backed by units of the 118th and 119th Regiments: A. Todorskii, *op. cit.*, p. 136.
17. See John F. Baddeley for a description of the 1832 campaign, *op. cit.*, pp. 276–7.
18. A. Todorskii, *op. cit.* p. 125. Chemical weapons used on a few occasions in Afghanistan in the 1980s had no more impact.
19. *Ibid.*, p. 140.
20. W.E.D. Allen and P. Muratoff, *op. cit.*, p. 525.
21. A. Todorskii, *op. cit.* pp. 146–8.
22. *Ibid.*, pp. 149–50.
23. Of the 105th and 106th Cavalry Regiments of the 11th Army.
24. Todorskii wrote that 5,000 men were killed in Daghestan and Chechnia during the whole of the Civil War and uprising. However, as the Red Army only arrived in Daghestan in the spring of 1920, we can safely deduce that the casualties were sustained during the uprising. A comparison of this figure with the semi-official data on Soviet soldiers killed in Afghanistan — about 10,000 in the ten years of

fighting — gives an idea of the intensity of the fighting in the North Caucasus.

25. A. Todorskii, *op. cit.*, pp. 159 and 173.
26. A. Takho-Godi, *op. cit.*, pp. 26–7.
27. A. Todorskii, *op. cit.*, pp. 54–5.
28. N. Samurskii, *op. cit.*, pp. 138–9.
29. See, on this subject, Alexandre Bennigsen and S. Enders Wimbush, *Mystics and Commisars: Sufism in the Soviet Union*, London: C. Hurst 1985.

THE CHECHENS AND THE INGUSH DURING THE SOVIET PERIOD AND ITS ANTECEDENTS

Abdurahman Avtorkhanov

On 15 January 1939 *Izvestiia* published the following information from the official Soviet news agency TASS in the article 'Quinquennium of Chechnia-Ingushetia' (Groznyi, 14 January):[1]

Five years ago, on 13 January 1934, two Caucasian peoples, endowed with a kindred language, culture and life-style, united to form an autonomous Chechen-Ingush *oblast*. On 5 December 1936, this *oblast* was transformed into an autonomous Soviet Socialist Republic. The history of Chechnia-Ingushetia is that of a decade long bloody struggle by a freedom-loving people against colonisers and the national bourgeoisie — the mainstay of tsarism. During the years of the Soviet regime Chechnia-Ingushetia was transformed beyond all recognition. By government deed, over 400,000 hectares of land were turned over for permanent use to the Republic's *kolkhoz*. 92.7 per cent of peasants' properties were unified into *kolkhoz*. An important petroleum industry was founded. New petroleum-producing regions were discovered: Malgobek and Gorskaia. Two refining plants and an engineering plant, 'Krasnyi molot' [Red Hammer], were built. Food processing and chemical engineering, in particular, together with both light and cottage industries, were newly created.

The culture of the Chechen-Ingush people, national in form and socialist in content, has flourished sumptuously under the sun of Stalin's Constitution. Before the Revolution, Chechnia-Ingushetia possessed just three schools. Today over 118,000 children are attending 342 primary and secondary schools. The higher education institutions — technicums and workers' universities — train hundreds of engineers, technicians and teachers every year. All these results have been achieved in the course of a stubborn struggle against the enemies of the people: Trotsykists, Bukharinists, bourgeois-nationalists, who are endeavouring to snatch from the workers the gains of the Great October Socialist Revolution.

In February 1944, exactly five years later, the entire population of

146

Chechnia-Ingushetia, literally in the course of twenty-four hours, were arrested and embarked in prisoners' convoys for transport to an unknown destination. Subsequently, two years and four months later, *Izvestiia* published an antedated *ukaz* of the Presidium of the Supreme Soviet of the RSFSR on the 'Liquidation of the Chechen-Ingush Soviet Republic and the Deportation of its Population', with no indication of the place of deportation. The *ukaz*, dated 25 June 1946, justifies the deportation as follows:

> Many Chechens and Ingush, incited by German agents, entered voluntarily into formations organised by Germans and, together with German armed forces, rose up in arms against the Red Army. Obeying German orders they formed gangs in order to attack the Soviet government from the rear. A large section of the population of the Chechen-Ingush Republic offered no resistance whatsoever to these traitors to the fatherland. For this reason the Chechen-Ingush Republic is being liquidated and its population deported.

Thus came to an end the centuries-old history of Chechnia-Ingushetia with the obliteration of the entire Republic from the map of the Soviet Union and the disappearance of the names 'Chechen' and 'Ingush' from the current vocabulary. However, the official reason given for the annihilation of these people — collaboration with the Germans — is based on the assumption of the ignorance of the Soviet people and a lack of information in the Western world. It is relevant here to point out two factors first, that during the Second World War not one single German soldier ever appeared on Chechen-Ingush territory, with the exception of a brief occupation of the frontier locality of Malgobek, where the population was Russian; and secondly, that it was materially impossible for Chechens and Ingush to join German formations since there was no compulsory mobilisation in Chechnia-Ingushetia throughout the entire existence of the Republic. The partial mobilisation during the Soviet war against Finland was cancelled at the beginning of German-Soviet hostilities. Moreover, the Chechens and Ingush were exempt from service in the Red Army. (The order of the High Command of the Red Army in February 1942 explains this exemption by the refusal of the Chechens and Ingush to eat pork on religious grounds.)

It is true that at the beginning of the hostilities the Germans captured, along with a 5-million-strong Red Army prisoner-of-war population, a few dozen Chechens and Ingush who later formed into a company within the framework of the North Caucasian Legion (in the summer of 1945, this company was handed over by the British to the Soviets in the region of Hanover). But it is in the first document quoted above that we find the key phrase revealing the reason for the deportation: 'The history of Chechnia-Ingushetia is that of a decade-long bloody struggle by a free-dom-loving people against colonisers. . . .' It is only thanks to this phrase that we can establish the historical truth.

It is well known that the Bolsheviks considered the struggle of oppressed peoples for their national liberation and independence as justifiable when it took place before the establishment of the Soviet regime. Any national liberation struggle in the Soviet Union, on the other hand, was not only condemned but mercilessly quelled. This does not mean, however, that nations which fought for their independence in tsarist Russia gave up this struggle under the Soviet regime. Quite the reverse: never in the history of pre-1917 Russia was the national problem more acute, and never were non-Russian nationalities more pitilessly repressed, than under Soviet rule. In tsarist Russia it was principally the non-Slavic peoples, Caucasians and Turkestanis, that struggled for independence. But in the Soviet period the national liberation movement was carried on across a broad front that included all Slavic and non-Slavic nationalities. As of old, the Caucasus was in the vanguard of this struggle led by the Chechen-Ingush people. That is why they were the first victims in this unequal, though just, struggle.

Historical background

According to the Soviet Union's Constitution of 1936, the territory (*krai*) of the North Caucasus consisted of the autonomous regions (*oblast*) of Cherkessia, Adyghe and Karachay, and the autonomous Soviet Socialist Republics of Kabardino-Balkaria, Northern Ossetia, Chechnia-Ingushetia and Daghestan. The Chechen-Ingush Soviet Republic occupied an area of 15,700 square kilometres with a population of 700,000. At the time of the deportation, which affected all Chechens and Ingush living in the Caucasus (including those resident in Daghestan and Georgia), and taking into account the normal increase in the population, this probably amounted to one million people. The Republic dealt mainly in agriculture, stock-breeding and the petroleum industries. Chechnia-Ingushetia was the second most important petroleum-producing area in the Soviet Union after Azerbaijan. At the start of the Second World War its average annual production was between 3 and 4 million tonnes.

In spite of the existence of distinct languages and dialects, the North Caucasian Mountaineers are essentially one people consisting of kindred tribes sharing a common history and culture. The historical unity of these tribes conditioned their common evolution and historical struggle for independence, best exemplified by the State of Mansur (1780–91), the State ('Imamate') of Shamil (1834–64), the Republic of the North Caucasus Mountaineers (1918–19), the North Caucasian Emirate (1919–20), and finally the Soviet Mountain Republic (1920–4).

Moscow became interested in the Caucasus after its conquest of the Kazan and Astrakhan Khanates in 1556. Ivan the Terrible even married a Cherkess princess, Maria Temrukovna, in 1561 to provide a basis for peaceful incorporation of the North Caucasus into Russia. However, the expected peaceful incorporation did not materalise. A few unsuccessful attempts to penetrate the North Caucasus were made by Boris Godunov (1606), after which attempts at conquest were abandoned and for a century no further move was made by Russia in that region.

In the eighteenth century, Peter I undertook a campaign to annex the whole of the Caucasus, but was forced to withdraw after suffering a serious defeat at the hands of the Mountaineers and the Azeris in 1772. Russian expansion in the Caucasus was renewed under Catherine II; her commander-in-chief, Suvorov, directed this new campaign, which provoked the first organised resistance of North Caucasians operating mainly from Chechnia and Daghestan. In 1785, Mansur Ushurma, a Chechen from Aldy, assumed the title of imam of all the Caucasian Mountaineers, a move which effectively united all the tribes of the North Caucasus: the Chechens, the Ingush, the Daghestanis, the Ossetians, the Cherkess and the Kabardians. For a time, Catherine considered the idea of ending the war against the Mountaineers by concluding a treaty of independence and friendship with them, but the intervention of Turkey on their side put an end to this plan. While admitting the possibility of Caucasian independence, the Russian government was not prepared to turn the country over to Turkish domination, and fighting continued more bitterly than ever. Finally, the movement came to an end when Mansur was captured in Anapa together with Mustafa, the Turkish Pasha.

However, the capture of Mansur did not mean the end of the Mountaineers' struggle. Under the leadership of Ghazi Mohammad, Hamza Bek and Imam Shamil, Daghestan and Chechnia made an appeal-to-arms uniting the mountain tribes. The struggle was crowned by the success of the Mountaineers. The North Caucasian independent state — the

'Imamate of Shamil' — was created in 1834 and lasted for thirty years, during which it fought without interruption for every inch of its territory.

Officially, the Caucasian war ended in 1859, when the active army in the Caucasus was increased to 300,000 men. In the summer of that year the new Commander-in-Chief of the Caucasian forces, Field-Marshal Prince Bariatinskii, had at his disposal a large concentration of fresh forces and modern military technology which enabled him to defeat Shamil. He was able to issue a triumphant note: 'Gunib is taken, Shamil is made prisoner, I congratulate the Caucasian army.' In 1864, the last component of Shamil's independent government, the Cherkess state, fell to the Russians.

In spite of the fact that the Mountaineers were vanquished, the Tsar's government felt compelled to pay homage to their aspirations of independence and love of freedom by granting them certain rights to internal self-administration. The proclamation, in the Emperor's name, to the Chechen people reads as follows:

I declare in the name of the Emperor

(1) that the Russian government leaves you forever absolutely free to profess the faith of your fathers.

(2) that you will never be forced into the army as soldiers or be transformed into Cossacks.

(3) that you are given a three-year exemption period from the date of ratification of this Act, after which you will be compelled to pay three roubles per household for the maintenance of your national administration services. However, the *aul* communities are free to distribute this tax among you as they think fit.

(4) that the authorities in charge of your government will exercise their authority according to the *shariat* and the *adat*. Judgment will be administered and decisions taken by popular courts composed of the best people.

The original was signed by Bariatinskii.[3]

However, fearing new revolts in the Caucasus the tsarist government decided to exile large groups of Chechens, Daghestanis, Ossetians and Cherkess to Turkey. These deportations took place in 1864. The procedure was harsh and there were many victims — also many protests in the West.

In 1877, a popular uprising headed by Ali-Bek Haji flared up in subjugated Chechnia and Daghestan. The ceaseless efforts of fifty years and the immense sacrifice made by Russia to subdue the North Caucasus were thus reduced to nought. However, thanks to an immense concentration of military force in a small territory (literally, fifteen soldiers for every one inhabitant of Chechnia), commanded by General Svistunov, the revolt was quelled after a year of warfare.

Twenty-eight leaders of the revolt, including Ali-Bek Haji, aged twenty-three, Uma Zumsoevski, aged seventy, and Dada his son, a guards officer, were court-martialled. The presiding general asked if they considered themselves guilty under the laws of the empire. Ali-Bek Haji replied on behalf of his companions: 'It is only before God and the Chechen people that we consider ourselves guilty because, in spite of all the sacrifices, we were not able to reconquer the freedom that God gave us!' They were sentenced to death by hanging. Before the execution the condemned were allowed to express their last wish. Uma Zumsoevski said: 'It is hard for an old wolf to witness the slaughter of his puppy. I ask to be hanged before my son.' The Tsar's court was not generous enough to grant this favour to the old man.

The struggle of the Mountaineers for freedom and independence became an important issue in Europe. Marx and Engels wrote in their famous *Communist Manifesto*: 'People of Europe! learn to fight for freedom and independence from the heroic example of the Caucasian Mountaineers.' Russian writers such as Pushkin, Lermontov and Tolstoy immortalised their struggle, condemning at the same time the cruel and inhumane methods of their Russian conquerors.

It is important to stress two characteristics of the social development of the Chechen-Ingush people which contributed to the intense conflict between the forces of the conquerors and the conquered. First (different in this respect from many other Caucasian regions), Chechnia and Ingushetia had never experienced either class antagonism or despotic government. Although the cultural-political development of the Chechens and Ingush had reached the same level as that of other Caucasian people (culture developed there on the basis of Arabic script), it knew no feudalism. Every Chechen and Ingush considered himself *uzden* (a freeman). Legal equality was an ancient law in this society.

Chantre, a French author, wrote in 1887:

'At the time of their independence, the Chechens formed several separate communities placed under the rule of a popular assembly. Today they live as people unaware of class distinctions. They are very different from the Cherkess whose gentry occupies a very high place.

This is the essential difference between the aristocratic Cherkess state and the wholly democratic constitution of Chechen and Daghestani tribes. It is this that determined the specific character of their struggle.[...] The equality among the population of the Eastern Caucasus is clear-cut. They all possess the same rights and enjoy the same social position. The authority with which they invest their tribal chiefs grouped within the framework of an elected council is limited in time and power . . . Chechens are gay and witty. Russian officers nicknamed them the French of the Caucasus.[4]

The German author Bodenstedt mentions the same circumstances and concludes that the 'Chechens have a purely republican constitution and equal rights.'[5] The second feature of the Chechen-Ingush is the immense significance they attach to the Muslim faith. Chechens are almost fanatically religious, and any attack on Islam arouses among them a profound reaction. It is these two characteristics that constitute the Chechen-Ingush specific way of life. They were in total opposition to the spirit and general trend of the tsarist conquerors' official policy.

The Russian Revolution of 1917 and the restoration of North Caucasian independence

After the declaration of rights promulgated by the Russian Revolution of 1917, the First North Caucasian Congress set up the Central Committee of the Union of the North Caucasus and Daghestan in May 1917. This Central Committee was to act as the provisional government of the North Caucasian independent state. In September of that year, the provisional constitution of the newly-formed state was ratified by the Second Congress. On 11 May 1918, after the Bolsheviks had seized power, the North Caucasian state declared itself entirely independent from the Russian Federation. Its status as such was recognised by Germany and Austria-Hungary and by Turkey, with which the North Caucasian Republic concluded an alliance on 8 June 1918. Its most important political figures were President Tapa Chermoev, the chairman of parliament Vassan-Giray Jabagi, the minister of foreign affairs Haidar Bammate and the ministers Pshemakho Kotsev, Abdul Rashid Katkhanov, Ahmet Tsalikov, Alikhan Kantemir and Aytek Namitok.

It was not the Bolsheviks but Denikin who dealt the first blow to the North Caucasian Republic. The White Russian movement — the 'Voluntary Army' — began its operation in Cossack territory in the North Caucasus. It was favourably viewed by some Mountaineers

*The Chechens and Ingush during the Soviet Period
and its Antecedents*
153

as a military and political movement directed against the Bolsheviks, but disillusion set in when its anti-national aspect became apparent. With the slogan 'for one indivisible Russia', Denikin decided to subdue the Caucasus. He considered the Mountaineers' desire to organise their political life as they saw fit as equivalent to 'national Bolshevism', which he deemed it his sacred duty to eliminate; hence his policy of burning down the *auls* and exterminating the rebellious Mountaineers.

After having dealt with serious resistance in Kabarda and Northern Ossetia, Denikin penetrated the territory of Chechnia-Ingushetia with the intention of breaking down the opposition of the Chechens and Ingush. He burned dozens of the largest centres of Chechnia-Ingushetia to the ground, including Ekazhevo, Dolakovo, Alkan-Yurt, Chechen-Aul, Ustar-Garday, Gudermes, Gherzel-Aul and Staryi-Yurt. The only result was to arouse a universal desire for revenge among the Chechen and Ingush population and to unite them. This is the reason why, instead of concentrating his forces against the Bolsheviks during the Moscow campaign, Denikin was forced to draw on his best detachments to fight against the Mountaineers. Indeed, he himself acknowledged later that no less than one third of his forces were kept busy in the Caucasus. The objective was to extinguish the 'seething volcano' — his own words when describing Chechnia-Ingushetia in his *Description of the Great Trouble.*

The independent Republic of the North Caucasus fell, and Denikin became a rather anxious master of his conquest. This was hardly surprising since already in September 1919, after the August revolt in Chechnia-Ingushetia, Sheikh Uzun Haji had liberated the mountains of Daghestan, Chechnia, Ossetia and Kabarda. The Sheikh then proclaimed the independence of the North Caucasus once more and established the 'North Caucasian Emirate'.

In February 1920, Denikin was forced to evacuate from the territory of the Emirate (the former Republic of the North Caucasus), and the Red Army made its entrance there in the guise of 'liberators'. The Bolsheviks had formerly recognised the government of Uzun Haji *de facto*[6] and assisted him in his struggle against Denikin; they had even placed at the disposal of the North Caucasian Emirate the 5th Red Army commanded by Nikolai Gikalo. The Emirate was now liquidated, and Sheikh Uzun Haji was offered the honorary post of Mufti of the North Caucasian Mountaineers. He died three months later thus ridding the Bolsheviks of a dangerous ally. Nevertheless, in August 1920 an anti-Soviet revolt flared up in the mountains of Chechnia-Ingushetia and

Daghestan under the leadership of Said Bek, Shamil's great-grandson. The movement lasted exactly one year until September 1921.

The Soviet Mountain Republic

On 20 January 1921, while Said Bek's uprising was still blazing, a Congress of Mountaineers was convened in Vladikavkaz. Moscow sent the People's Commissar for Nationalities, Stalin, to the Congress. Stalin explained to the Congress the policy of the Soviet government regarding nationalities, and proclaimed an amnesty for all those who had participated in the revolt of Said Bek on condition that the movement would cease and the authority of the Soviet government would be recognised. Furthermore, he declared that the Soviet government recognised the internal sovereignty and independence of the Mountaineers. In the name of his government, he recommended the creation of a unique 'Soviet Mountain Republic' (*Gorskaia Sovetskaia Respublika*), endowed with a large measure of autonomy so that the old dreams of the Mountain people might come true and their own independent government become a reality.

The constitutional assembly of the new Republic made their recognition of the Soviet government conditional on the *Shariat* and the *adat* being officially acknowledged as the basic constitutional laws of the Republic of the Mountain, and that the central government should not be intervening in their internal affairs; also on the lands of the Mountaineers, of which they were deprived by the Tsars, being given back to them. Stalin accepted both conditions, after which the delegates officially recognised the Soviet government.[7] The Soviet Mountain Republic was proclaimed as a result of this agreement between the Mountaineers' representatives and the Soviets. It comprised Chechnia, Ingushetia, Ossetia, Kabarda, Balkaria and Karachay. Daghestan was declared an independent Soviet Republic. Thus was created a completely unnatural Soviet Republic with a Soviet emblem on its banner and a *Shariat* constitution. The Bolsheviks directed that portraits of Shamil and his *naibs* should replace those of Lenin and Politburo members in all administrative institutions, schools and public places. Several Cossack settlements (*stanitsa*) were transferred into the Russian interior on the orders of Stalin and Ordzhonikidze, and the lands were returned to the Chechens and Ingush (including those that the population had previously seized).

The new leaders of the Mountaineers were radical intellectuals who had supported the Bolsheviks from the first days of the Russian Revolution, having been attracted by their promise to give nations the right to self-determination and secession. During the Civil War, this intelligentsia had naturally preferred the internationalist Lenin to the champion of the Great Russian State, Denikin. The requirements of this radical communist intelligentsia were very modest: they wanted complete domestic autonomy in the North Caucasus in the guise of a Soviet Mountain Republic within the RSFSR. Ordzhonikidze and Kirov, future members of the Politburo, lived at that time in the territory of the mountains and supported the claims of local communists. After the end of the Civil War, it was the members of this native communist intelligentsia who were placed at the head of the Mountaineers: Samurskii, Korkmasov, Dalgat, Mamedbekov, Takho-Godi in Daghestan; Elderkhanov, Kurbanov, Tokaev, Oshaev, Arsanukaev in Chechnia; Malsagov, Ziazikov, Albagashiev, Goigov in Ingushetia; Takoev, Mansurov, Butaev, Ramonov in Northern Ossetia; Eneev, Katkhanov, Kalmykov in Kabardino-Balkaria; Kurdzhiev in Karachay; Hakurati in Cherkessia. The government of these '*padishahs*' was a period of maximum political peace and harmony between the various Caucasian nations, and popularity of the Soviet government among the Mountaineers. Furthermore, this was the time of the NEP (New Economic Plan) regime 1921–8 which did not give rise to any serious national or political disruption in the country, except some isolated acts of provocation emanating from the GPU. At that time the Soviet authorities were engaged in punishing their individual enemies, past and present; as yet there were no attempts at reprisal against whole nations.

The *padishahs* and their constituents were allowed to voice their opinions, which were taken into consideration by Moscow. Moreover, the Bolsheviks pursued a most flexible and prudent policy in the Caucasus — everything was done to reinforce the belief of the North Caucasians that they had really achieved their long-desired independence. Immediately after the insurrection of Said Bek Shamil had been quelled, Lenin addressed a special letter to the communists of the Soviet Mountain Republic in which he urged all North Caucasian communists 'not to copy our tactics but to adapt them to Caucasian conditions'.

Stalin forgot Lenin's words when he began his 'all-out offensive of socialism on all fronts'. When the infamous *ezhovshchina* was unleashed throughout the Soviet Union, the Caucasian old guard was not spared. All the Mountain *padishahs* were arrested on the charge of bourgeois-nationalism. Some were executed and others deported. Lenin's renowned national policy, when applied by Stalinists, turned into the most shameless form of colonial oppression. To ensure the success of this policy, it was essential to transfer 'autonomous sovereignty' from Caucasians to the Moscow *Cheka* (secret police). The first official act in the course of this gradual, though systematic, process was the liquidation of the Soviet Mountain Republic which ceased to exist in 1924, the Soviet government having already created six autonomous regions: Karachay-Cherkess (12 January 1922), Kabardino-Balkar (16 January 1922), Adyghe (27 July 1922), Chechen (20 November 1922), Ingush (7 July 1924), and Northern Ossetian (7 July 1924).

Soviet leaders in Chechnia-Ingushetia

The first act of the internal government organisations in Chechnia and Ingushetia, after they were endowed with the status of autonomous regions, was general disarmament. Not only did the Soviets confiscate existing personal weapons but they also imposed on every house the obligation to hand one firearm to the authorities; to carry out this assignment the Chechens and Ingush bought weapons from Red Army soldiers and from the *Chekists* themselves. The disarmament itself, albeit a normal procedure in peace time, was interpreted as preparation for a forthcoming repression and as an attempt to deprive them of the rights granted by the *Shariat* constitution. To mitigate this impression, leaders of the Soviet government paid several visits to Chechnia-Ingushetia. Thus Kalinin, the Soviet President, visited several *auls* where he delivered propaganda speeches on the theme of friendship between the Chechens and Soviets.[8] He was followed in 1925 by Rykov, President of the *Sovnarkom* (Council of People's Commissars) and heir to Lenin, and Chicherin, People's Commissar for Foreign Affairs. In Groznyi (which had become the capital of Chechnia) Rykov and Chicherin, accompanied by K. Voroshilov, the commander of the North Caucasian Military District, and Mikoyan, secretary of the *kraikom* of the Bolshevik Communist Party of the USSR (VKP[b]), delivered speeches assuring the Chechen-Ingush population that the Soviet government was firmly resolved to fulfil their hopes and to serve the interests of the Caucasian Mountaineers. Rykov declared that the time of persecution was definitely over and that from 'now on, the freedom-loving heroic Mountaineers will know only happiness and prosperity'.

Later came Bukharin and Lunacharskii, the People's Commissar for Education. In brilliant propaganda speeches, they sang the praises of the Caucasians and the indestructible 'friendship of the peoples of the USSR' declaring that the Soviet government was called upon by history to save the Mountaineers. Nevertheless, it was decided to operate this salvation not in Bukharin's but in Stalin's style. Collectivisation began.

Collectivisation and armed insurrection

Socially, economically and psychologically the Chechens and the Ingush were the least prepared among the population of the Soviet Union to face the onslaught of compulsory collectivisation. Exactly a year before it began, the *kraikom* and the Central Committee decided to convene a 'Regional Conference of the Poor' in Groznyi. The resolutions of the conference stated that the main task of the Party and Soviet authorities was to raise the level of prosperity of the Chechen peasantry by various measures of assistance: credit to peasants, and provision of tools and seeds together with allocations of additional plots of land to those needing them. The Chechens were urged to take advantage of generous government assistance to develop their agricultural economy.

Naturally, not a word was said in the Party instructions or in the conference resolutions on the subject of the *kolkhoz*. Nevertheless, in the autumn of 1929, the Chechen *obkom* received a telegram signed by A.A. Andreev, a member of the Politburo and secretary of the *kraikom* of the Bolshevik Communist Party of the Soviet Union, stating that the North Caucasus was the first territory in the Soviet Union where complete collectivisation of the rural economy would be introduced, beginning with the liquidation of *kulachestvo* as a class. Andreev indicated the practical measures to be taken and added that collectivisation would be implemented in all the national regions, Chechnia included. At first the Chechens did not attach much importance to Andreev's telegram. However, representatives' of the *kraikom* and the Central Committee later arrived in the *auls*, and proceeded to confiscate personal and real estate from some peasants who were arrested as *kulaks* and deported with their families to Siberia. From others they seized possessions that were to be turned over to the *kolkhoz*.

The whole of Chechnia exploded and rose as one. It is impossible to describe accurately the nightmarish events which followed, so we will limit ourselves to the main points. The most important and the best organised revolts took place in Goiti (led by Mullah Ahmet and Mullah Kuriev), in Shali (led by Shita Istamulov) and in Benoi (led by Iaroch and Hodja). The insurgents occupied all the rural and regional institutions, burned official archives, and arrested the staff of the regional government, the chiefs of the GPU included. In Benoi they seized the petroleum refineries and instituted a provisional government that presented the following demands to the Soviets:

(1) Illegal confiscation of peasant property, i.e. 'collectivisation', must be stopped.

(2) Arbitrary arrests of peasants under the pretext of fighting *kulachestvo* must cease.

(3) The GPU chiefs must be recalled from Chechnia and replaced by elected civil officers of Chechen origin whose right to prosecute would be limited to criminal elements.

(4) The 'popular courts' imposed from above would be liquidated and the institution of *Shariat* courts, as foreseen by the constitutional congress of the Soviet Mountain Republic in Vladikavkaz in 1921, reinstated.

(5) The intervention of regional and central authorities in the internal affairs of the 'Chechen Autonomous Region' had to be stopped, and all the economic and political decisions taken by the Chechen Congress of elected representatives as foreseen in the status of 'autonomy'.

The insurgents' leadership sent these requests directly to Moscow stating that only when they were given satisfaction on all of them would they agree to disarm and recognise Soviet authority. A government delegation from Moscow came to Groznyi in order to 'peacefully liquidate' the insurrection. It comprised K. Nikolaev, a member of the Central Committee of the Communist Party (b); Ryskulov, vice-Chairman of the *Sovnarkom* of the RSFSR, and other high-ranking officials. A local peace commission was set up which included three religious leaders Shamsuddin Haji, Sultan Mullah, Mullah Ahmed Tugaev; D. Arsanukaev, and Hasman an old Moscow Bolshevik, respectively chairman and secretary of the Regional Party Committee. The peace commission was empowered to engage in direct negotiations with the leaders of the insurgents; in Shali it declared to them that the responsibility for recent events lay with the local executives who had not acted in keeping with Party and government instructions, and it promised that the authorities in question would be severely punished once the fighting stopped.

As to the insurgents' claim regarding the re-establishment of autonomous status, it was dealt with by the commission's 'Declaration to the Chechen People' which stated that 'Chechnia's internal matters will be settled in future by the Chechen people'. The insurgents accepted these explanations and agreed to return to their homes while awaiting the execution of the promises made by the Soviets. At the same time, the governmental commission published a telegram stating that a special

GPU detachment would come to Shali to arrest and punish rural and regional leaders. People felt reassured when the detachment arrived and arrests were made among the local leaders. The GPU detachment completed operations against the Soviet executives in three days, and on the fourth day, towards one o'clock in the morning, it surrounded the house of the former leader of the insurgents, Shita Istamulov. He was taken by surprise, but in response to an ultimatum to surrender he and his brother Hassan opened fire. At dawn, when help came to Shita, part of his house was ablaze and Hassan was badly wounded. Some hundred Chechen horsemen surrounded the GPU detachment besieging Shita's house, and after an hour of fighting the GPU force of about 150 men was practically annihilated. Shita Istamulov appealed to all Chechens to join in a holy war for the re-establishment of the imamate of Shamil and the eviction of 'infidels' from the Caucasus. In response to this call Shali, Goiti and Benoi rose up in arms once again, and at the same time revolts flared up in Daghestan, Ossetia, Kabarda (Bekseneks), Balkaria and Karachay, all proclaiming the same national-religious slogans. It is difficult to establish whether there was any connection in the organisation of these uprisings, but their national and ideological bond was obvious. The slogans of *ghazawat* were common to all the fighters for the Mountaineers' independence: Mansur, Hamza Bek, Ghazi Muhammad and Shamil.

In the middle of December 1929, regular detachments of the Red Army began to arrive at the Chechen border. Towards the end of the month, Belov, commander of the North Caucasus Military District, sent the following forces against the insurgents: four infantry divisions, the 28th Combat Division from Vladikavkaz, the Vladikavkaz Infantry School, the Krasnodar Cavalry School, three artillery divisions and two regiments of border guards taken from the Turkish and Iranian border. Furthermore, three squadrons of the GPU forces were brought in the operation: from Groznyi, Vladikavkaz and Makhachkala. They were commanded by Kurskii, the vice-chirman of the regional GPU. Due to the concentration of such large forces on the relatively small territory of Shali-Goiti (150,000 inhabitants) whose local conditions did not favour defensive war, both insurgent centres were conquered towards the middle of January 1930: Goiti was vanquished after the complete annihilation of the insurgents' general staff, including Kuriev and Ahmet Mullah, and Shali after an orderly retreat of Istamulov's forces to Upper Chechnia, in the mountains.

The losses of the Reds were heavy. In the Goiti battles practically the whole 82nd Infantry Regiment was annihilated. Near Shali, Belov lost a whole division. At the end of March 1930, he received reinforcements from Transcaucasia and embarked on a campaign in the mountains, his objective being to capture the last fortress held by the insurgents: Benoi. In April 1930, after two months of fierce fighting with heavy losses, Belov entered Benoi but found the place empty: all the inhabitants, women and children included, had been evacuated to remote hiding places in the mountains. The victorious Belov sent a negotiator to the insurgents offering honourable peace conditions to all those who would return of their own free will and surrender their weapons. The insurgents replied that they would return to their *auls* only when Belov and his army left.

Meanwhile, an abrupt change had occurred in the country's policy. Stalin and the Central Committee were re-examining the failure of the *kolkhoz* movement. A special decree of the Central Committee condemned the leftist deviators responsible for collectivisation and declared that the *kolkhoz* would be transformed into voluntary unions. In national regions such as Chechnia and Ingushetia, *kolkhoz* were banned altogether as premature. Only 'comrades' associations' (TOZ — *tovarishchestvo obrabotki zemli*) were allowed to be set up to cultivate the land. The Chechen Party leaders (Hasman, Zhuravlev and Arsanukaev) were dismissed from their posts as leftist deviators. Armed forces were withdrawn from Chechnia and large quantities of industrial goods, at very low prices, were sent there. Amnesty was declared in the name of the central government for all the leaders and participants in the insurrection. The insurgents returned to their *auls*. Shita Istamulov (who had formerly been a Red guerrilla fighter) returned to Shali, and on orders from above was even appointed to the post of president of the Rural Consumers Cooperative.

In the autumn of 1931 Baklakov, chief of the regional GPU, invited Istamulov allegedly to hand him the official amnesty act from Moscow. Baklakov gave him the document with one hand while firing the entire charge of a Mauser pistol with the other. Though badly wounded, Istamulov had time to stab Baklakov to death before being killed by a guard stationed outside. Istamulov's brother Hassan organised a new 'gang' which hunted and killed *Chekists* to avenge the murder of Shita until 1935.

The killing of Shita marked the beginning of a large-scale GPU operation in Chechnia to eliminate the '*kulak* counter-revolutionary elements and mullah-nationalist ideologists'. According to the lists drawn up by the regional GPU of Groznyi and Rostov, and confirmed by the government of the Soviet Union, about 35,000 men were arrested. They were judged and convicted by an 'Extraordinary Commission of Three' created by the GPU for this purpose, presided over by the GPU chief G. Kraft. It is hard to determine the percentage of those who were shot, but not many regained their freedom.

Uprising in Ingushetia

In 1926 T. Elderkhanov, President of the Central Executive Committee of Chechnia, and his assistants Khamzalov and Sheripov were dismissed from their posts, accused of associating with Ali Mitaev, a well-known political dissident arrested in 1923 for planning an insurrection with leaders of the Georgian revolt. For similar reasons I. Malsagov, President of the Ingush Regional Executive Committee, and I. Ziazikov, Secretary of the Regional Committee of the GPU, were also replaced. Chernoglaz, a Russian from Moscow, replaced Ziazikov as secretary of the Ingush *obkom* — an appointment which, in the opinion of the Ingush population, was a breach of their autonomy. They sent a delegation to Moscow with a request to reinstate Ziazikov; in Moscow it was hinted that Ziazikov was worthless while Chernoglaz was dependable. The argument of the Ingush that they preferred 'a bad homegrown communist rather than a good imported one' was ignored.

The take-over by Chernoglaz was immediately marked by a sharp policy change in the regional administration. Repressions in villages began on an unprecedented scale. The campaign started with an attack on religion and the activities of the 'reactionary clergy'. In Vladikavkaz, then the capital of both Ossetia and Ingushetia, Chernoglaz announced the institution of a 'Regional Union of Unbelievers of Ingushetia' and proclaimed himself its honorary president. *Serdarlo*, the Ingush-language newspaper, was instructed to encourage mass recruitment for the 'Union of Unbelievers'.

More was to follow: some of the mullahs were summoned to the GPU and forced to sign anti-religious declarations stating that they refused to perform the service of the cult — 'an anti-popular reactionary activity' — and inviting the Ingush to join the 'Union of Unbelievers'. However, only a small number of mullahs did sign and those who yielded explained to their compatriots that they had signed only to avoid death or a life sentence of exile. Chernoglaz then instructed his regional assistants to 'pass from idle work to acts in their struggle against Kunta

Haji'. This Sufi *tariqat* was well established in Ingushetia, incorporating at the time nearly 50,000 members.

The first to react to the instructions of Chernoglaz was Ivanov, chief of the regional GPU of Nazran: in the summer of 1930 he came to the village of Ekazhevo, which had been burned down in the past by Denikin who had declared it a 'Red *aul*'. Ivanov asked the president of the village council to convene an immediate meeting with the local mullah; his orders were carried out. He explained to the mullah that crops were being gathered but that there was nowhere to store the grain in the *aul*. 'You must turn the *aul's* mosque into a granary and as from today discontinue religious services.' The interpreter scarcely had time to translate Ivanov's speech when uproar broke out. People shouted: 'Kill the *gaiour*! Stab him to death!' The president of the council struggled vainly to restore order but it was only thanks to the mullah's intervention that things eventually calmed down. He declared to Ivanov: 'The action you suggest would offend not only the people but God. Therefore I would fear God were I to carry out your orders.' The council president then made an offer: 'We will find another granary. Any Ingush would offer his own house rather than see the mosque close down.'

These words were approved by all present, but Ivanov was adamant that he needed not just any house but the mosque. Pandemonium broke out again. Sensing danger, Ivanov left the meeting, but it was already too late. That very day he was killed near Ekazhevo by Uzhakhov, a member of the Kunta Haji *tariqat*. To avenge his death, five people, including the mullah and Uzhakhov, were shot and about thirty Ingush were deported to Siberia as 'members of the counter-revolutionary *kulak* gang'.

The conclusions that Chernoglaz drew from this event were erroneous: he considered that the killing of Ivanov was the expression of a general anti-Soviet plot in Ingushetia which he decided to unmask. But how does one set about unmasking something that is non-existent? Here again the GPU proved helpful.

In the autumn of 1930 a mysterious 'representative of Japan' turned up in Ingushetia. He visited large *auls*, contacted Ingush authorities and arranged clandestine interviews, during which he gave information about Japan's war plans with the Soviet Union. The headquarters of the 'Japanese representative' were in the house of a former tsarist officer, Razhab Evloev, in Dolakovo. After an 'inspection tour' of the *auls*, the 'Japanese representative' organised a meeting of delegates from several *auls*, to which he also invited influential Ingush known for their anti-

Soviet attitude. It is worth noting that Razhab Evloev was trusted by the Ingush since, as a former tsarist officer, he could not be a Soviet supporter. All those present were known to each other and to the Ingush population as trustworthy people. Among them were Haji Ibragim Tashkhoev, Mullah Issan Geliskhan Shibilov, Chada, Said Shibilov, Rans Dalgiev, Murad Uzhakhov and others (from the *auls* of Nazran, Dolakova, Bazorkino and Galashki). During the meeting, the 'Japanese representative' and Razhab Evloev asked all those attending to swear an oath on the Quran, promising to keep the discussion secret and never betray each other or the 'representative of Japan'. After the ceremony the 'representative' explained the situation: allegedly in the near future, Japan would declare war on the Soviet Union. Other powers would side with Moscow, but Japan was supported by people oppressed by the Bolsheviks, and according to him, almost all the Caucasian peoples, with the exception of the Ingush, had promised their support. He stated that he had been empowered by his government to invite the Ingush to join the common 'Liberation Front of the People'. The 'Japanese representative' spoke for a long time, persuasively and very logically. He declared that Japan wanted to help her allies by supplying them with money and weapons before the war started. To show the Ingush that these were not empty promises, he had brought with him money and a quantity of weapons. At the end of his speech he asked whether his audience accepted the 'plan for the liberation of Ingushetia'. They replied in the affirmative and he nominated all those present to be commanders of 100 men each. These commanders received Japanese weapons and Japanese military shoulder-straps as signs of distinction. Money, it was promised, would be sent at the start of the clandestine military operations, and battle orders at the beginning of the war.

The 'Japanese representative' left highly satisfied with the success of his mission. The Ingush buried the weapons and straps while awaiting the opening of hostilities. But instead of war Ingushetia was flooded with GPU troops. In the course of twenty-four hours, arrests were effected in almost all the large *auls*, and all the 'Japanese general staff' conspirators were taken. The weapons and straps were easily found to serve as 'material evidence'. Razhab Evloev and the 'Japanese' himself remained free; the latter turned out to be a Mongol from a Central Asian *oblast* GPU. Twenty-one men were shot and 400 deported without trial or further investigation. Almost all the senior staff of the Vladikavkaz *oblast* GPU were decorated with the highest Soviet orders. Among those honoured was an Ingush agent of the GPU.

After this coup, Chernoglaz gained great prestige with the Central Committee. His knowledge of the Ingush was limited to what he had read in old Russian geography manuals. (Denikin wrote in his *Description of the Great Trouble*: 'Old geography manuals speaking of the Ingush say: "The Ingush occupations are stock-herding and plundering." And he continues: 'During the Civil War, however, the second occupation had priority over the first.')

Chernoglaz, thus enlightened, thought that a semi-clandestine counter-revolutionary organisation, unknown to the Soviet government, had developed in Ingushetia under the guise of the Sufi brotherhoods (the *tariqat* of Kunta Haji, Batal Haji and Sheikh Deni Arsanov). Therefore, immediately after the 'Japanese operation', he gave instructions for the arrest of all the chiefs of the *tariqat* who had already faced deportation before the Revolution. These arrests grieved the Ingush, and Moscow received dozens of complaints against Chernoglaz. A special delegation, which included friends of Ordzhonikidze and Kirov, paid a visit to Kalinin in Moscow requesting the recall of Chernoglaz in order to restore peace. But all the petitions were subsequently sent to Chernoglaz himself 'for investigation'. These investigations usually ended in the arrest of those who had signed 'the counter-revolutionary slander inspired by mullahs'. However, the flow of complaints was not interrupted.

Chernoglaz then decided to visit the countryside and explain to the Ingush that he had no intention of pampering them even though some had been Red guerrillas in the past. His first visit was to Galashki where he delivered a speech, after which an old man — Bekmurziev — spoke up and said, to the approval of the audience:

'Twenty five years ago, on the very square where we are now assembled, Colonel Mitnik, who was then, as you are today, the governor of the Ingush, presented us with an ultimatum in the name of the Sardar [Governor General of the Caucasus]: we were to give up the weapons that we did not have. Mitnik himself was a good man, but the Tsar's government was bad. That is why I killed him on this same spot with a dagger like this one (the old man showed his dagger). I was sentenced to penal servitude for life, but twelve years later the Revolution liberated me. The Soviet government is good, but you, Chernoglaz, are a bad man. I do not want to kill you. Instead, I am giving you wise advice: go away from Ingushetia while you still have a head on your shoulders. People here are furious with you. I swear they will kill you.'

The old man spoke in Russian, warmly and convincingly like a youth. Instead of meditating on his wise counsel, Chernoglaz ordered the 'old bandit' to be arrested and proceeded to another *aul*, Datlakh. Here the same performance was repeated. The same day, near Galashki, in a place where the road cuts through a little wood, Chernoglaz was shot in his car. Two other officials of the Regional Committee who accompanied him were released unharmed. Chernoglaz's headless body was left on the road beside the bullet-riddled car. The Ingush carried his head away.

The Ingush population paid dearly for the assassination. Idris Ziazikov, former secretary of the Ingush Regional Party Committee, was the first to be arrested and charged with having organised the murder. His wife, relatives and friends were also arrested. In the *auls*, arrests were made from the GPU 'lists of corrupt elements', on which were registered the names not only of 'former bandits' but also of 'future' ones. The ringleaders of the plot against Chernoglaz — Ziazikov first and foremost — were tried in Moscow by the Supreme Court of the RSFSR. Among them figured those who had actually committed the murder. At the time of the killing, however, Ziazikov was in Moscow attending lectures on Marxism organised by the Party. Nevertheless, he was accused of having provided the moral and political preparation of his successor's murder.

The Ingush explained the murder of Chernoglaz by his policy of deliberate provocation in Ingushetia. An exchange between the court and one of the accused gave rise to a well-known anecdote. Asked by the President of the Court what had become of the head of Chernoglaz, the Ingush replied: 'Chernoglaz never had a head at all. Had he had one, he would never have come to Ingushetia.' All the prisoners, Ziazikov included, were sentenced to death. On the personal intervention of Ordzhonikidze and Mikoyan, Ziazikov's sentence was commuted to ten years' imprisonment. The others were executed.

The NKVD creates a 'nationalist centre of Chechnia'

Peasant revolts in the mountains of Chechnia occurred every spring as though carefully pre-planned. As to guerrilla warfare it was a permanent phenomenon. The revolts were induced not only by a passionate longing for freedom but also as a result of provocation by *Chekists*. They practised the tsarist system of taking *amanat* (hostages) to induce 'bandits' to surrender but on a much larger scale. The former Caucasian administration freed the *amanat* when the bandit gave himself up, whereas there is not a single case in the history of Soviet Chechnia-Ingushetia of an *amanat* being freed after the surrender of the 'bandit'. When the latter gave himself up voluntarily, he was shot despite solemn promises to spare his life. As to the hostages, they were all — men, women and children — sent to Siberia. As a result of the code of deceit which ruled the activity of the *Chekists*, people stopped believing the claims of the Soviet government. There is a Chechen saying that can be translated as 'lying like the Soviets'. But deception, which had become second nature to the Soviet administration, impaired only the credibility of their regime and was a much lesser evil than the deliberate provocation of the *Chekists*, to which the Chechens and Ingush were particularly vulnerable. Here is one instance. The Regional Party Committee directed by Egorov, a Muscovite, decided to organise a pig-breeding farm in Dargo. His Chechen-Ingush colleagues advised him against this enterprise, knowing that this would irritate the Chechens who, being Muslims, do not eat pork, but without success. Egorov accused his colleagues of nationalist prejudices: 'If Chechens do not eat pork, so much the better for the pigs. No one will steal them.' The farm was set up and survived for twenty-four hours: pigs were brought during the day and at night the Chechens killed them. Naturally, not one was stolen. Psychologically, this act was easy to understand. The Chechens considered that by bringing pigs into a Muslim village where no one had ever seen them before, the authorities had committed a gross blasphemy.

Pigs were never again brought into the mountains, but in response to the killing of the pigs, the NKVD arrested thirty 'bandits' and deported them to Siberia. There are thousands of examples of such pointless provocation. Until 1930 the victims of the NKVD were only from the *auls*. It is true that many intellectuals of the old school who might have presented a danger for the Soviet administration in Chechnia had been sent away from the Caucasus — men such as T.E. Elderkhanov, former member of the State Duma, A. Mutushiev, member of the Moscow College of Lawyers, M. Krumov and the brothers Matsiev. Other members of the Chechen and Ingush intelligentsia had emigrated abroad, among them Tapa Chermoev, Vassan-Giray Jabagi, Ibragim Chulikov, General Safarbi Malsagov and Captain Sozryko Malsagov. Others remained who had recognised Soviet authority and even had Communist Party cards, but were nevertheless distrusted by the NKVD. According to *Chekist* logic, all the culprits and organisers of anti-Soviet revolts had to belong to a unique 'national centre' representing, according to the same logic, 'internal' and foreign emigration.

The idea of unmasking this mythical centre was so tempting that it was supported by the whole North Caucasian NKVD, and personally supervised by Kurskii (who later committed suicide when he was assistant to the NKVD chief, Ezhov). The Chechen regional section of the NKVD, led by its chief G. Kraft, created this 'counter-revolutionary centre' so expertly and plausibly that even many Chechens believed in its existence. It was established through GPU surveillance of prominent Chechen citizens, specifically Magomet Matsiev, manager of the Regional Office for Supplies (*Sevkatsnab*) and member of the Communist Party;[9] Magomet Abdul Qadirov, legal expert of the Chechen Regional Executive Committee, not a Party member but formerly a civil servant in the tsarist administration; Isa Kurbanov, responsible for the scientific sector; Khalid Batukaev, Professor of Theoretical Mechanics at the Petroleum Institute of Groznyi; and his father Ahmat Batukaev, a former Red guerrilla, although neither he nor his son were members of the Party. Also under surveillance were Edil Sultan Beimurzaev, a non-Party member, formerly a civil servant in the tsarist administration, and his two sons aged fourteen and eighteen; Khalid Shamilev, director of the Finance Department, a non-Party member and former officer of the White Army; Magomet Sataev, a Party official; Yusuf Chermoev, a non-Party member and former petroleum industrialist; and Mustafa Dombaev, an engineer and member of the *Komsomol*. Some agents of the NKVD were given the task of arranging meetings between these people and various suspects from the *auls*. Moreover, some of them such as M. Matsiev and Kurbanov were officially appointed by the Vice-Chairman of the regional NKVD to conduct 'peaceful negotiations' with Makal Gazgireev, a well-known anti-Soviet guerrilla chief, to persuade him to give himself up in return for his life. Although Gazgireev was formerly a friend of Matsiev and Kurbanov, he prudently declined to take advantage of the NKVD's generosity. Later it was established that the meeting was organised by Kurskii himself in order to accuse them of conspiring with 'bandits'.

At the same time, the NKVD instructed its agents abroad to watch the émigrés, in particular those connected with Tapa Chermoev. With this objective a former White Army officer, Visa Kharachoev, was sent abroad under an assumed name. We do not know whom Kharachoev met and how he set about his mission, but it is known that letters began to arrive from Istanbul, Paris and London. The letters were written to Matsiev, Kurbanov and Beimurzaev among others and delivered in Groznyi to NKVD intermediaries. The author, in most cases, was Tapa Chermoev.

In the autumn of 1932 the whole group was arrested. Mass arrests followed in the regions of Gudermes and Nozhay-Yurt; in all 3,000 men were detained. They were accused of having organised a 'counter-revolutionary national centre of Chechnia in preparation for an armed uprising'. Speaking at the regional Party Conference in 1934, the Secretary of the Regional Committee, Evdokimov, quoted the 'letters of the millionaire Chermoev'. He claimed that in his letters Chermoev urged those who shared his ideas to prepare for an armed uprising with money and weapons supplied by Western powers — the British in particular.[10] Today we have proof that Chermoev's letters were forged by the NKVD. But it was precisely these letters which served as material evidence against the 'national centre'. Almost all those arrested were convicted by the NKVD courts. Abdulnadirov, Shamilev, Kurbanov, Mosta-Haji, Sataev and Beimurzaev, all members of the 'centre', were shot. Others were condemned to ten years' imprisonment. It is impossible to estimate how many rank-and-file members were executed. The Order of the Red Banner was awarded to Kurskii and Fedotov, Pavlov, Kraft, Mirkin, Vassiliev and Tregubov as a reward for the discovery of this mythical 'plot'. Hence the theory whereby 'bandits' existed not only in the mountains and forests of Chechnia but also among scientists, in the industrial workshops, in the offices of civil servants and even among the Party staff prevailed. The fantastic reports of the *Chekists* that Chechens and Ingush were busy day and night preparing a 'liberation campaign' of the whole of the Caucasus were believed.

Although the Soviet authorities had renounced their principles on the nationality problem, notwithstanding the harshness of Soviet laws and the cruelty with which they were carried out, Chechens and Ingush might have bowed to their fate had it not been for these deliberate provocations. Chivalry, noble feelings, hospitality, honour, faithfulness in friendship, a spirit of self-sacrifice for the common good, courage in war, modesty in everyday life and yet vindictiveness bordering on inhumanity when facing a treacherous enemy — such are the characteristics of the Caucasian Mountaineers as described by classic Russian writers such as Pushkin, Lermontov and Tolstoy. The former conquerors of the mountains, Russian princes and noblemen, were themselves endowed with many of these qualities, but the Russians and *Chekists* were absolutely devoid of them. Let us take a commonplace example. A Russian might refer to the unfortunate mother of an adversary with abuse of all kinds. In reply, he will hear the same insults and there the matter will end. But the Chechen who has insulted his foe must draw his dagger to protect his life. With Chechens and Ingush abuse is punishable by death. Such is the code of honour. According to a Chechen saying, 'A wound by the dagger can be cured by a doctor, but a wound by words can be cured only by the dagger.'

These characteristics were now described as 'bourgeois-nationalist prejudices' and condemned to disappear for the sake of 'communist re-education'. Even the famous *kinjal* or dagger, that ancient and obligatory part of Caucasian national costume, was outlawed and banished on pain of severe punishment as for a criminal act.

The NKVD and the myth of the bandits

As a general rule, not one of the chiefs of the Chechen-Ingush GPU-NKVD was a Chechen. All were appointed from Moscow, and their knowledge of the people over whose destiny they presided was limited to reference-books composed by tsarist authorities. Total ignorance of the psychology, traditions and history of the native people was compounded by an amoral, or simply criminal mentality in the case of Deuch, Abulian, Pavlov, Kraft, Raev, Dementev, Ivanov and Riazanov. The avowed objective of each new chief was to be decorated. As a result, they were interested not in the pacification of Chechnia-Ingushetia but rather in the continuation of the war with the Soviets. We have already seen how the 'national centre of Chechnia' was organised. Let us now see how individual 'bandits' were created.

In autumn of 1933, at Geldegen in the Shali region, an elderly peasant Ibragim Geldegenskii was accused of 'assisting gangs' although both the NKVD and the people knew him to be a man of unimpeachable character. An active member of the *kolkhoz*, he had been a Red guerrilla fighter during the Civil War under the command of Sergo Ordzhonikidze. When, during the occupation by the White Army, Ordzhonikidze took refuge in the mountains of Chechnia and Ingushetia, Ibragim Geldegenskii served as his personal guard. Because of his courage Ordzhonikidze nicknamed him 'Zelimkhan of Geldegen'.[11] In 1919, Ordzhonikidze sent Ibragim on several secret missions to Astrakhan to carry messages across the White lines to Shliapnikov, the commander of the 11th Red Army. To thank him Shliapnikov offered Geldegenskii a watch engraved with his name, and Ordzhonikidze a Mauser pistol, a 'weapon of honour', bearing his name. When the war ended Ordzhonikidze left for Moscow while Ibragim returned to his native *aul* and enlisted in a *kolkhoz*. Time passed and things changed. The watch engraved with Shliapnikov's name stopped working and Ordzhoni-kidze's 'weapon of honour' was confiscated by the *oblast* NKVD. Ibragim was indignant: he went to Rostov to complain to Evdokimov himself. He showed the letter signed by Ordzhonikidze stating that he had been rewarded with the gift of the 'weapon of honour' and that he was allowed to carry it at all times. The NKVD confiscated the letter with a polite explanation: 'You have no weapon and therefore you do not need the letter either.'

Losing all hope, Ibragim threatened the *Chekists* with Moscow's and Ordzhonikidze's intervention. The NKVD replied: 'Good speed to you, but know that sensible people do not waste time complaining about the NKVD.' Ibragim went to Moscow. At the Kremlin command post he registered as Zelimkhan Geldegenskii and 'Ordzhonikidze's friend'. It would seem that Ordzhonikidze had not forgotten the Caucasian tradition of hospitality. He welcomed Ibragim as simply and warmly as Ibragim used to receive him years ago in the mountains of Chechnia. Ibragim told him what had happened, and Ordzhonikidze promised to take the necessary measures. Ibragim returned to Chechnia. A few days later, his Mauser and the letter were returned from Rostov. His victory was a humiliating blow for the NKVD. From that moment on Ibragim's downfall was assured. He was constantly watched and surrounded by a network of plots and provocations. *Agents provocateurs* were sent to see him with suggestions to kill the regional NKVD chief, but Ibragim steadfastly refused.

Later, he received a visit from a man claiming to be a Daghestani mullah who explained that he was making a pilgrimage to Arti-Kort, a holy place near Vedeno, and that before he had left Daghestan his friends had recommended Ibragim Geldegenskii as a trustworthy man and a pious Muslim. The mullah quoted several Daghestani names that Ibragim remembered from the time of the Civil War. The mullah seemed a highly learned Arabist and a very religious man, which duly impressed Ibragim, and he had with him a whole set of theological books. After three days the mullah left, presenting Ibragim with a Quran as a reward for his generous hospitality. The next day the *Chekists* came and searched Ibragim's house, where they found the Quran with a compromising letter in Arabic in its binding. The NKVD took Ibragim away with the letter and the Quran.

During the investigation that followed, Ibragim explained in what circumstances and by whom the Quran had been given to him and said that he knew nothing about the letter. The *Chekists* claimed that his visitor was not a Daghestani but an 'Anglo-Turkish' spy and that the letter promised to help Ibragim organise a Chechen uprising. A few other peasants from Ibragim's village, together with all his near relatives, were arrested as members of his 'counter-revolutionary' organisation. During the examination, held at night, they were tortured in the office of the NKVD magistrate in Groznyi. Ibragim jumped from the second floor into the river Sunja and managed to escape.

A year later, in the autumn of 1934, the villagers of Geldegen witnessed two officers of the NKVD, Slavin and Ushaev, pouring petrol on the severely wounded Ibragim and burning him alive. This public execution provoked profound indignation, not only among the simple masses but even inside the Chechen government. H. Mamaev, President of the Chechen Regional Executive Committee and a member of the Central Executive Committee of the Soviet Union; Groza (a Russian), President of the Regional Council of Professional Unions; and Ia. Ediev, Secretary of the Regional Committee of Shali, sent a written protest criticising the behaviour of the NKVD to the Secretary of the North Caucasian Committee of the Communist Party and to the President of the *Ispolkom*, and as a result all were dismissed from their posts. Mamaev and Ediev were accused of nationalism and the Russian Groza of right-wing opportunism. Slavin and Ushaev were temporarily transferred to the NKVD of Central Asia, and both were decorated there with the Order of the Red Banner for work accomplished in Chechnia. In 1937 Ushaev was recalled to Chechnia and appointed to the post of President of the Supreme Court of the Chechen-Ingush Republic. That same year, one of his relations served him poisoned food from which he died.

Chechen-Ingush delegation to Ordzhonikidze

The threats and vehement complaints of the population finally induced the puppet government of the Chechen-Ingush Republic to inform the central government of the real situation. The opportunity arose when Ordzhonikidze was resting in Pyatigorsk, the health resort of the North Caucasus, in the spring of 1935. The government's delegation was composed of the President Ali Gorchkhanov, the Second Secretary of the Party Regional Committee Vakhaev (no Chechen was ever appointed to the post of First Secretary), Goigov, Mekhtiev, Okuev, two former guerrillas and Civil War companions of Ordzhonikidze: Kh. Ortzhanov and Albert Albogachev, and a few elders, also former guerrillas. They came to Pyatigorsk and were received by Ordzhonikidze with typical

Caucasian hospitality. Knowing Chechen-Ingush traditions, Ordzhon-ikidze was surprised that the former guerrillas had no daggers. When the reason was explained to him, he replied 'A Chechen without a dagger is like a European without a necktie', and promised to raise the subject in Moscow.

At the beginning of the conversation, Ordzhonikidze told his visitors that he wanted to know the whole truth about the discontent in Chechnia-Ingushetia and the measures they recommended to remedy the situation. The representatives reported everything in great detail — about the *kolkhoz*, the machinery and tractor stations, the roads, schools, hospitals and petroleum — but they remained silent about the principal grievance, the NKVD. The Chechen-Ingush government knew full well that the NKVD was the main cause of the evil, and that as long as any *Chekist* continued to wield more power than the Chechen-Ingush prime minister, there could be no improvement. But they were afraid to speak out, and they were right; Ordzhonikidze would soon return to Moscow whereas they would remain at the mercy of their own NKVD. (It should be noted that the NKVD had 400 cadres in the Republic, of which only four were Chechen or Ingush: S. Albagachiev, U. Mazaev, I. Aliev and U. Elmurzaev. Nor did the rank and file of the NKVD contain a single Chechen or Ingush.)

Ordzhonikidze became indignant when the delegation informed him that saddle-horses were confiscated after the setting-up of the *kolkhoz*: 'You have been over-zealous, comrades. It is a crime to deprive Chechens and Ingush of their saddle-horses, as the Mountaineers are famous for their horsemanship. No one can outshine their *djigits*. Yes, comrades, you have been over-zealous,' he concluded. He promised to speak with the 'master' in Moscow and to present the Executive Committee and the *Sovnarkom* with a set of proposals aimed at improving the situation.

A month after Ordzhonikidze's return to Moscow, the central press published two decrees. The first, signed by the Presidium of the Central Executive Committee of the Soviet Union, stated that 'daggers may be worn only as part of the national costume', while the second, issued by the Central Committee and the *Sovnarkom*, stated that as an exception to the statutory regulations members of the *kolkhoz* in Chechnia-Ingushetia were 'authorised to have and to tend their own saddle-horses'.

Although these decisions improved the moral and political situation of the Chechen and Ingush population, the spirit and methods of *Chekist* policy in the *auls* did not change. In Moscow the authorities did not know — or rather did not want to know — that the causes of the tragedy did not lie in the nature of this population or in its aversion to authority, but in the vicious effects of political provocation. That is why the good intentions of the Soviet government were cancelled out by the subsequent provocations, although after the visit of the Chechen-Ingush delegation to Ordzhonikidze the *Chekists* behaved more prudently.

The period extending from the end of 1935 to the beginning of 1937 was calm. True, some NKVD officials were murdered, but these were generally old scores being settled. Even the guerrilla movement in the mountains took on a defensive character. It should be noted that it was always the NKVD officials who supplied weapons and ammunition to the guerrillas. The main suppliers, well known in Chechnia-Ingushetia, were Semikin, Poghiba and Nikolskii, who were later prosecuted.

The leader of the guerrilla movement for nearly fourteen years was 'Major' Saadullah Magomaev. His orders were that Russian civil servants — except the *Chekists* — were to be spared, but that no mercy was to be shown to Chechen-Ingush civil servants if they were communists: 'The Russians are against us because it is their service duty. Honour to men engaged in service but death to scoundrels.'

A famous incident created a sensation in the Republic. In the spring of 1940 Smoltsin, the Secretary of the Regional Party Committee for Industry and Transport, was sent on a mission to the region of Galanchozh, most of which was in the hands of Saadullah's guerrillas. He was accompanied by three men and a Chechen Party worker. In the forest, between Shallazh and Yalkhoroy, near the mountain ridge, they were surrounded by guerrillas. The *Chekists*, understanding the situation, left their horses and fled into the forest, but Smoltsin panicked and was taken prisoner along with his Chechen guide. In view of the prisoners' importance, they were judged by Saadullah himself. At his trial, Smoltsin acknowledged his high-ranking position within the Republic's administration, and stated that he was on a government mission. The Chechen claimed that it was his duty to accompany his chief. The court decided that Smoltsin, as a Russian communist, was to be set free but that the Chechen was to be shot for treason. Smoltsin was released and reached the republican capital safely whereupon he was promptly arrested by the NKVD, this time as a 'traitor to the fatherland'.

Proclamation of the Chechen-Ingush Republic and visit to Stalin's mother

As already stated, all was peaceful in Chechnia-Ingushetia in the second half of 1935 and throughout 1936. As a result of the promulgation of the new Soviet Constitution on 5 December 1936, the Chechen-Ingush Autonomous Region was transformed into the 'Chechen-Ingush Autonomous Soviet Socialist Republic'. In all the *auls* the event was celebrated with special popular entertainments. In the course of these festivities, Chechens and Ingush expressed their gratitude to the authorities who had justified their trust in them by creating the autonomous republic. After the promulgation of the 'Constitution of the Chechen-Ingush ASSR', defining the sovereign rights of the people, this gratitude turned to enthusiasm. The establishment of the Republic was interpreted by the majority of the population, especially the intelligentsia, not only as an extension of the people's rights but also as a long-hoped-for end to the despotism of the NKVD.

Women shared in the joy of the population. Chechen women did not usually take part in politics and public life but on this occasion, in the spring of 1937, they sent a 'women's delegation of the Chechen-Ingush Republic' to Tbilisi, led by Aminat Islamova. Their aim was to speak to Keke Dzhugashvili, Stalin's mother, to express their gratitude towards her son for his 'fatherly care for the Chechen-Ingush people'. The delegation brought rich gifts of local handicrafts. Keke received the delegates in great style in the former palace of Vorontsov-Dashkov. To their warm praises of her son she replied: 'My wish is that every mother should have such a son.' She assured the Chechen women that she would ask her son to continue his 'caresses' to the 'brothers *Kistebi*' (the Georgian name for Chechen-Ingush). The 'caresses' and the real meaning of 'Stalin's constitution' were revealed to the Chechens and Ingush during the summer in the course of a grandiose *Chekist* military operation executed throughout the Soviet Union: *Ezhovshchina*, an epidemic of persecution, originated by Ezhov, which spread to the Chechen-Ingush mountains, on a scale that no human imagination could have conceived.

General operation of 1937

The 'General Operation for the Removal of Anti-Soviet Elements' was carried out on the night of 31 July–1 August 1937 throughout Chechnia-Ingushetia. People listed by the NKVD were transported in lorries to the republican capital, Groznyi. First, the two NKVD prisons in Groznyi were filled: the 'inner prison' for the hardened counter-revolutionaries (about 1,000) and the 'external prison' to which about 4,000 people were sent. Others were jailed elsewhere: 5,000 in the central garage of Grozneft, 3,000 in the club bearing the name of Stalin near Bashirov mill, and 300 in the premises of the Republic's militia. During that night in July and in the ensuing months, nearly 14,000 men were arrested, representing 3 per cent of the Republic's population. Naturally, the 'citizens' rights', so emphatically stressed in both the Soviet Constitution and of that of Chechnia-Ingushetia, were shamelessly violated during the arrests and sentencing. The prosecutor signed one order of arrest for all the accused and all of them were condemned after one and the same trial conducted by an 'extraordinary *troika*' of the Chechen-Ingush NKVD: Egorov, First Secretary of the Regional Committee; Dementiev, the NKVD chief; and Porubaev, the special prosecutor of the Chechen-Ingush ASSR NKVD. All were sentenced in compliance with the NKVD recommendations, some to death, others to concentration camps. It is impossible to say exactly how many were shot, but every night there were mass executions in the cellars of the NKVD to the accompaniment of the roar of motor-cars outside.

As it would have been impossible to carry out the death sentences pronounced by the *troika* within the assigned time, a special 'execution hall' was established for the extermination of large groups. It was situated in the northern part of the NKVD building facing the Sunja river. The *Chekists* called it the 'relay chamber' because the doomed prisoners taken there were told that they were being sent to Siberia by 'relay-stages'. The relay chamber was made of reinforced concrete and hermetically sealed from the outside world. Revolving firing positions were fitted into the walls and the ceiling from the exterior. The bodies were carried off in lorries under cover of darkness, and taken to a mass grave in a forest at the foot of the Goriachevodskaia mountain.

As a result of this operation, thousands of Chechens and Ingush joined the guerrilla groups. In the regions of Galanchozh, Gudermes and Kurchaloy, guerrillas killed the chiefs of the regional NKVD sections. In September, they derailed a military train between Groznyi and Nazran.

At the beginning of October 1937, Shkiriatov, candidate member of the Politburo, President of the Party Collegium of the Central Committee and Ezhov's deputy, came to Chechnia-Ingushetia with a large *Chekist* staff. An enlarged plenum of the Chechen-Ingush Party Committee was summoned to meet on 7 October in the Lenin House of

Culture in Groznyi. Besides the members of the plenum, the meeting also comprised leading city and regional workers who had been personally invited to take part. In the course of this plenum Shkiriatov ordered the arrest of all the Chechen and Ingush members of the Regional Party Committee, and they were arrested immediately in the plenum hall itself. Shkiriatov's orders were then extended to all Chechen-Ingush official workers from the President of the Republic down to the President of the *selsoviet* (village councils). Throughout October and November all the secretaries of the Party regional committees were arrested, as well as the President of the Republic A. Gorchkhanov. Also arrested were the presidents of regional executive committees, of which there were twenty-eight, almost all the presidents of rural councils, and the *kolkhoz* and Party members who had organised them. In the course of the liquidation of the 'bourgeois-nationalist henchmen', civil servants of government, urban, regional and rural institutions were also arrested.[12]

The general psychology of these arrests was clearly expressed by the chief of the regional NKVD of Gudermes, Gudasov, when one of his somewhat inexperienced assistants asked him ingenuously 'How can we arrest a man if we have no evidence against him?' He replied: 'We can always find evidence provided he wears a Caucasian hat!' We may also note that among the twenty-three chiefs of the regional NKVD there was one Chechen, Goitiev, who was arrested during this campaign. Chechens and Ingush who had been living outside the Republic were also indicted. They included D. Tokaev (member of the Central Committee of the Azeri Communist Party), Kh. Oshaev (Director of the North Caucasian Mountain Pedagogical Institute), M. Omarov (instructor of the North Caucasian *kraikom*) and Idris Ziazikov, who was still serving time from a previous conviction.

Arrests continued up till November 1938, when the case against the 'bourgeois-nationalist centre of Chechnia-Ingushetia' was ready. 137 people, all formerly responsible cadres of the Republic, were prosecuted under various clauses: bourgeois-nationalism, counter-revolution, insurrection, Bukharinist-Trotskyist anti-Soviet terrorism, espionage and sabotage. In legal terms this meant that they were tried under Article 58 of the criminal code: (1) treason to the fatherland; (2) preparation of armed uprising; (7) detrimental activity (*vreditel'stvo*); (8) terrorist acts; (9) subversion; (10) anti-Soviet propaganda; (11) membership of an anti-Soviet organisation; (14) sabotage.

According to the prosecution, the centre developed this widespread counter-revolutionary activity in alliance with other nationalist centres of the North Caucasus: Daghestan, Ossetia, Kabardino-Balkaria, Karachay and Adyghe-Cherkessia. The prosecution also claimed that the objective was to 'establish a North-Caucasian federal republic under the protection of Turkey and England'. To coordinate their activity with that of other national republics, the bourgeois-nationalist centres of the North Caucasus were supposedly in contact with the 'Muscovite internationalist centre' through their representatives, Korkmasov and Samurskii for Daghestan, Oshaev, Avtorkhanov and Ziazikov for Chechnia-Ingushetia, Takoev for Ossetia, and Kurdzhiev for Karachay. For the Party affiliation and education of the arrested members see the accompanying Table.

PARTY AFFILIATION AND EDUCATION OF SPECIAL ARREST OPERATION, NOVEMBER 1938 (total number: 137 person)

Period when a member of Bolshevik Communist Party of the USSR			
Until 1917	*1917–21*	*1921–7*	*1927–38*
2	6	39	90

		Age	
Over 40	*30–40*	*25–30*	*Under 25*
20	35	52	30

		Education	
Higher special education	*Higher Communist*	*Secondary*	*Primary*
10	53	36	50

The following conclusion that can be drawn from this table are, first, that all the arrested members of the 'bourgeois-nationalist centre' belonged to Stalin's school (with the exception of eight people belonging to Lenin's Guard); secondly, that the great majority (82 people out of 137) were under thirty years old (that is of *Komsomol* age); and thirdly that over one-third (52 men) had been educated in a communist VUZ (Higher Educational Institution) and Stalin's KUTVa (Communist University of the Workers of the East).

Investigation into the 'bourgeois-nationalist centre' lasted exactly three years. As one court alone could not have presided over a case involving 137 persons, it had been divided during the preliminary investigation into three groups: (1) the Soviet and Party section (Gorchkhanov, Salamov, Bakhaev, Okuev, Tuchaev and others; (2) groups not belonging to the Party and cultural-ideological figures (Zhaidarov, Matsiev, Avtorkhanov, D. Malsagov, Mamakaev and others); and (3) the terrorist group (Saparov, Ermolov, Tovbulatov and others). In this last group the *Chekists* included, logically, only the youngest of the accused. The investigations were conducted under torture, as was the custom throughout the Soviet Union, and in the course of the investigations D. Machkuev, former president of the *oblast* Executive Committee; M. Gisaev, former director of cultural propaganda; and Idris Ziazikov, former secretary of the Ingush *obkom*, were tortured to death. Unable to endure the torture any longer, M. Islamov (president of the Planning Commission of the Republic) and M. Bektemirov (secretary of the Party Regional Committee) opted for suicide. Ninety per cent of the accused were forced to invent and sign confessions to crimes they had never committed.

The surreal character of these confessions is best highlighted in the 'sincere statement written in his own hand' by A. Salamov, former vice-president of the Republican government. He confessed that Britain had sent, via Turkey, the following material to help the uprising: fifty guns for mountain use, 1,000 machine-guns, 200,000 rifles, 5 million cartridges, and 10,000 shells and grenades. Moreover, Britain had also promised to support the uprising from the air. As Salamov could not possibly have had any knowledge of where such weapons were buried, he continued to be tortured.

Finally, when the accused appeared for court-martial at the North Caucasian military district, only one man out of the 120 survivors pleaded guilty, mullah Ahmad Tuchaev. The others declared that the crimes of which they stood accused were a fabrication and that their confessions were false. They displayed their scars, their broken teeth and their injuries (one of them had been castrated during the interrogation). They declared that their confessions had been made under torture in the hope of hastening either judgment or death. There was no evidence, material or otherwise, to support the accusations other than the confessions. Since all the accused but one had recanted the charges, it would have been logical to postpone the case and order further investigations, but the Court was aware that those it had to judge were guilty only because of their nationality and maybe of excessive trust in the ideals of

Lenin and Stalin's national policy. The first group were sentenced on the basis of Tuchaev's deposition. A. Salamov, A. Gorchkhanov and Tuchaev himself were sentenced to death. It was then that the secret of Tuchaev's confessions was revealed: from his death cell he sent a petition for reprieve to Kalinin stating that he had confessed to the crimes because the NKVD had promised to liberate members of his family and spare his own life.

Moscow commuted the death penalty for the three men. Others were given a shorter term of imprisonment; for others the sentences were confirmed. The 'terrorist group' were liberated by the court-martial. As to the 'cultural-ideologists', the court did not judge them. They were left to the NKVD administrative court. The liquidated government cadres were replaced by imported officials who neither knew the language nor had any idea of the customs and history of the people entrusted to their care. The link that existed between the people and the authorities was broken when the intelligentsia was destroyed. *Chekists* were given the monopoly of authority in the Chechen-Ingush Republic, which was to be liquidated five years later.

Chechens and Ingush banned from the Red Army

By the start of the Second World War the Chechen-Ingush Republic was deprived of its leadership, and the nation crushed and deeply resentful. Nevertheless, when the Soviet authorities issued a call to fight for the Fatherland, the Chechens and Ingush supplied two divisions of volunteers, one active and one reserve.

Before the Revolution, there was no obligatory military service in Chechnia-Ingushetia. However, a number of Chechens and Ingush served as individuals in the Tsar's army and provided some brilliant officers. The small Ingush tribe supplied only high-ranking officers. There were seven Ingush generals and two Chechen generals. One of the latter, General of Artillery Erikhsan Aliev, commanded the second West Siberian Corps from 1901 to 1905. During the Russian-Japanese war he became Commander-in-Chief of the whole Russian front, replacing General Linevich who had left the army.

In the First World War the Chechens and Ingush supplied a regiment each to the Wild Division, famous for its bravery in the Carpathian battles. Russian Guards officers deemed it an honour to serve in this Division commanded by the Tsar's own brother, Grand Duke Mikhail Alexandrovich. The Wild Division was the first to fight the Bolshevik uprising in Petrograd during the famous Kornilov campaign.

After the German invasion in July 1941, the Soviet government did not allow the Chechens and Ingush to create their own native formations. When mobilised, they were incorporated individually into Russian detachments. Since they did not speak Russian, they served as 'mute soldiers', and commanding officers forced them to eat the same food as the other soldiers: pork. This detail was largely responsible for the mass desertions from the Red Army and for the Soviet government order that Chechens and Ingush were not to be accepted into the Red Army and that those already serving were to be dismissed. However, on the advice of General Supian Mollaev (a Chechen), Colonel Abadiev (an Ingush), Major Visantov, Captain Akhtiev and others, the Soviet government allowed the Chechen-Ingush Republic to incorporate volunteers into military formations. Two divisions were formed. One was incorporated into the southern front soon after the Red Army had evacuated Kerch. The commander of the southern front, Marshal Budenny, deployed two divisions in Krasnodar; one of them was the newly-arrived Chechen-Ingush division, and the other had just arrived from Kerch after a precipitate retreat. Inspecting the troops, Budenny said to the Russian division: 'Look at these Mountaineers. Their fathers and grandfathers, under the leadership of the great Shamil, fought bravely for twenty-five years to defend their independence against tsarist Russia. Let them be an example to you and show you how one fights for the Fatherland.'

But neither the active nor the reserve Chechen-Ingush divisions were accepted into the Red Army. They did not even have an official serial number. They formed a 'Wild Division' indeed. Their uniforms were supplied by the Chechen-Ingush Republic, which also provided them with rations. Encouraged by Marshal Budenny's praise, the officers asked him to accept Chechens and Ingush within the regular formations and to arm them properly — the only weapons the division had were swords and, occasionally, rifles of various makes. Many went barefoot. Budenny promised to think about their request. While the Marshal was thinking, the Germans crossed the Don and the Chechen-Ingush division found itself, without tanks or artillery support, confronted by the fury of the Germans advancing towards Stalingrad. On 4 August 1942, German tanks rolled over the bodies of many soldiers from this division. A few were taken prisoner, while others, together with the general staff, succeeded in breaking through the German lines and retreating. Despite the collapse of the whole southern front, the Chechen-Ingush population was blamed for this defeat.

1940 — Israilov's insurrection

The guerrilla movement which had survived for the previous twenty years in the mountains of Chechnia and Ingushetia gained momentum during the war. The Soviet government decided that this was due to German support. The movement was led at the time by well-educated and politically sophisticated people such as the lawyer Mairbek Sheripov and the writer Hassan Israilov. This allowed the NKVD to accuse the guerrillas of being under German orders although the Germans did not once send weapons to the insurgents even when they were at the frontier of the Chechen-Ingush Republic. Only spies and propaganda material crossed the border, a normal activity in wartime. Most important, Israilov's insurrection had already started in the winter of 1940, when Stalin was still an ally of Hitler.

During the previous decade the leadership of the insurrection had gradually passed from the mullahs and sheikhs to a new Soviet-educated generation, well able to understand the intricacies of Soviet colonial policy in the Caucasus. Soviet and Party chiefs could only make a career in the Caucasus on one condition: their complete ideological and practical support for Stalin's colonial policies against their own people. Many agreed to engage in this labour of treason and collaboration that spelt disaster for their nation, although it did not save them ultimately: the Soviet authorities dealt with their staff in the same manner as Soviet intelligence dealt with its burned-out agents: having absorbed what they had to offer, it destroyed them. But there were others who rejected the tempting prospects of an illusory personal career and preferred to lead their people in their difficult, indeed almost hopeless struggle for freedom. Such were the young nationalist leaders Hassan Israilov and Mairbek Sheripov.

Hassan Israilov was born in 1910 in the village of Nashkhoi in the Galanchozh region, Chechnia, the youngest of six brothers. In 1929 he finished secondary school in Rostov, and the same year, when already a member of the *Komsomol*, he joined the Communist Party. However, he did not take an active part in politics and devoted himself entirely to his passion for literature. He wrote poetry and plays, and became a permanent correspondent of the Moscow periodical *Krestianskaia Gazeta* (Farmer's Newspaper). His articles, vigorous and spirited, dealt with a single subject: the plundering of Chechnia by the local Soviet and Party leadership. Compelled to narrate the truth (as far as this was possible under Soviet administration), Israilov expertly criticised Soviet laws while seeming to defend them from the abuses of the local administration. Naturally, such a literary career could not remain unpunished. In the spring of 1931, he was arrested and condemned to ten years' imprisonment for counter-revolutionary slander and 'connections with a gang'. Three years later he was freed and reinstated into the Party after it had been proved that some of the officials he had denounced were indeed guilty. After his release, he went to Moscow to study at the Communist University of Workers of the East (KUTVa). Two books he had written in prison were published.

In Moscow Israilov gradually abandoned poetry for active politics. Together with other Chechens and Ingush, he sent a declaration to the Soviet authorities, stating that 'if the government persisted in its policy, the unavoidable result would be a general popular uprising'. They asked for a change of policies and demanded the dismissal of Egorov, the First Secretary of the Party Regional Committee, and Raev, the People's Commissar for Internal Affairs. The Soviet government sent this declaration to the local authorities and as might have been expected it resulted in a second arrest for Israilov and his friends. However, when at the beginning of 1939 Raev and Egorov were themselves arrested 'as enemies of the people', Israilov was set free again.

In January 1940 Bykov, the new secretary of the Regional Committee, summoned Israilov and suggested that he should present a petition for his reinstatement into the Party. Israilov promised to think about this. A week later, the *obkom* received the following answer: 'For twenty years now, the Soviet authorities have been fighting my people, aiming to destroy them group by group: first the *kulaks*, then the mullahs and the "bandits", then the bourgeois-nationalists. I am sure now that the real object of this war is the annihilation of our nation as a whole. That is why I have decided to assume the leadership of my people in their struggle for liberation.' He continued: 'I understand only too well that Chechnia-Ingushetia — indeed, the whole of the Caucasus — will find it difficult to get rid of the yoke of Red imperialism. But a passionate faith in justice and the hope that the freedom-loving people of the Caucasus and of the world will come to our assistance inspires me in this enterprise which you may consider foolhardy and senseless but which I believe to be the only possible path. The brave Finns are proving that this great empire built on slavery is devoid of strength when faced with a small freedom-loving nation. The Caucasus will be a second Finland and we will be followed by other oppressed nations.'

The insurrection spread. At the beginning of February 1940, Hassan Israilov was in control of Galanchozh, Sayasan, Chaberlo and part of the Shato region. The guerrillas' weapons were captured from the punitive detachments. After most of the mountain regions had been cleared of the Bolsheviks, a national congress was convened in Galanchozh. It proclaimed the establishment of a 'Provisional Popular Revolutionary Government of Chechnia-Ingushetia' with Israilov at its head.

The agreement between the Soviets and Finland dealt a blow to Israilov's morale. However, he did not lose hope that other Caucasian nations would support him or that Stalin would be eliminated in the course of the war. When the Soviet-German hostilities began, the span of Israilov's insurrection widened, aiming to liberate the whole of the Caucasus and proclaim its independence.

In February 1942, when the Germans were near Taganrog (500 km. from Chechnia-Ingushetia), Mairbek Sheripov, the brother of a renowned Chechen revolutionary hero, led an insurrection in Shato and Istumkala and joined Israilov, thus uniting the general staff of the rebels. Being aware of the methods used by Rosenberg and Himmler in 'liberated Ukraine', they published an 'Appeal to the Chechen-Ingush People' in June 1942, stating that Caucasians would receive Germans as guests only on condition that they recognised Caucasian independence. For its part the general staff of the German army in the Caucasus issued a special order to the troops underlining that the German soldier had to behave in a way that was different from that accepted in the Ukraine and other Soviet regions. Another noteworthy declaration was that of the North Caucasian National Committee to the *Ostministerium* at the end of 1942 to the effect that if 'the liberation of the Caucasus meant the exchange of one coloniser for another, then the Caucasians would only consider this a new stage in the national liberation war'.

During the war, the Bolsheviks' rearguard operations were much more deadly than their action in the front line. As is well known, in 1941–2 Soviet military aircraft were completely inactive in the front line against the enemy. On the other hand, they bombed their own rear savagely. In the spring of 1942, there were two Soviet air-raids over the Chechen-Ingush mountains. In some *auls* (Shato, Istumkala and Galanchozh) the number of dead was greater than that of the living. While Stalin shelled his own people, not a single German had set foot on Caucasian soil, and when the Germans finally came to the Caucasus in the summer of 1942 they never penetrated into Chechen-Ingush territory.

It is of course understandable that the Chechens and Ingush, who had been methodically exterminated by the Soviet authorities, should have held the latter in profound contempt. Still, not all the population took part in the insurrection. One could imagine that women, children, the very old, Chechen-Ingush communists, officers of the Red Army and the privileged categories of the Republic such as NKVD agents were not guilty of crimes against the Soviets. Nevertheless, Stalin faithfully executed the orders of Nicholas I to exterminate the Mountaineers, albeit after a delay of more than a century — an unprecedented happening in the history of war. All Chechens and Ingush, Balkars and Karachays were deported from the Caucasus in 1943-4. For years nothing was known about where they had been sent, or if any of them had survived somewhere in Siberia or Central Asia.

How they were deported

The following is an unemotional account of the deportation by a student who witnessed it:

> In 1943 I arrived from Kokand to Groznyi with the Petroleum Institute which had been evacuated to Kokand in 1942 at the time of the German attack.
>
> No real *kolkhoz* had been established in Chechnia though members of *Zagotzerno* [grain production], of *Zagoskot* [livestock production], and even *kolkhoz* presidents were present in the *auls*. It seemed that the peasants remained independent.
>
> Gangs were active in the mountain *auls*. After the liquidation of the Chechen-Ingush Republic, the newspaper *Groznenskaia Pravda* wrote that since the establishment of the Soviet government, the gangs of Chechnia-Ingushetia had killed nearly 20,000 Red Army troops and Party members.
>
> During the war, when the Groznyi Military School was evacuated to the Chechen mountains, the guerrillas killed 200 students.
>
> At the end of 1943 there were rumours in the city of the projected deportation of Chechens and Ingush, but these rumours were mere whispers. In the second half of January and the first half of February 1944, special detachments of the NKVD began to arrive in American Studebaker lorries. The newspapers published an appeal to the population: 'Let us make an example of our roads and bridges', and 'let us help our dear and beloved Red Army in its manoeuvres in the

mountains!' Thus the army occupied the mountains and each *aul* was supplied with its own garrison.

Then came the day of the Red Army: 23 February 1944. In the evening the Red soldiers built blazing fires in the village squares and there was singing and dancing. The unsuspecting villagers came to see the festivities. When they were assembled in the squares all the men were arrested. Some of the Chechens had weapons and there was some shooting. But resistance was rapidly eliminated. The men were locked up in barns and then a hunt began for those who had not gone out. The whole operation was effected in two or three hours. Women were not arrested but were told to pack their belongings and get ready to leave the next day with the children.

At the same time, in Groznyi, students and housewives were mobilised. In the evening of 23 February, the director of the Institute came to the students' quarters and told us to assemble at 6 a.m. near the building of the Institute. We were to take some extra underwear, and food for three days. The students of the Pedagogical Institute also showed up. When we had assembled near the Institute we saw many Studebakers half-filled with Red Army soldiers. Then, according to a carefully prepared plan, we were stationed among the *auls* by groups of twenty to thirty men. When we arrived in the *auls* we were surprised by the silence. Half an hour after our arrival the lorries were filled with the men arrested the previous day and the women and children. They were then transferred to freight cars in Groznyi. All Chechens and Ingush, without exception, were taken away. The Daghestanis were left: there were seven or eight of them in our *aul*.

The students' task was to take care of the farms until the arrival of immigrants from Kursk and Orel regions. We had to assemble and feed the livestock, store the grain, take care of stocks, and so on. Things were different in the mountain *auls*: after the livestock had been evacuated, the *auls* were set on fire in order to deprive the 'bandits' of their means of subsistence. For days one could see *auls* burning in the mountains. At the same time, an amnesty was promised to those who had escaped to the mountains if they returned. Some of them did return but they were also deported.[12]

According to other eye-witnesses, groups of Chechens and Ingush were immediately shot. It was only the men, women and children whose loyalty inspired no doubts even in the NKVD who were deported. Only women were allowed to take some hand-luggage.

The journey was no less tragic. The men transported in prison freight cars were deprived for days not only of food but even of water. Because of these privations and the lack of medical care (the freight-cars were so full that people were sitting on top of each other), there were mass epidemics. Jewish refugees from Central Asia reported that typhus had already started on the journey, killing half the prisoners. The authorities tried to localise the epidemic to the Chechens and Ingush in order to get rid of them in a 'natural' way. The local population were strictly forbidden to help the dying by giving them food, water or medicine. Even simple displays of humanity were forbidden under threat of arrest. The present writer's efforts to discover even an approximate percentage of the Chechens and Ingush who had died or were executed in the course of this nightmare proved to be in vain. Eye-witnesses sometimes quoted such a high figure that one refused to believe that so frightful a slaughter could have happened. However, none of the witnesses I interviewed spoke of less than 50 per cent deaths.

Other North Caucasians, Balkars and Karachays were treated in exactly the same way. The Balkars (120,000 men) and Karachays (170,000 men) were Turkic peoples who had never recognised the Soviet government. They had fought heroically, together with other North Caucasians, for their faith and independence. The Germans passed through their territory and were received — as in the Ukraine, Belorussia and Smolensk in the early years — as guests. Their arrival was viewed as liberation from Bolshevik despotism — a desire shared by all the people of the Soviet Union.

The motive given by the Soviets to justify the deportation — collaboration with the Germans during the war — was ridiculous. As already mentioned, the Germans never penetrated the territory of the Chechen-Ingush Republic during the War, and since the Chechen-Ingush were never enrolled in the Red Army, they could not serve in Vlassov's army. As to the government's claim that anti-Soviet detachments were active deep within Chechnia-Ingushetia, this is absolutely true. As the Soviet government was well aware from the experience of the Russian empire, armed resistance against a foreign conqueror was an old-established tradition in those parts long before Hitler or Stalin appeared. Indeed the Imamate of Shamil fell only sixty-three years before the installation of the Soviet government. It was for their secular and just pursuit of freedom and independence that the Chechens and Ingush were destroyed and their republic was liquidated. On a small stretch of land in the Caucasus two worlds came face to face: a colossal police despotism and an enclave of true human aspiration. The struggle between good and evil, between democracy and totalitarianism, was being enacted in the Caucasian mountains for decades while the outside world remained largely ignorant and indifferent. Furthermore, the strategic position of the Caucasus made it imperative for the Bolsheviks to finish the task which the tsarist conquerors had left unfinished: to create in the Caucasus a new colonising force combining military and police functions and incorporating subjugated natives who would be obedient in defending Soviet imperialist interests.

The annihilation of the Chechen, Ingush, Karachay and Balkar people marked the beginning of a grand operation of destruction and deportation of all the Caucasian populations. A number of Daghestanis, Ossetians, Kabardians and Cherkess were also deported and replaced by colonisers. Daghestan and the Georgian shore of the Black Sea were in jeopardy too, and group expulsions in Azerbaijan, Armenia and Georgia served to liquidate the remaining nationalist elements. The Bolsheviks thus managed to drive the first serious wedge in the relations between the peoples of the Caucasus. The wealth of the region (petroleum, zinc, manganese and other minerals) further added to its misfortune. The Soviet administration nationalised these riches and transformed them into centres of hard labour for the local population, the colonisers acting as slavers. This provoked further hostility between Russians and Caucasians.

Exile and return

Thus the history of Chechnia-Ingushetia was written off for thirteen years. How did the Chechens and Ingush behave during their exile? According to Solzhenitsyn's observation in Kazakhstan, 'Only one nation refused to accept the psychology of submission.' This applied 'not to individuals, nor to insurgents, but to the nation as a whole: the Chechens . . . They alone in the Dzhezkazgan camp endeavoured to support the Kengir uprising.' He noted that 'no Chechen ever tried to be of service or to please the authorities. Their attitude towards them was proud and even hostile.' They despised the natives and deportees who submitted to the authorities, plundered cattle, and 'respected only rebels'. He further remarked that 'the strange thing was that everybody feared them and no one prevented them from living as they liked. The authorities who had owned the country for thirty years could not force them to respect their laws.'[13] Thus it was only as regards plunder that

Chechens were faithful to Marxism-Leninism. As prescribed by Marx they 'expropriated the expropriators', or more simply, according to Lenin's advice they 'plundered the plunderers'. But not even Stalin could force them to obey his laws.

In the course of the 20th Congress, Khrushchev, presumably on the initiative of Mikoyan who had formerly been in charge of the North Caucasus, rehabilitated the Mountaineers and the Kalmyks. On 9 January 1957, the Chechen-Ingush ASSR and the autonomy of the Balkars, Karachays and Kalmyks were re-established. The other deported nationalities, the Crimean Tatars and the Volga Germans, remained in their zones of deportation, although officially they were decreed 'free', a sign of the Kremlin's indifference to the all-important nationality question. Furthermore, there were indications that, up till the end, the Soviet government considered as justified the deportation of the peoples it allowed to return to their fatherland, namely the Chechens, Ingush, Karachays and Balkars, and these nations are periodically reminded of this. 'Witnesses' among the Chechen-Ingush are produced who argue that Stalin was right to expel them from their homeland. One such witness was Kh. Bokov, awarded the title of 'Candidate of Historical Science' for his efforts. Bokov sought to prove that Stalin's deportation had saved the Chechens and Ingush from a worse fate — Hitler's genocide. He made extensive use of a forged document claiming that the *Wehrmacht* had issued an order on 8 December 1941 stating: 'When Groznyi, Malgobek and other regions have been taken, we will be able to introduce the needed garrisons into the mountains without difficulty. When the region is sufficiently pacified, all the Mountaineers will be exterminated. The population of the mountains is not very large so that about ten of our *Sonderkommando* will be able to annihilate all the males in a short time.'[14] The implication was that the 'evacuation' saved the Chechen and Ingush population from total extermination by Hitler.

Bokov made a brilliant career in his Republic. First nominated to the post of Second Secretary of the *obkom*, he later became President of the Republic and Chairman of the Presidium of the Supreme Soviet of the Checheno-Ingush Autonomous Republic. When *perestroika* was already well under way, the journal *Kommunist* (no. 2, 1988) commissioned him to write an article, and this appeared with the title 'How to Form Internationalist Convictions'. Although he did not dare to reproduce the forged *Wehrmacht* document a second time, he repeated the old accusations against his people, adding 'The Chechens and Ingush are expanding the sphere of activity of Islam, opening new mosques, stubbornly preserving "reactionary traditions", deliberately observing religious festivals, and exciting local nationalism as a result of which Russians are running away from the Republic.' He also says:

> The Great Patriotic War was a severe ordeal for all the nations of the USSR. The sons and daughters of the Fatherland defended it with weapons in their hands . . . However, the real face of anti-Soviet elements was also unmasked . . . Traitors and enemies of the Soviet authorities were active here [in Chechnia-Ingushetia]. They formed terrorist gangs, committed acts of sabotage and murdered Party and Soviet activists . . . Their dirty crimes were among the causes of the tragedy which befell the Chechens and Ingush — their mass expulsion from their homeland. Yes, there were traitors, indeed there were many of them. (p. 89).

As might be expected of a true internationalist, Bokov addresses dithyrambic praises to the 'elder brother'. With a crude lack of sensitivity, the *Kommunist* article claims that 'Russian people are displaying towards the Caucasian population the care that an older brother might take of a younger one' (p. 90), a statement as tasteless as dancing the lively *lezghinka* at a funeral. North Caucasians were driven to certain death in special camps in Kazakhstan where half of them died of hunger, cold and typhus. One more instance of such care and the North Caucasians would now survive only in our memory, as was the fate of the Ubykhs and Nogay Turks, exterminated during the conquest of the Caucasus.

On 17 June 1988 *Komsomol'skaia Pravda* published an interview with a Moscow economist, Professor Ruslan I. Khasbulatov, a native of Chechnia-Ingushetia (at the time of going to press Chairman of the RSFSR Supreme Soviet), which we quote below. The interview highlighted the shortcomings in national relations in the North Caucasus:

> 'I spent my childhood in the extreme north of Kazakhstan, in a small village called Poludino where Chechens were transported in February 1944 as 'special emigrants'. The village was multinational. Besides my mother, two older brothers and my sister, there were a few families from our village to which we were related, together with some thirty Volga German, Korean and Tatar families. The majority nationality was Russian. We lived there for ten years, during which time I do not recall a single national conflict despite the fact that we

were deportees. Why did we not suffer the same violence in this remote village as we did from the state? Judge for yourself: since I was five or six years old, I tried to help my mother and family like the other boys. My mother was working as a milker in the *kolkhoz*. As for me, I did what I could like the others: I drew water from the well, watered the cattle, cleaned the cowsheds in the winter, looked after calves in temperatures of minus 40 C, and so on. Everybody in the village was in the same boat — equally poor — with hardly enough bread to eat. Wages were notably low . . . The mothers of other boys worked side by side with mine and they also sweated blood. They were Russian, Kazakh, German and Korean. My first teacher, Vera Vladimirovna, walked 5 kilometres every day to come to our house. Why did she do it for a boy from a 'criminal' family when she could easily have avoided it? Remembering her, I realise that she was giving us a lesson in internationalism and kindness. My memory of superiors is associated with two sergeants and the president of the *kolkhoz*. They were severe but just. They did not victimise my mother — on the contrary they encouraged her by saying she was the best milker. Naturally this was equality among beggars but it was enough to avoid national conflicts.'

Interviewer: 'What else besides economic problems causes outbreaks of nationalism? What is the nature of such outbreaks?'

Khasbulatov: 'There are many causes. I cannot attempt to analyse them all. However, it is important to maintain a Leninist approach and never, whatever the circumstances, make a whole nation into a scapegoat. This has been overlooked by our provincial Dantons and republican Robespierres. They incriminate entire nations while putting beyond the reach of criticism the 'leadership' whose foolish acts offend national pride.

'Take for example *Groznenskii Rabochii* of 26 January 1988 reporting on a plenum of the Party *obkom*. The plenum was convened to discuss *perestroika*. Instead of analysing the present situation, the newspaper turned to the 'troubled times' of the tragic year 1944, describing at length how the enemy — the Chechens and Ingush — stabbed the Red Army treacherously in the back, the numbers of gangs and rebels, their weapons and so on. Even I, though I never lived in Chechnia-Ingushetia, find this disagreeable reading. How much more so would those who live in the Republic?

'Let us settle the question of the "gangs". They appeared as a result of the fabrications of Beria, Stalin and their local parasites. Thus was created the criminal idea of the "guilt" of the nation and its collaboration with the enemy. But truth prevailed and the people were fully rehabilitated. However, thirty years have passed and rumours about gangs are still being spread. They have acquired a life of their own as local militants push their dishonest articles in the central press. I believe this 'firing' campaign to be a recurrence of local Stalinism aimed at browbeating and frightening. Could this be the reason why the local Chechen and Ingush leaders are pathologically scared of being accused of nationalism? They cannot and do not want to use their native languages in the press and television. They are even proud of this deficiency. Needless to say the [local] Russian leaders are totally ignorant of the native languages. One must assume then that Comrade Kolbin, who learned Georgian when serving in Georgia and later Kazakh, had more time on his hands than the bureaucrats of Chechnia-Ingushetia.'

In another interview the Russian scholars L. Drobizheva and Iu. Poliakov in *Izvestiia* (22 March 1988), noting that in the Soviet Union 'we are past masters at hiding the truth regarding the nationality problems', reveal that it is possible to write about 'Chechen and Ingush gangs' and the way they had 'treacherously betrayed the Red Army', but not about the re-establishment of the Republic since this would necessitate a mention of its previous liquidation. Even in the period of *glasnost* and denunciation of Stalinism, people who claimed to be internationalists wrote incredible nonsense about the Chechens and Ingush. Stalin — who is accused of all sins, be they his own or those of others — is loudly justified for deporting the North Caucasians. One could almost say that a second genocide, this time a spiritual one, was taking place up to the late 1980s. It was implied that since time immemorial, the Chechens' favourite pastime was to butcher the Russians, and sadly the Russians believed it. N. Startseva explained why in an article in *Literaturnaia Gazeta* on 3 August 1988, entitled 'The National Disease': 'People of various nationalities — Russians, Ukrainians, Armenians, Tatars — live side by side with the Chechens and Ingush but know little about their concerns. They are deprived of the possibility to learn about the traditions, culture and the day-to-day problems and existence of the natives.' She wrote further:

Literature unmasks Stalinism and uncovers the psychological mechanism that forced people to believe that which seemed unbelievable, as well as the process by which they persuaded and deceived themselves

. . . It is natural to look for a plausible explanation . . . Thus G. Murikov in his review of A. Pristavkin's novel *Nochevala tuchka zolotaia*[15] writes in the Leningrad review *Zvezda* (no. 12, 1987): 'Children were brought to the rich and fruitful lands of the Caucasus . . . made available after the expulsion of the Chechens.' Why were they deported? Murikov replies: 'Mass collaboration with the Germans and treason — a most heinous offence — were the reason for such a radical act.' Naturally some succeeded in hiding. And thus a movement similar to that of the Basmachi flared up.[16]

Startseva's refutation was logical: 'Before justifying Stalin's decision which caused the death of hundreds of thousands of innocent people, it would do no harm to look at military maps of the Caucasus for 1942–4 which would clearly show that the territory of Chechnia-Ingushetia had never been occupied. This in itself is reason enough to exclude the possibility of "mass collaboration" with the enemy.' She concluded: 'I was impressed by the words of the poet Hussein Satuev whom I met in Groznyi: "There must be truth. Our people have experienced the hideousness of the personality cult. We are still crying on our stones. Why should we die twice? When lies are written about a nation it dies again." ' She ended with a question which may not be answered for a long time to come: 'Has everything been done to rehabilitate those who returned from exile and to give them equal opportunities to develop creatively like other nations?'[17]

The Central Committee decree of 25 June 1946 which justified the genocide of Stalin and Zhdanov *a posteriori* was a mockery of historical facts. Stalin himself, writing for *Pravda* in 1918, praised the revolutionary spirit of Chechnia led by Aslanbek Sheripov, the commander of the Chechen Red Army killed by the Whites in 1919 during the battle of Vozdvizhenskaia. These facts are well known to historians. General Denikin, as mentioned earlier, wrote that during his advance on Moscow he had been forced to leave one-third of his army in the Caucasus because the Chechens and Ingush had concluded an alliance with the Bolsheviks. Stalin disappeared long ago, yet the new thinkers of the Kremlin, who are perfectly aware that Chechens and Ingush did not and could not collaborate with the Germans, still encourage the propagation of Stalin's concepts on 'counter-revolutionary nations'. As a result the younger Russian generation knows nothing about the history of the non-Russian peoples — or for that matter about its own.

NOTES

1. The information provided in this chapter was researched for a special memorandum to the United Nations in 1948. While Stalin was still alive, the memorandum was published in Russian under the title *Narodoubistvo v SSSR*.
2. Friedrich Bodenstedt, *Die Völker der Kaukasus and ihre Feiheitskampfe gegen die Russen*, part 2, 1855, Berlin.
3. See Memoirs of Major-General Musa Kundukhov, published in *Caucasus*, May 1936, no. 5.
4. Ernest Chantre, 'Recherches anthropologiques dans le Caucase'. Paris, 1887, part IV, p. 104, in A. Sanders, '*Kaukasien*'.
5. *Die Völker des Kaukasus . . ., op. cit.*
6. Ideologically, the Emirate was conservative and pro-clerical, and therefore much more right-wing than the government of Chermoev. Nevertheless, the Emirate maintained the tactics of a united front with the Bolsheviks against Denikin. Inaluk Arsanukaev Dyshninskii, who acted as the Prime Minister of Uzun Haji, was much more to the left than the latter. He was killed for this reason in 1921 by the Bolsheviks in the streets of Groznyi; the local paper announced that he had been 'killed by bandits'.
7. Cf. stenographic reports of the First Congress of the Soviet Republic of the Mountains, Vladikavkaz, 1921.
8. Cf. M.I. Kalinin, *Za eti gody*, Moscow, 1923.
9. Although he came from a family of merchants, he commanded the Chechen Red Army during the Civil War.
10. The legend of the British coming to free the Caucasus was prevalent among the Chechens. Any Chechen would have supported this eventuality through reference to the religious authorities of the pre-revolutionary era. I last heard it mentioned in the summer of 1942: 'We are ready to stake our lives on it: it is not the Germans who will come but the *Ingiliz*, and they will not come from the West but from the East.' That was the belief of the majority. At that time the Germans were near Chechnia, on the western shore of the Terek! I do not know the origin of this legend, but the Chekists believed it as firmly as did the Chechens. This being so, every Chechen 'bandit' and every national uprising was ascribed to the British intelligence service. It is truly ironic that whereas for eighty-five years after the time of Shamil, first the tsarist authorities and later the Chekists accused the Chechens of being Anglophiles, yet it was as Germanophiles that they were deported in 1944.
11. Zelimkhan, a Chechen *abrek* (bandit of honour), was famous throughout Russia before the First World War.
12. *Prometheus*, no. 3, March 1949.
13. A. Solzhenitsyn, *Arkhipelag Gulag*, Paris: YMCA Press, pp. 420–1.
14. *Sovetskaia Rossiia*, 13 June 1970.
15. 'A golden cloud slept', opening line of a well-known poem by Lermontov.
16. The Basmachi war was a popular uprising which engulfed Central Asia and threatened the Soviets' control over the region. The movement was at its height between 1918 and 1924, but pockets of resistance survived till 1936.
17. The suppression of native-language teaching is another tool used against the

Caucasians. The writer Rasul Gamzatov, a member of the Presidium of the Supreme Soviet of the USSR, wrote on the 'distortions' prevailing in his native Daghestan. Gamzatov, in an interview with *Izvestiia* (29 March 1988), blamed not Russian bureaucrats but their local proxies: 'In Makhachkala there is not a single kindergarten, school or course teaching the language of our ancestors and no possibility to organise such courses because the teachers' colleges no longer train their students for the Avar, Darghin or Lak languages . . . I am sure that no one in Moscow intends to suppress the teaching of national languages, literature and history in pedagogical schools.' But Gamzatov is mistaken. The Avar language, for one, is that of the great Daghestani imams who fought Russia for over half a century to preserve Caucasian independence. One cannot teach the true history of the Caucasus without speaking of them. As Gamzatov himself admits, 'up till now the theme of Shamil was forbidden in Daghestani literature . . . On orders from the local authorities in Daghestan, people continue to look in vain for facts which would support the thesis of the voluntary annexation to Russia . . .' Gamzatov is a Caucasian blessed with great poetic talent and author of a remarkable book *My Daghestan*. Yet he keeps a stubborn silence about the fate of his countrymen although he risks nothing and is considered by Gorbachev an 'old friend'. However, Anatolii Pristavkin, a Russian writer mentioned earlier, published a novel on the deportation of the North Caucasians. Semen Lipkin, another Russian writer of great courage and humanism, wrote a striking book on the Caucasian tragedy, *Dekada*, risking prison or internment in a psychiatric ward. *Dekada* was published in 1980 by a small Russian publisher in New York, and remained almost unnoticed. See on this subject Michel Heller, 'Decades et decennies' in *Turco-Tatar Past: Soviet Studies presented to Alexandre Bennigsen*, Paris: Editions de l'Ecole des Hautes Etudes, 1986.

INTERNATIONALISM, NATIONALISM
AND ISLAM

Fanny E.B. Bryan

Atheism failed to win the hearts of the North Caucasians. Seventy years after the victory of a regime that claimed to have permanently abolished the social and economic bases of religion, the practices and rituals of Islam had been maintained substantially intact. For all Muslims in the North Caucasus, believers or not, Islam continues to form the essential part of their way of life.

Soviet anti-religious propagandists fostered the view that the survival of Islam rested mainly on its historical roots, its role in the national past. In part this was true. The young Muslim intelligentsia, even if officially indifferent to the practice of religion, observe the religious customs; there is a substantial literature depicting Islam as an aspect of the national patrimony. But in the North Caucasus the role of Islam is not limited to its being an expression of the national patrimony. To be accepted as a Chechen, an Ingush or a Daghestani, it is necessary to establish one's *bona fides* with an appropriate attitude toward Islam. It is not the national identity that implies one's attitude to religion, instead, one's attitude toward Islam is an inseparable aspect of one's national identity.

Historically, the North Caucasus has served as a barrier to Russian (and Soviet) expansion. The barrier takes at least two forms, one relating to geography, the other to people. The North Caucasus contains a major and formidable chain of mountains, which has formed a natural geographical barrier. But the *people* who inhabit the region also constitute a barrier, despite different impressions that might emerge at first glance. Although a disparate group, consisting of several distinguishable ethnic sub-groups and a myriad of languages and dialects, these peoples are bound together by Islam, a religion that by its very nature permeates the whole of life.

Some of the material to be presented here is not new. Thus, for example, the nexus of Islam, Sufism and nationalism in the North Caucasus has been developed elsewhere.[1] But some of the evidence relating to this nexus, and the specific forms it has taken, have emerged since *glasnost*. This chapter addresses several issues: first, the role of Islam in the North Caucasus, with a description of its outward manifestations in the region, along with a discussion of the post-*glasnost* shift toward increased activism; secondly, the role of Sufi *tariqat* in maintaining the strength and purity of Islam, with conjectures regarding their role as prime movers in recent years; thirdly, a discussion of several of the important issues that form the content of nationalist initiatives and dissent; and finally, a review of developments in anti-Islamic propaganda and agitation.

Islamic Omnipresence

It comes as no surprise that Islam enters virtually every facet of life; that, after all, is the nature of the religion. Even so, its omnipresence in the North Caucasus is surprising in view of the environment within which Islam existed during the seventy decades following the Revolution. What is more, Islam is no longer satisfied with mere survival. Similar to developments elsewhere in the Islamic world, Islam in the North Caucasus is on the offensive.

The Soviet press left us in no doubt as to the widespread presence of Islam in the North Caucasus. It is present everywhere: in the mountain areas, in the lowlands, in the cities and in the industrial centres. According to Soviet authors, the level of religiosity was revealed by the attachment of the population to religious rites, especially religious marriage, religious burial, prayers on family occasions, and the celebration of religious holidays. Soviet sources were agreed that new civilian secular rituals had not been able to replace religious rituals despite official efforts to that end. Either civilian and religious rites coexisted, or civilian rites and holidays had been taken over by the Muslim clerics. Indeed, there was concern that Islam in the North Caucasus had the capability of permeating all aspects of everyday Soviet social life.[2]

Religious weddings are observed throughout the Muslim regions of the former Soviet Union, even by those calling themselves non-believers. A survey conducted in Daghestan and published before the beginning of *glasnost* indicated that 65 per cent of marriages were celebrated according to the religious ritual.[3] In recent years, as many as 80 per cent of the marriages in the cities of the North Caucasus and in the mountain regions have followed the religious customs.

Mixed marriages in the North Caucasus strictly follow the *Shariat*, that is Muslim men marrying non-Muslim women. The reverse — the marriage of a Muslim woman to a non-Muslim man — is a sin and a dishonour. In a society in which the clan structure remains an important reality, as in Daghestan and Chechnia where vendettas are frequent, girls have little possibility of transgressing that law. Satisfactory statistical data concerning mixed marriages are very difficult to find. One such source covers marriages in Daghestan in 1973, and although the data are now quite old, they give an idea of the small number of Muslim women marrying non-Muslim men. The percentages were as follows: Avar 0.17, Darghin 0.9, Lezghin 0.9, Kumyk 1.1, Lak 1.5, Tabassaran 0.2, Nogay 2.0, Agul, Tsakhur and Rutul nil. The percentages of Muslim men marrying non-Muslim women are Avar 2.7, Darghin 1.6, Lezghin 3.1, Kumyk 6.0, Lak 5.0, Tabasaran 3.5, Nogay 3.7, Agul, Tsakhur and Rutul nil.[4] One of the most widespread attacks against Islam is that it prevents mixed marriages and teaches national exclusiveness.

In the *auls* women are judged according to how they follow the prescriptions of Islam and national traditions. A non-Muslim wife of a Daghestani or a Chechen will find life difficult and perhaps even impossible. In the same way her sons, if not circumcised and not carrying Islamic names, will have a difficult time being accepted or finding wives. Children of mixed marriages or spouses from non-Muslim nationalities are sometimes refused burial in local Muslim cemeteries.[5]

Funerals in the North Caucasus are automatically conducted in the presence of religious figures irrespective of the rank or Party affiliation of the dead person. Either secretly or openly, a religious figure will read the prayers for the dead at the graveside; such a ceremony would occur even for professors who had spent their lives lecturing on atheism. *Komsomol*, Soviet and Party cadres openly participate in religious burials, offering the excuse that religious funerals accord with the wishes of relatives. In Chechnia-Ingushetia, in the case of the members of a Sufi brotherhood, the burial ceremony is organised and conducted by the *tariqat*, the family being merely present. Iu. Aidaev, a member of the Chechen-Ingush *Oblast* Party Committee, wrote in *Pravda* on 8 August 1986 that responsible Party workers of the districts of Achkho-Martan, Nozhay-Yurt and Nazran could not remember an instance of a civil funeral rather than a religious one. Each of these districts has a strong Sufi presence. Achkho-Martan and Nozhay-Yurt districts are Naqshbandi centres, and the district of Nazran is the spiritual centre of Batal Haji (Qadiri) *tariqat*.[6]

In the North Caucasus the Ramadan fast is widely if not strictly observed. In some villages of Daghestan no wedding or other ceremony is performed during Ramadan, and dining halls close for 'refurbishment'.[7]

The main religious festivals, *Uraza Bayram* (feast marking the end of Ramadan), *Kurban Bayram* (feast of the sacrifice) and the *Mawlud* (birthday of the Prophet), are celebrated by the overwhelming majority of the population of Daghestan and Chechnia-Ingushetia. Soviet literature on the holy places indicated that pilgrims are numerous during periods associated with religious festivals, especially at the time of *Kurban Bayram*. In Chechen and Ingush *auls* and towns where the *tariqat* are present, *zikr* is performed every day during Ramadan and on the last day for *Uraza Bayram* in the main town centre.

The authorities complain that conservative religious opinion has grown to the point that those who do not observe the prescriptions of Islam are persecuted. Thus, in rural areas of Daghestan and Chechnia-Ingushetia, where public opinion is strongly in favour of Islam, it is impossible to exercise free choice. Religious rites must be observed. As a consequence, members of the intelligentsia, Party members, *Komsomols* and even anti-religious propagandists often lacked the courage to show their atheistic convictions. They were reluctant to alienate their fellow-countrymen or to be accused of betraying their national culture. Atheism was viewed as treason to the faith of their forefathers.

Islamic Activism

Traditionally anti-religious propaganda always represented believers as semi-literate, uneducated and generally old people from backward mountain regions, who did not participate in socially productive work and thus did not contribute to the building of communism. However, after *glasnost* the propaganda presented a different picture.[8] The contemporary North Caucasian believer was viewed as a well-educated and modern person. The propagandists admitted that 'new believers' consisted of professional people and intellectuals in all fields, including scientists, who might be found in both urban and industrial centres. Even worse, members of the political elite, Party and Soviet cadre — among them anti-religious propagandists — frequently participated in religious celebrations.

References to Islam in the North Caucasian press after 1987 revealed the bewilderment and helplessness of the authorities. It was common for retired Party members to abandon professed atheist ideals and return to the mosques. Anti-religious activists were liable to turn their coats and become religious propagandists. Teachers whose task was to develop a materialistic outlook in their pupils did not oppose Muslim clerics who took over the children's religious education; indeed, they often encouraged them. In increasing numbers, university students, the future élite of the country, were admitting that religion served a positive function in society or, at the minimum, was not harmful and therefore did not need to be combated.

Taking advantage of *glasnost*, Muslim religious dissent underwent a change. From a latent opposition it became an active movement clearly on the offensive against the system. The movement was on two levels. On one level North Caucasian believers were making material demands that would permit them to practise their religion freely, and on another believers sought an open ideological confrontation with the officially-sponsored doctrine. Moreover, the unofficial religious leadership in Daghestan and Chechnia-Ingushetia also appeared to be taking the lead in the political opposition movement, which would have made these developments different from those in other republics.

In a series of religious demonstrations in Daghestan in the spring and summer of 1989 (in Buinaksk on 14 May 1989, in Makhachkala on 15 May and 20–23 June 1989, and in Groznyi on 30 July 1989), a number of demands were made by the demonstrators.[9] First among these demands was the authorisation to build new mosques, in particular a cathedral mosque in the capital Makhachkala. Demonstrators asked for allocations of land in the centre of cities for this purpose. They wanted their mosques to be in plain view, not on back streets. In Kizilyurt, for example, believers threatened a general demonstration if their mosque could not be located on precisely the plot of land on which a Palace of Culture was scheduled to be built.[10] Old mosques were being restored throughout the North Caucasus. According to unofficial sources, some 200 mosques are already functioning now in Daghestan alone with or without official authorisation. Daghestani official sources claimed that there were twenty-eight official mosques in the Republic before 1989, but that numerous Muslim religious associations had been officially registered since then. Private sources tell us that permission was given to reopen only seventeen mosques.[11] It should be noted that believers did not ask the state for money; the mosques were to be built or restored with private funds. Other demands included the election of mosque councils by believers instead of by appointment from above; the right to print religious texts in Arabic on a printing press in the town of Buinaksk; and the teaching of Arabic in schools as a foreign language.[12]

In their ideological fight, North Caucasian believers challenged atheists to open debate. The latter were called on to explain why Islam should be considered harmful if believers and the religious establishment were loyal to Soviet power, if they encouraged work, and if they participated in the construction of society alongside non-believers. They insisted that they should not be treated as second-class citizens and denied their constitutional guarantees. Believers pointed out that atheists engaged in large-scale anti-religious propaganda on radio, television and in the press; they argued that believers should not be forced to listen to this outpouring without being given the right to express themselves and their own world view in print. North Caucasian anti-religious propagandists admitted that militant believers had studied atheistic literature as well as religious literature, and in consequence were able to force atheists into blind alleys with questions they themselves could answer better than the anti-religious propagandists.

One of the issues of the debate was the question of morality. For years the anti-religious literature compared communist morality favourably to religious morality, but by the end of Communist Party rule the roles were reversed. Privileged, haughty, swaggering, profiteering, money-grabbing and corrupt Communist Party leaders who preached atheism were asked now to defend their moral values. An honest mullah is better for society than a bad communist, a believer wrote in the Party press of Daghestan.[13] The controversy also focused on the spiritual emptiness of communism. With the passage of time the shining horizon of Lenin's socialism had faded, leaving nothing to fill the soul.

The argument around morality had an unexpected development in the North Caucasus when the head of the official Spiritual Board of the North Caucasus and Daghestan, Mufti Mahmud Gekkiev, was dismissed from office under the pressure of believers who accused him of immoral behaviour. His removal followed a burst of religious activity in Daghestan.[14] Gekkiev was dismissed in mid-May of 1989 by an unauthorised assembly of believers gathered in the town of Buinaksk. The next day the assembly and demonstrators proceeded to Makhachkala where they occupied the main square of the capital, demanding to talk to government officials and to officials of the Religious Board. Representatives from neighbouring North Caucasian republics and nationalities were among the demonstrators, who later stormed the *muftiat* in search of the Mufti, his secretary and his accountant, threatening to put them on trial forthwith. The assembly elected the imam of the town of Tarku as temporary acting mufti. Subsequently, the Council for Religious Affairs of the Council of Ministers of the Soviet Union was forced to confirm the decision and accept the *de facto* disbanding of the Muslim Religious Board of the North Caucasus. The leaders of the demonstrators, who called themselves the 'Initiative Group', formed an unauthorised council to oversee the activities of the *muftiat*, and its members travelled around the Republic visiting mosques, organising meetings and assemblies, and 'exhorting believers to actions contrary to Soviet law'. Follow-up demonstrations were staged at Makhachkala in June 1989 and at Groznyi in July.

Within the Marxist understanding of religion, the religious revival is inexplicable. It was painful for anti-religious propagandists to explain it as an internal phenomenon. Soviet anti-religious specialists were reluctant to acknowledge the need for spiritual succour. 'Science', wrote a Soviet specialist of Islam, 'has not yet elucidated the reasons for the reproduction of Muslim rituals and traditions under socialism. Nor has it explained the attraction for Islam felt by people known to be unbelievers or the identification of religion with nation in people's consciousness.'[15] Aside from the generalised belief that Islam is an integral part of the nation, the main reason given by Soviet anti-religious specialists for the revival of Islam in the North Caucasus was the intense activity of the Sufi *tariqat*. Religious propaganda from abroad, especially from Iran and the conservative Arab states, was also singled out as an influence on the Islamic rebirth in the Soviet Union. However, strong Iranian or Arab influence in Daghestan or Chechnia-Ingushetia was an unlikely explanation. Historically, such influences have never been important. Beyond that, the North Caucasus has never needed a religious example.

The role of the tariqat

For much of the past two centuries, Islam in its Sufi form played a prominent role in the North Caucasus in the face of Russian domination. The Sufis continued that role in response to the advance of communism during the Soviet period and there is no doubt that Islam's persistent entrenchment in the North Caucasus is largely a result of the activities of the Sufi *tariqat*,[16] which were not destroyed in the great anti-religious drives of the 1920s and 1930s, but went underground. In recent years they have emerged openly, taking an increasingly active role. Their efforts in the North Caucasus are directed toward organisation and recruitment, education and self-management. They attempt to maintain religious intensity through proselytising and religious instruction and, beyond that, collect taxes and administer the *Shariat* law.

Sufi *tariqat* remain on the fringe of the political system, yet they are very influential. In Chechnia and Ingushetia, according to private sources, most of the new informal groups and political parties are formed by either committed members, followers or sympathisers of the *tariqat*. Thus although the *tariqat* are not engaged yet in political activities as organisations, their influence on the new political developments has been predominant.

The work of the *tariqat* relating to religious education has been done through a network of illegal mosques, underground religious schools, holy places and shelters for pilgrims barely disguised as hostels and *chaikhana* (teahouses). In Daghestan and Chechnia-Ingushetia the Sufis have at their disposal a large body of religious propagandists, and are able to conduct their religious work in a number of ways. Bennigsen and Lemercier estimated the number of Sufi adepts in the North Caucasian Republics of Daghestan and Chechnia-Ingushetia as *ca*. 200,000. Kh. Bokov wrote that in the Chechen-Ingush ASSR there were '60,000 able-bodied people who completely escape socially productive work. These people belong to the *murid* groups which provide them with work and moral satisfaction.' With increasing openness the *tariqat* preached at large gatherings in cemeteries, at holy places and during group services and ceremonies organised on the occasion of Muslim festivals. They engaged in these activities notwithstanding Soviet law on cults, which strictly forbade religious proselytising as well as religious meetings outside the legal houses of prayers. Furthermore, in recent years details have emerged of women Sufi adepts in the North Caucasus who, according to the Soviet press, 'speak publicly, openly intruding into the spiritual life of other families'.[17]

Another Sufi tactic involves modelling themselves on the methods of *agitprop*. With this approach, Sufi missionaries go from home to home to conduct regular private discussions with individuals and families in which they act as consultants on a variety of questions. Intimate meetings such as these are geared toward preserving and deepening religiosity among the believers and winning over non-believers.

The propagation of religious dogma among children and teenagers was especially worrying for the Soviet authorities. The rapid growth in the number of unofficial Quranic schools in the North Caucasus has resulted from the special efforts of the Sufi clergy to spread religious influence among the upcoming generations. In those schools children are taught the fundamentals of Islam and Arabic. Religious teaching is reinforced by 'field trips', group visits to holy places, *mazars*. These are usually in areas associated with an historical event or person, typically connected with resistance to the Russians. But they can be anywhere, and most cemeteries in the mountains are considered *mazars*. Quranic schools take pupils at a very tender age, with organised teaching beginning with pre-school children from the age of three or four.

Religious schools exist in various settlements, most of them in the strongholds of *muridism* in the mountain regions of Daghestan and Chechnia-Ingushetia. Some Quranic schools, however, are known to exist in areas that could be more easily supervised by the Soviet authorities, such as the middle mountains and lowlands of the Darghin and Kumyk areas of Daghestan, which are also Sufi strongholds. Their presence has been reported in the towns of Usisha and Tebekmakhi of the district of Akusha, in Khasavyurt and in Gubden. There is a Shia *madrassah* in Derbent, and there are several small 'private' schools run by mullahs in Makhachkala. In Chechnia, religious schools have been reported in Nazran in the Ingush region. A fairly large illegal enterprise producing religious books in Arabic was uncovered in 1985 in Baku, which was filling book orders from Khasavyurt and Nazran.[18] The *madrassahs* are of varying sizes; some have been registered officially since 1989, others at the time of writing are not registered. Aside from children living in the immediate area, many urban families send their children to 'relatives' in the mountains to learn the Quranic tradition.

The Soviet press in the North Caucasus was wont to accuse Muslim clerics of hunting for youngsters' souls. It is a fact that the *tariqat* direct much energy toward individual work with teenagers. According to a 1978, pre-*glasnost* survey conducted among young believers of the Chechen-Ingush ASSR, 51 per cent of those questioned acknowledged belonging to a specific *tariqat*.[19] Ties are often established that develop into a *murshid-murid* (master-disciple) relationship.[20] For some time it has been known that both the Naqshbandi and the Qadiri *tariqat* in Daghestan and Chechnia-Ingushetia allow children to participate as spectators in the *zikr* ceremony. Mention has been made in the press of the existence of children's brotherhoods (in Chechnia).[21]

Another important aspect of the proselytising activities of the *tariqat* before the end of Communist rule was the distribution of Muslim Sufi underground (*samizdat*) literature to which the North Caucasian media made a growing number of references.[22] Written Muslim *samizdat*, whether published or in manuscript form, reproduced religious texts of high intellectual and theological content, consisting of extracts from the Quran, classic authors of Islam such as al-Ghazali, writings of Sufi sheikhs and Daghestani Arabist scholars of the sixteenth to nineteenth centuries, writings of North Caucasian and Tatar *jadid* (reformist) theologians, and so on. Sufi teaching and learning are based on such texts from manuscripts hidden and preserved since the Revolution. There was also a *samizdat* literature for a larger public. Often in the form of chain letters, this literature gave explanations of elements of the Islamic faith — such as the importance of prayers and fasting. Some of those chain letters were reproduced by children and circulated in schools.[23] The brotherhoods do not reject modern means of communication. For example, they make extensive use of tape recorders to distribute religious hymns, mystical poems, admonitions and sermons — some in Arabic originating from the Middle East.

For years Soviet anti-religious experts observed that Sufi communities in the North Caucasus had been able to remain outside the Soviet political system and, at the same time, retain an independent, self-supporting, non-sovietised way of life. Sufis have always been accused of isolating themselves from Russians, of refusing to learn Russian, of avoiding — when they existed — all Soviet organisations dominated by Russians (such as pioneers, *Komsomols*, the Communist Party and trade unions), and of escaping military service. The adepts of the Vis Haji (Qadiri) *tariqat* even regard speaking Russian as a sin. The Batal Haji and Vis Haji (both Qadiri) *tariqat* practice endogamy within their respective *tariqat*.[24] However, the latest information from Chechnia-Ingushetia indicates that the *tariqat* — at least the largest: Kunta Haji, Bammat Giray and Ali Mitaev — are spread throughout the Republic irrespective of clanic affiliation. With *glasnost*, increased information became available on the management of those communities, their court system and their economic and financial operation. According to Bokov, the Chairman of the Chechen-Ingush Presidium in 1988, political, social and economic life in Chechnia-Ingushetia is still regulated by the clans.[25] The clanic *taip* and sub-clanic (*nek'e* or *gar*) formations serve as bases for Sufi recruitment, and the clan elders are generally the Sufi religious authorities. Bokov went on to observe that the *kkhel*, the outlawed clanic religious tribunal composed of religious authorities or Sufi sheikhs and clan elders, operates everywhere. People turn to the *kkhel* to obtain a judgement or reparation according to the *Shariat* law or to get a judgement correcting decisions of the Soviet courts.[26] Sufi tribunals can apply severe judgments, going as far as the death penalty for unworthy adepts.[27]

An old accusation against the *tariqat* was that they did not consider the stealing of state property to be a sin, but a more recent one is that they advocate the private ownership of land and free enterprise. The authorities used to complain that, on the initiative of Muslim clerics, there were cases of private plots of land in a number of regions of Daghestan being distributed according to former, pre-collectivisation, ownership. The *tariqat* were thus viewed as the keepers of the old traditional social order. It would be interesting to know the extent to which the *kolkhoz* system was ever implemented in the high mountain regions of the North Caucasus. Following *glasnost* rumours emerged suggesting that it never was introduced properly. The sources do not indicate the regions of Daghestan in which the redistribution of land takes place.[28]

The *zakat* and the *sadaqa* are the basis of the financial independence of the *tariqat*. This allows them to make improvements to the land by constructing irrigation canals, wells, small bridges and so forth.[29] Funds are also used to embellish cemeteries and to provide special facilities for ablution around the holy places. Many new cult places have arisen recently in a number of regions, notably along the main highways. At the time of *namaz* (prayer), buses stop near those 'roadside Meccas' where collective prayers are organised. Special facilities are often provided nearby. The *tariqat* also fund religious propagandists whose full-time work is to proselytise. In addition to expenditure based on their own financial resources, Sufis are accused of actively interfering in the expenditure of state money.[30]

Soviet anti-religious propagandists recognise that the efforts of the *tariqat* in Daghestan and Chechnia-Ingushetia have always been geared toward maintaining the level of religiosity. And they recognise that the *tariqat* have been very successful. It seems that even the geographic location of the *tariqat* in those two republics has changed little since the pre-revolutionary period. The districts in Daghestan most often identified by Soviet sources as having well-organised *murid* groups are Charoda, Gergebil, Gumbetov, Gunib, Khunzakh, Levashi (mixed Avar/Darghin), Sovetskii, Tliarata, Tsumada and Untsukhul in the Avar territory; Botlikh and Akhvakh in the Andi territory; Babayurt, Buinaksk, Kaiakent, Khasavyurt, Kizilyurt, Kizliar, Lenin, Izberbash and Kaspiisk along the industrial coastline in the Kumyk territory; Akusha, Dakhadaev, Sergokala and Tsudakhar in the Darghin territory; Akhty, Magaramkent and Kasamkent in the Lezghin territory; Agul, Tabasaran, Novo-Lakskii; and finally in cities such as Makhachkala and Derbent. In the Chechen-Ingush Republic the districts identified as having a strong Sufi presence are Achkho-Martan, Dargo, Groznyi, Gudermes, Kurchaloy, Malgobek, Nazran, Nozhay-Yurt, Shali, Shelki, Sunja, Urus-Martan and Vedeno. The communities with a strong Sufi presence before 1917 have retained their Sufi allegiance. Even so, the situation is not static, but continues to evolve in favour of the *tariqat*. muridism is no longer identified with rural, traditional Islam. From their mountain strongholds the *tariqat* have descended into the lowlands, the cities and the industrial coastline. With the movement to the cities, *muridism* has become increasingly politicised. Moreover, it is the most extremist *tariqat* that are gaining ground.[31]

The press in the North Caucasus has made it clear that the spiritual and temporal influence of the Sufi sheikhs is spreading, and that their communities have become increasingly active. Aside from having taken into their hands the regulation of all religious affairs, at least in rural areas, they were accused of 'interfering in the social life of labour collectives and of meddling in public affairs that have nothing in common with the religious feeling of the believers'.[32] The Soviet authorities complained that the word of a mullah or of the leader of the *murid* group had greater authority in some villages than the word of the local Party leader.

Religious demonstrations in Daghestan in the spring and summer of 1989 indicated that religious freedom had become a major issue. The Soviet press hinted and private sources confirmed that they were organised and led by Sufis. In the May 1989 demonstration in Makhachkala, the demonstrators performed collective prayers in front of the *obkom* building. The prayers were *zikr*, consisting of loud prayers and dancing. The 'Initiative Group', which oversees the Spiritual Board, consists of 'religious leaders.' In the North Caucasus religious leaders are themselves Sufis. It is not surprising therefore that the Soviet media accused the Sufis of progressively taking over the official administration of the Spiritual Board.

Nationalism

Nationalism in the North Caucasus is centred in Islam, and in searching through their own national past, the Muslim intellectuals constantly encounter the legacy of Islam and Sufism. This legacy is an aspect of their cultural, intellectual and mystical background. It is also a prominent part of their militant holy war tradition, symbolised by the Naqshbandiya and Qadiriya and their centuries-long resistance to Russian domination. In this section we try to lay out the agenda within which much of the nationalist controversy has been framed which shows clearly that the integrating force of these concerns is Islam.

The nationalist agenda. The history of the Caucasian war was reinterpreted several times in Soviet historiography. In the first decades of the Soviet regime, Bolshevik historians were concerned to denigrate the tsarist past. Incorporation of non-Russian people into the Russian empire was termed an absolute evil by Pokrovskii and his school. Shamil and his *murids* were depicted as heroes, and their movement as progressive. The religious element of their struggle was ignored or rationalised. In the 1930s, with the rise of Russian nationalism within the Communist Party, Pokrovskii's theory of absolute evil was abandoned for that of the lesser evil. While the misdeeds of the tsarist regime were not necessarily denied, the incorporation of non-Russians began to be reinterpreted as a progressive phenomenon since it brought them into contact with the advanced Russian people.

After the Second World War and the deportation of some of the North Caucasian nations, the theory of lesser evil was abandoned and opposition to the Tsarist conquest was declared reactionary. A resolution condemning Shamil and his movement was adopted by the Central Committee of the Communist Party in 1949.[33] After Stalin's death, the debate on Shamil was reopened by the journal *Voprosy Istorii* in 1956. Once again the progressive role of the Russians in the North Caucasus was upheld, and furthermore any idealisation of Shamil's muridism was declared an anti-Soviet manoeuvre.[34] Since then periodic attempts have been made, generally by North Caucasian historians, to rehabilitate Shamil — without great success. In 1983, a North Ossetian historian, M.M. Bliev, came up with a new interpretation of the Caucasian war,[35] which argued that tsarist colonial policies could not be the reason for that war, because the North Caucasus was unaware of them. Instead, the roots of the war were the aggressive expansionist raids of Daghestani and Chechen tribes into neighbouring Russian allies: Georgia, Transcaucasia and Ossetia.[36]

After the beginning of *glasnost* the main issues discussed by the North Caucasian intellectuals related to Islam and Sufism, at least in their historical role. The intelligentsia wanted a rehabilitation of Shamil and his movement, along with a realistic reappraisal of the Russian conquest, and the historical rehabilitation of muridism. They used *glasnost* and *perestroika* in an effort to set matters straight. In late 1988, the deputy director of the Institute of History of the Academy of Sciences of the Soviet Union gave in to a pressure campaign by North Caucasian intellectuals, and officially condemned past attempts to vilify Shamil as tendentious. A spirited vindication of Shamil was published in the

Party press of Daghestan in an article by the jurist A. Khalilov; this was
the most enthusiastic appraisal of Shamil to appear in the Soviet Union
since the 1930s.[37] Khalilov's portrait of Shamil and his movement was a
radical change from the past official version which presented Shamil and
his Mountaineers as savages, plunderers and bandits, bloodthirsty
fanatics and aggressive expansionists. Khalilov professed passionate
admiration for Shamil, stressing that his government was strong and
progressive. The ideology of the Mountaineers could only have been
religious, but Shamil's attitude to the *Shariat* law was creative. He had
all the qualities required of a statesman, a legislator and the leader of a
national liberation movement. He was wise, an able administrator, a
fearless warrior, a talented commander, a great religious scholar and an
Arabist. He was dedicated to his people and their freedom, intolerant of
lawlessness, strict in matters of discipline and a hater of injustice. He was
modest, considerate, kind and tolerant toward other religions.

Another controversial theme relates to the actual date of the
annexation of the North Caucasian territories. The traditional historical
view has always been that Chechnia, for example, was annexed by the
Russian empire in 1859 after Shamil's defeat. However, in 1979 Soviet
historiography came up with a new version whereby Chechnia and
Ingushetia became part of Russia between 1762 and 1781 at their own
request. The rewriting of Chechen-Ingush history was the latest in a
long line of reinterpretation of the history of the non-Russian peoples.
These revisions were started after the Second World War in order to
promote the myth that enmities had never existed among the Soviet
nations, as proof of their voluntary entry into Russia. Already in 1970,
M.M. Bliev advanced the thesis that virtually all the people of the North
Caucasus had become Russian subjects voluntarily by the end of the
eighteenth century.[38]

An All-Union conference on the nineteenth-century national liberation movement of the North Caucasian Mountaineers was held in
Makhachkala in June 1989, and its proceedings give an idea of the extent
to which opinion in the North Caucasian republics was united in reject-
ing the official Soviet interpretation of the history of their countries.[39]
The progressive nature of the annexation of those areas to the Russian
empire is denied, as is the supposedly voluntary entry of Chechnia and
Ingushetia in the Russian empire. Russian colonial policies in the North
Caucasus are advanced as the main reasons for the struggle of the
Mountaineers. Muridism is presented as an ideology that served to

cement the anti-colonial national independence movement of the Mountaineers, and for the first time Russians are cast in the role of villains. Another historical issue taken up by North Caucasian intellectuals is the uprising of 1877 in Daghestan and Chechnia, led by the *tariqat*. This was unequivocally condemned by both Russian and Soviet historiographies. But in the spirit of *glasnost* the uprising began to be reinterpreted as a progressive movement. Also, the history of the massive purges of the 1920s and 1930s in the North Caucasus was reinvestigated and the deportation in 1944 of a number of North Caucasians — Chechens, Ingush, Karachays, Balkars, Muslim Ossetians, and some of the Avars and Cherkess — surfaced as a topic of discussion.

The local authorities also began to redefine their national heroes. National communist leaders were rehabilitated, one example being Samurskii who joined the Bolshevik Revolution but disappeared in Stalin's purges accused of national deviation. However, the communist leaders who were executed during the purges did not seem to be adequate national favourites for modern North Caucasians. Instead, the most attractive national heroes are those Muslims, mostly Sufis, who resisted Russian and Soviet expansion in the region. But although Shamil began to be rehabilitated, those who fought during the Soviet period were not. The official Soviet view of other Sufi leaders who led the revolts in the 1920s and 1930s — such as Najmuddin of Hotso, Uzun Haji, Mohammad of Balakhany, Arsanukay Khidirlezov and Salsa Haji Yandarov — continued to be that they were utter villains and political bandits.[40] In the popular imagination their memory remained vivid, as continual pilgrimages to their tombs and *mazars* made clear.

In the anti-religious attacks against the holy places, propagandists drew considerable attention to the increasing number of shrines in the North Caucasus associated with Muslims who resisted Russian and Soviet expansion. The tombs of some Naqshbandi and Qadiri sheikhs, who were executed by the Soviet authorities in the 1930s for 'counter-revolutionary activities' or as 'adversaries of socialism', have come to be venerated as holy places. Some of these tombs did not become destinations for pilgrimages until the 1980s. A new category of holy places has also been identified: tombs of foreigners who fought for the defence of Islam on North Caucasian soil.[41] Thus after seventy years, those who joined the Bolsheviks were not venerated as martyrs even if they had eventually been executed. The saints and martyrs are those who fought and died for their faith combating Bolshevism. It is significant that the North Caucasian intelligentsia are most interested in the rehabilitation of Shamil, the reinterpretation of the uprising of 1877–8 and, when possible, a review of the twentieth-century uprisings. All these events and personalities have an important religious component. The rehabilitation of such national leaders as Samurskii has no doubt been considered a good thing. Samurskii's writings, if re-edited, will be read with interest by the Daghestani intellectuals. But his rehabilitation has not had the same importance for the Daghestanis as that of Sultan Galiev for the Volga Tatar intelligentsia.

Soviet sources complained that the paramount interest of the young North Caucasians lies in their own national history, their national culture and political developments in the Muslim world abroad. Increasingly Soviet propagandists denounced the national arrogance of the Daghestanis and the Chechens and their aggressiveness in the defence of their national religious tradition.[42] Singled out were Muslim preachers — which was not new — and intellectuals — which was new. The intense pro-internationalist campaign of the last few years of communist control was particularly directed toward the intellectuals. Anti-religious propagandists even acknowledged that rising nationalism is a reaction against too many 'white spots' in national history, too much slander against the past. It was the view of the anti-religious propagandists that interest in the national past is dangerous because it gives too much importance to Islam and emphasises it as a political factor in history as well as in the contemporary world.

North Caucasian resentment of the Russians for robbing them of their national history is doubled for the Daghestanis by the forced loss of their Arabic patrimony. In the nineteenth century, it was considered that the best literary Arabic was spoken in the mountains of Daghestan. Daghestani Arabist scholars were famous, attracting students from the whole Muslim world. The *lingua franca* before the Revolution was Arabic. Then, in the 1920s and 1930s, the main thrust of the anti-religious campaign was to eradicate Arabic, a religious language, and to replace it with Russian. The finest flower of Arabist scholarship disappeared in Stalin's purges.

It was thought that among Soviet Muslims the Daghestanis (together with the Volga Tatars) demonstrated the best command of the Russian language, but that belief has been shaken. Many in the Soviet press complained of the weak knowledge of Russian among the Daghestanis.[43] What then is the *lingua franca*? Daghestan has nine official languages and many unofficial ones. One mountain valley can speak a language not understood in a neighbouring valley. In 1983, a delegation of the Muslim Spiritual Board of Central Asia and Kazakhstan visited the *jami* mosques of Khasavyurt, Buinaksk and Derbent (Sufi strongholds), and delivered sermons in Arabic. The delegation was surprised by the large number of people who could follow the sermons and theological discussions in Arabic.[44] Such evidence, along with reports from private sources, suggests that the use of Arabic as a *lingua franca* has not totally ceased. Some recent Arab travellers to Daghestan claim that they have seldom heard such pure literary classical Arabic as in Daghestan. The art of composing instant poetry, long forgotten among the Arabs, has been kept alive there. Kumyk, used as a secondary *lingua franca* before the Revolution, is also still in use. Until recently, preserving the Arabic tradition was a chief responsibility of the *tariqat*; however, because Arabic scholarship is a Daghestani tradition, it has become an issue with the nationalists as well. In fact, the teaching of Arabic has become an issue with all the national fronts and groupings in the Muslim republics, where a number of newspapers and magazines devote a section to the teaching of the Arabic language.

As pointed out, nationalism in Daghestan and Chechnia-Ingushetia is centred in Islam in its Sufi form. Sufism in the North Caucasus is at the confluence of religious and national currents. For North Caucasians the exaltation of the memory of Shamil and other *ghazis* who fought the Russians has both a religious and a national meaning. In addition, contrary to the situation in many other countries, the Sufi orders in the North Caucasus have always had control over the fundamentalist trends.[45]

Anti-religious propaganda and internationalism

In view of the strengthened currents of nationalism and Islam's increasingly activist stance, it is relevant to assess the responses of those who, under the Soviet regime, were charged with the responsibility of eradicating religion. The anti-religious effort made important adaptations, shifting away from anti-religious attacks toward promoting internationalism.

The anti-religious propaganda organisation in the Soviet Union was a formidable machine, or at least it seemed so until *glasnost*. The task of combating religion was shared by all state organisations, both within government and within the Communist Party. Specifically in charge of anti-religious propaganda were the syndicates of workers (*profsoiuz*), the republican branches of the Marx-Engels-Lenin Institute, the *Komsomol*, the republican ministries of culture, the Communist Party regional (*obkom*), district (*raikom*) and city (*gorkom*) committees, and all educational establishments.

From the Second World War onwards, anti-religious propaganda was centralised in and orchestrated by the Association for the Diffusion of Political and Scientific Knowledge (*Znanie*). This association had republican, regional and district branches. A number of special new institutions were created, some quite recently, to combat religion, especially Islam, and these additional institutions were particularly numerous in Muslim territories. The mass media and cultural institutions were also involved in anti-religious work, including radio, television, theatre, the periodical and non-periodical press, exhibitions, museums, libraries and so forth. These were supplemented by anti-religious clubs, along with the widespread use of lectures and one-on-one private discussions.

In spite of the impressive deployment of resources, anti-religious activity was finally in utter disarray in the North Caucasus as well as in other Muslim republics. We read of the problems of anti-religious propaganda in the press and of the need for *perestroika* in ideological work — whatever that may have meant. The authorities in the North Caucasus openly admitted that Party and Soviet workers refused to conduct anti-religious work. Few wanted to associate with the atheist propagandists, who by their ignorance, their formalism and their brutality compromised all anti-religious work.

Following *glasnost* we learned that proper atheistic education did not exist in some areas of the North Caucasus for a long time. The impressive statistics on the number of anti-Islamic lectures read and the number of atheist councils, circles, clubs, private discussions and so on existed only on paper. For example, a Daghestani teacher, S. Gadzhiev, told of his experience as an anti-religious propagandist in a village of the district of Buinaksk, a Sufi stronghold. As a native of a different locality, he was assigned the task of organising an atheistic circle for teachers. This circle, which he was never able to organise, was regarded as the most advanced in the Buinaksk district (*raikom*) of the Party. The republican organisation of the *Znanie* society sent journalists to interview Gadzhiev and a colleague who was also a senior teacher considered to be a propagandist-atheist, but who in fact was a believer. Thus, through the *Biulleten' Ateista* published by the *Znanie* society, Gadzhiev's non-existent atheist circle was cited as a model throughout the Republic.[46] It is plausible to believe that there were many such examples. We learned of propagandists threatened with rough treatment if they dared to slander

Islam, and of lecturers going to a club to deliver an anti-Islamic lecture and finding it closed. Propagandists in charge of private discussions with believers never approached the subject of religion. Even the existence of institutions was falsified. For example, no school of Scientific Atheism functioned in Daghestan in the latter half of the 1980s.[47]

From 1988, North Caucasian propagandists complained of a lack of support, and charged local authorities with leniency in addressing short-comings in atheistic work. Many accused the authorities of closing their eyes to the violation of laws on cults, and there were complaints that the judiciary was too indulgent toward violators. Another complaint was that propagandists received no help from the authorities in obtaining information that would be of value in forming an accurate picture of the religious situation.

For the first time the lack of success of the atheistic propaganda was attributed to atheism itself. Atheistic propaganda as applied to Daghestan and Chechnia-Ingushetia was formulated in the 1920s and 1930s during the years of civil war and constant uprising, but it did not correspond to the needs of a later period. From 1987 important changes were made in the anti-Islamic propaganda in the North Caucasus. Traditional attacks against Islam in the periodical press diminished considerably; in fact, they all but disappeared. Anti-Islamic propaganda took refuge in the propaganda for internationalism. Because Islam has the effect of reinforcing national differences and promoting a sense of ethnic exclusiveness, it was viewed as likely to work strongly against the development of a sense of oneness in the Soviet Union. Thus, anti-Islamic education was called internationalist education. And, as any reader of the North Caucasian press can testify, it became a major subject of discussion.

Prospect for the national movement

With *glasnost* the potential political danger of the revival of Islam, in Muslim territories in general and in the North Caucasus in particular, achieved official recognition in the Soviet press. A number of Soviet specialists on Islam accepted the premise that Islam was more dangerous for Communism than for Western democracies.[48] They agreed that Soviet Muslim territories were particularly vulnerable, and pointed out that bureaucratic methods to eradicate Islam had proved counter-productive. Their solution for dealing with the religious revival was through a politically pragmatic approach. They advocated the legislation of all unofficial religious organisations — unregistered mosques and Quranic schools, the refuge of 'fanatics' and 'extremists'. Only if all religious societies were registered and brought 'within the framework of the law . . . will it be possible to suppress any attempt to utilise religion against society'.[49] Legalisation of religion was not the first attempt by the Soviets to use political cooperation with religious institutions in their pursuit of revolutionary goals. Such was Lenin's flexible policy toward Islam in Central Asia during the Basmachi war and Stalin's cooperation with Mufti Rasulaev during the Second World War. This did not constitute a major policy shift, but rather a change in tactics. If a person's activities were regarded as prejudicial to the state or society he could be subject to prosecution. Within this context, the *tariqat* in the North Caucasus continued to be considered criminal.

National front movements and political parties in Daghestan and Chechnia-Ingushetia are likely to be strongly influenced by the *tariqat*. In the North Caucasian republics and especially Daghestan, Islam can provide a basis on which the multi-ethnic populations can come together. Islam gives the multiple ethnic groups of the North Caucasus a dimension without which they would be only small separate groupings. The pan-Islamic character of the Sufi message gives absolute priority to Muslim identity over a narrow national one. Having made full use of the failure of Communism to provide an attractive ideology and a viable economy, the *tariqat* are poised to take a more active role in the North Caucasus. Because of their well-organised structure, they can rapidly become an efficient political machine. With *glasnost*, sources hinted at the fact that the *tariqat* enjoyed the sympathy, if not the active support, of the leading intelligentsia and Communist Party cadre. It is most probable that national fronts will be led jointly by the *tariqat* and the nationalist intelligentsia. If that were to happen, the fronts would present a strength that the revolt in 1920 in Daghestan and Chechnia lacked. During that revolt most of the intellectuals sided with the Bolsheviks.

The goals of national fronts are not difficult to anticipate. Total independence is certainly the ultimate dream of the North Caucasians, especially the conservative Muslims. Already in 1977, a Daghestani propagandist affirmed that part of the clergy and some representatives of the Daghestani intelligentsia 'tried to isolate themselves within their nationality . . . and to obtain the autonomy for their people'.[50] The Central Asian, Transcaucasian and Baltic Republics are now independent states. The Volga Tatars and Bashkirs are seeking to free themselves from the tutelage of the Russian Federation, and to acquire equal status with the Republics of the Commonwealth of Independent States, while Chechnia has already unilaterally declared independence. Certainly, all the North Caucasian autonomous republics have the same aspirations. Atheistic propaganda has been stopped in the Russian Federation since the banning of the Communist Party and the collapse of the Soviet Union. However, the nationalist issues which were being debated before the failed *coup* of August 1991, and which form an integral part of the message of the Sufi *tariqat*, remain a topic of great actuality, especially those linked to the annexation of the North Caucasian territories by Russia. This is natural since they are of direct relevance to the future integrity of the Russian Federation. Thus many of the accusations used by the official anti-religious propaganda in the past continue to be levelled against North Caucasian Muslims by the Russian press in Moscow — the old label of 'anti-Soviet' has merely become 'anti-Russian'. Similarly, the argument in favour of 'internationalism', a notion now discredited, has been replaced by propaganda in favour of 'democracy' as interpreted in Moscow, which is contrasted to the supposed political 'extremism', 'fascism' and 'Islamic fundamentalism' of the religious and national liberation movements of the North Caucasus.

NOTES

1. A. Bennigsen and C. Lemercier-Quelquejay, *Le Soufi et le Commissaire*, Paris: Seuil, 1986.
2. P. Magomedova, 'Prishlos' po serdtsu — budet zhit', *Sovetskii Dagestan*, 1988, no. 4, p. 35. From the mid-1970s anti-religious propaganda concentrated on eradicating religious rites.
3. M.V. Vagabov, *Islam i Sem'ia*, Moscow Nauka, 1980, p. 133.
4. Percentages are calculated from data found in S.S. Gadzhieva, and Z.A. Iankova, *Dagestanskaia Sem'ia Segodnia*, Makhachkala, 1978, table 5.
5. S. Murtazalieva, 'Uchityvaia mestnye osobenosti', *Sovetskii Dagestan*, 1982, no. 5, p. 49.
6. Iu. Aidaev, 'Harmful Survivals in the Chechen-Ingush ASSR', *Pravda*, 1986.
7. G. Gadzhiev, 'Komu na ruku nasha lozh', *Sovetskii Dagestan*, 1988, no. 2, p. 17.
8. See among others: Kh.Kh. Bokov, 'Formirovat' internatsionalisticheskie ubezhdeniia', *Kommunist*, 1988, no. 3, p. 93; and G. Gadzhiev, 'Komu na ruku . . .', pp.16–18.
9. May demonstrations in Buinaksk and Makhachkala were reported in the Soviet press: K. Magomedov, 'Tak chto zhe proiskhodit?', *Dagestanskaia Pravda*, 9 July 1989. See also the Western news reports: SWB SU/0460 i, 18 May 1989; and *Keston News Service*, no. 326, 25 May 1989. Information concerning later demonstrations in Makhachkala and Groznyi come from independent sources.

10. K. Magomedov, 'Tak chto zhe proiskhodit?', see also T. Aliev, 'Ispoved' veruiushchego', *Sovetskii Dagestan*, 1989, no. 3, p. 26.
11. Reported by foreign visitors to Daghestan.
12. See SWB SU/0460 i, 18 May 1989; *Keston News Service*, no. 326, 25 May 1989; and *Central Asia and Caucasus Chronicle*, 1989, vol. 8, no. 3, p. 18.
13. T. Aliev, 'Ispoved' . . .', p. 26.
14. Events narrated by K. Magomedov in *Dagestanskaia Pravda* (see footnote 9) and confirmed by independent sources.
15. Talib Saidbaev comments on an article by Igor Beliaev, 'Islam i politika', in *Literaturnaia Gazeta*, 10 June 1987.
16. The history and currently situation of the Sufi *tariqat* in the Soviet Union and North Caucasus were documented by A. Bennigsen and C. Lemercier-Quelquejay in *Le Soufi et le Commissaire*, Paris: Seuil, 1986. A somewhat different version of this book was published in English: A. Bennigsen and S. Enders Wimbush, *Mystics and Commissars*, London: C. Hurst, 1985.
17. A. Bennigsen and C. Lemercier-Quelquejay, *Le Soufi* . . ., p. 129, pp. 122–3 (English version, *Mystics* . . ., p. 56, pp. 67–9). Kh. Bokov, 'Uroki istorii', *Nauka i Religiia*, 1987, no. 5, p. 6. S. Murtazalieva, 'Uchityvaia mestnye . . .', p. 48.
18. See S. Murtazalieva, 'Uchityvaia mestnye . . .', p. 48: and M.A. Okulov, 'Kogda net kontrolia', *Bakinskii Rabochi*, Feb. 3, 1985.
19. V. Iu. Gadaev, 'O kharaktere religioznosti sel'skoi molodezhi', *Kharakter religioznosti i problemy ateisticheskogo vospitaniia*, Groznyi, 1979.
20. S. Murtazalieva, 'Uchityvaia mestnye . . .', p. 47, gives a description of the behaviour of some Sufis with young people. Her narrative is a very precise description of the personal relationship between a master and his disciple within a *tariqat*.
21. Kh.Kh. Bokov, 'Formirovat' . . .', p. 91.
22. For a discussion of religious *samizdat*, letters, messages, theological treatises, songs and moral treatises of Sufi character circulating in Daghestan and Chechnia see M.A. Abdullaev, *Nekotorye voprosy teologii islama*, Makhachkala, 1973, pp. 59–62, and 105–7; and A. Bennigsen and C. Lemercier-Quelquejay, *Le Soufi* . . ., pp. 141–8 (English version *Mystics* . . ., *op. cit.*, pp. 88–93).
23. S. Murtazalieva, 'Uchityvaia mestnye . . .', p. 47.
24. See for example: Kh. Kh. Bokov, *Ateisty v nastuplenii*, Groznyi, 1968; I. Makatov, *Religioznye gruppy Amaiia i Kunta Khadzhi*, Makhachkala, 1965; Kh. B. Mamleev, *Reaktsionnaia sushchnost' miuridizma*, Groznyi, 1968; A.V. Avksent'ev, *Islam na severnom Kavkaze*, Stavropol', 1973, p. 100.
25. Kh.Kh. Bokov, 'Uroki Istorii', p. 6.
26. M.A. Mamakaev, *Chechenskii taip (rod) v period ego razlozheniia*, Groznyi, 1973, p. 78; and Kh. Kh. Bokov, 'Uroki istorii', p. 6, and 'Problemy internatsional'noi obriadnosti, obychaev i traditsii v natsional'nykh otnosheniiakh razvitogo sotsializma', *Nauchnyi Kommunizm*, 1982, no. 6, p. 45. Bokov gives the example of a man who denounced some members of his clan to the police, and the families of the accused turned to the *kkhel* tribunal for reparations. The *kkhel* tribunal ordered the denouncer to pay the lawyers of his victims and to reimburse all expenses incurred by their families.
27. Kh.B. Mamleev, *Reaktsionnaia* . . ., p. 38.
28. I. Makatov, 'V ushcherb interesam obshchestva i lichnosti', *Sovetskii Dagestan*, 1986, no. 6, p. 39.
29. It is customary for the families of believers and non-believers alike to distribute the

sadaqa, the voluntary contribution to the mosques or the *tariqat*, during religious celebrations such as marriage, burial, *pominki* and religious holidays. See D. Ikhilov, 'Perezhitki drevnikh verovanii i puti ikh preodoleniia', *Sovetskii Dagestan*, 1981, no. 4, p. 31; and I. Makatov, 'Delo slozhnoe i tonkoe', *Sovetskii Dagestan*, 1985, no. 1, p. 40. Also the *tariqat* collect the *zakat* from their adepts. See S. Murtazalieva, *'Bor'ba idei* . . .', p. 55; I. Makatov, *Religioznye gruppy* . . ., *op. cit.*, p. 19; Kh.B. Mamleev, *Reaktsionnaia* . . ., p. 25; and A.M. Tutaev, *Reaktsionnaia sekta Batal Khadzhi*, Groznyi, 1968, p. 19. The *zakat* is the legal alms, one of the five pillars of the faith outlawed during the Soviet period.

30. S. Murtazalieva, 'Uchityvaia mestnye . . .', p. 49. A. Magomedov, 'Ob etom pisat' ne priniato', *Sovetskii Dagestan*, 1986, no. 5, p. 75, writes that in the cemeteries of Daghestan tombs often have large and expensive funeral stone monuments with inscriptions in Arabic; G. Gadzhiev, 'Komu na ruku . . .', p. 17.

31. Ismailov and Murtazalieva indicate that the combative Kunta Haji (Qadiri) *tariqat* is gaining ground in the traditional Naqshbandi territory of Upper Daghestan. According to Murtazalieva, the extremist Vis Haji (Qadiri) *tariqat* is also gaining in Upper Daghestan: Sh. Ismailov, 'Vyshe uroven' ateisticheskoi raboty', *Sovetskii Dagestan*, 1982, no. 1, p. 4; S. Murtazalieva, 'Bor'ba idei i sovesti', *Sovetskii Dagestan*, 1981, no. 2, pp. 53 and 55. Makatov and Murtazalieva also claim that the Kunta Haji *tariqat* is gaining ground among Kumyks of the lowlands. The majority of the Kumyks are city-dwellers and industrial workers. They have always prided themselves on being religiously tolerant and progressive: I. Makatov, *Ateisty v nastuplenii*, Moscow, 1978, p. 118; S. Murtazalieva, 'Bor'ba idei . . .', p. 53. Makatov indicates that the extremist Naqshbandi Amay group is moving into Northern and Eastern Daghestan, especially into Makhachkala: I. Makatov, 'V ushcherb interesam . . .', p. 38.

32. See for example G. Gadzhiev, 'Komu na ruku . . .', p. 18; I. Makatov, 'Delo slozhnoe . . .', p. 42, and 'V ushcherb . . .', p. 37.

33. The official public condemnation came in the report of U.P. Sukhotin, 'Ob antinauchnoi otsenke dvizheniia Shamilia v trudakh istorikov ANSSR' to the Presidium of the Academy of Sciences of the USSR in September 1950.

34. S.K. Bushuev, 'O kavkazskom miuridizme', *Voprosy Istorii*, 1956, no. 12, pp. 72–9.

35. 'Kavkazskaia voina: sotsial'nye istoki, sushchnost', *Istoriia SSSR*, 1983, no. 2, pp. 54–75.

36. See an analysis of Bliev's article by A. Sheehy, 'Yet Another Rewrite of the History of the Caucasian War?', *RL Research Bulletin*, 30 Jan. 1984.

37. A. Khalilov, 'Shamil' v istorii i pamiati narodov', *Sovetskii Dagestan*, 1988, no. 5, pp. 31–7; a letter written by A.N. Sakharov, deputy director of the Institute of History of the Academy of Sciences of the Soviet Union, is reproduced at the beginning of Khalilov's article.

38. See the documentation of this process in L. Tillett, *The Great Friendship*, Chapel Hill, N.C.: Univ. of North Carolina Press 1969; M.M. Bliev, 'K voprosu o vremeni prisoedineniia narodov severnego Kavkaza k Rossii', *Voprosy Istorii*, 1970, no. 7, pp. 40–56. In the case of Chechnia his thesis did not find wide acceptance at the time. At a 1978 conference in Groznyi, specific guidelines were given to historians by the Academy of Sciences of the Soviet Union and by the Party to reinterpret the history of Chechnia-Ingushtia's entry into Russia. The new version of Chechen-Ingush history was officially produced at another conference in Groznyi in 1979. The published text was signed by no less than five historians. See

N.K. Baibulatov, M.M. Bliev, M.O. Buzurtanov, V.B. Vinogradov, and V.G. Gadzhiev, 'Vkhozhdenie Checheno-Ingushetii v sostav Rossii', *Istoriia SSSR*, 1980, no. 5, pp. 48–63. The article was analysed by A. Sheehy in 'Another Chapter in the Rewrite of History: the Voluntary Incorporation of Checheno-Ingushetia', *RL Research Bulletin*, 30 Sept. 1982.

39. *Narodno-osvoboditel'noe dvizhenie gortsev Dagestana i Chechni v 20–50kh godakh XIX v. Vsesoiuznaia nauchnaia konferentsiia 20–22 iiunia 1989 g.*, Makhachkala, 1989. A religious demonstration was staged in Makhachkala during the All-Union Conference.

40. For the first time, however, Soviet literature recognises that the uprising of 1920 lasted four or even five years. See Kh.Kh. Bokov, 'Uroki istorii', p. 4. In official Soviet historiography the uprising lasted from 1920 to 1921, when it was eradicated.

41. M. Kurbanov, and G. Kurbanov, 'Sviataia prostota', *Sovetskii Dagestan*, 1987, no. 4, pp. 36–7. The article was analysed by A. Bennigsen, 'Islam and Politics in Daghestan', *RL Research Bulletin*, 20 Nov. 1987. The foreign fighters are mostly Turks but include some Arabs, referred to by the authors as 'foreign invaders' and 'enemies and torturers of the Daghestani people'.

42. Kh. Kh. Bokov, 'Formiravat' . . .', p. 90. 'During the last three years, out of 62 teachers and 250 medical workers who came to the Chechen-Ingush ASSR from other areas of the USSR, 49 teachers and half of the medics left the Republic because they could not stand the nationalism and the hostility of the Chechens.' There was no new Russian migration to Daghestan and an out-migration of non-Muslim nationalities from Chechnia.

43. See, for example, G. Gamzatov, 'Russkii iazyk — nashe internatsional'noe dostoianie', *Sovetskii Dagestan*, 1981, no. 1, p. 41; A. Agaev, 'Dagestantsy: narod, natsiia ile drugaia obshchnost'?' *Sovetskii Dagestan*, 1985, no. 3, p. 14; and 'Armiia revoliutsii, armiia naroda', *Kommunist*, 1988, no. 3, p. 57.

44. A. Pirnazar, 'Theologians Exchange Experience', *Muslims of the Soviet East*, 1983, no. 4, p. 8.

45. A. Bennigsen and C. Lemercier-Quelquejay, *Le Soufi* . . ., *op. cit.*, p. 14, (English version, *Mystics* . . ., p. 4). The accusation of Wahhabism leveled at some of the leaders of the religious demonstrations in Makhachkala in the summer of 1989 made little sense in the North Caucasian context. And the accused deny being Wahhabis; see K. Magomedov, 'Tak chto zhe proiskhodit?'.

46. See, for example, L. Avshalumova, 'Chto nam nuzhno', *Sovetskii Dagestan*, 1988, no. 1, p. 31: G. Gadzhiev, 'Komu na ruku . . .', pp. 16–18; and M. Muslimov, 'Esli byt' otkrovennym', *Sovetskii Dagestan*, 1988, no. 4, pp. 26–7.

47. P. Magomedova, 'Prishlos' po serdtsu . . .', p. 34.

48. See I. Beliaev, 'Islam i politika', *Literaturnaia Gazata*, May 13 and 20, 1987; T. Saidbaev, comments on Beliaev's articles, *Literaturnaia Gazeta*, June 10, 1987; 'Novoe myshlenie: svoboda sovesti, uroki proshlogo pri vzgliade v budushchee', *Literaturnaia Gazeta*, 18 May 1988; and M. Muslimov, 'Esli byt' . . .', p. 30. Beliaev implied that there was an Islamic infrastructure in the Soviet Muslim territories; this, both religious and national, could be a destabilising network. Muslimov suggests that Beliaev underestimates the problem, and that the Islamic infrastructure was more widespread than Beliaev thought, at least in the North Caucasus.

49. 'Novoe myshlenie . . .'.

50. S. Gadzhiev, 'Pitaiushchii natsionalizm', *Sovetskii Dagestan*, 1977, no. 2, p. 51.

AFTER THE PUTSCH, 1991

Marie Bennigsen Broxup

The putsch in Chechnia-Ingushetia

On 19 August 1991, the putsch by Yanaev's junta sealed the fate of communism and rang the death knell for the Soviet empire as we knew it. On hearing the news, the Pan-National Congress of the Chechen Peoples[1] (hereafter the National Chechen Congress), a broad-based movement uniting nationalist and democratic forces in the Chechen-Ingush Republic, issued the following appeals[1] from its chairman, the forty-six-year-old retired Air Force general, Dzhokhar Dudaev:

TO ALL THE WORKING PEOPLE OF THE REPUBLIC

In accordance with the *ukaz* of the President of the RSFSR of 19 August 1991, the Executive Committee of the Pan-National Congress of the Chechen Peoples calls you to declare an indefinite general political strike from 21 August on all the territory of the Chechen-Ingush Republic and to display civil disobedience until the arrest of the criminal junta.

Decree of the Executive Committee of the Pan-National Congress of the Chechen Peoples of 19 August 1991

Having considered the actions of the so-called Government Committee for the State of Emergency in the USSR, the Executive Committee of the Pan-National Congress of the Chechen Peoples hereby proclaims:

(1) that the action of the Committee for the State of Emergency is a *coup d'état* by a group of government criminals and a very serious crime against the peoples and the Constitution;

(2) that in the present situation the *ukaz* of the President of the RSFSR be followed;

(3) that any actions by the KGB, MVD [Ministry of the Interior] and Army in support of the Committee for the State of Emergency are illegal and against the interests of the people;

(4) appeals to the population of the Chechen Republic to show endurance, determination and courage in defending democracy and human dignity;

(5) calls the population to a campaign of civil disobedience;
(6) considers the arrest of Z. Yandarbiev, chairman of the Vainakh Democratic Party and Deputy Chairman of the National Chechen Congress, to be a violation of the law and of human rights. The responsibility for this act, which is in breach of the *ukaz* of 19 August 1991 of the President of the RSFSR, lies with the First Deputy Chairman of the Supreme Soviet of the Chechen-Ingush Republic, A.N. Petrenko.

Appeal of the Executive Committee of the National Chechen Congress to the MVD of the Chechen-Ingush Republic

Dear brothers, officers, sergeants and soldiers of the MVD of Chechnia-Ingushetia!

The hour has come when every honest man and citizen, whatever his national or social background, must make his choice according to his honour and conscience.

In the country the Armed Forces and law-enforcing organs have made their choice which has allowed a transition to democratic reforms without bloodshed. However, the local authorities show furious opposition towards the progressive forces. The most absurd rumours are being spread in order to provoke inter-national and inter-tribal clashes and to slander the crowds of demonstrators, describing them as hungry for power.

Let us not be fooled yet again by a corrupt pro-communist clique.

The Executive Committee of the National Chechen Congress appeals to you personally to follow its instructions and to come to the defence of democracy in order to avoid bloodshed in our Republic.

An appeal was also sent by General Dudaev to all the Chechens and Ingush serving in the Soviet armed forces exhorting them to disobey the orders of the junta.[2]

Three days later, on 22 August 1991, at a rally of the democratic groups held on the main square of Groznyi, the leadership of the Republic was condemned for its total lack of trustworthiness and ambiguous behaviour during the *coup*. Included in the condemnation were the Supreme Soviet, its chairman Doku Zavgaev, the Council of Ministers, the Procurator's Office, the KGB, the MVD and generally all the official bodies of executive power. The participants passed a resolution succinctly postulating their immediate political aims: (1) to secure the resignation of Zavgaev; (2) to disband the Supreme Soviet; (3) to transfer all powers in the transitional period pending new elections to the Executive Committee of the National Chechen Congress; (4) to disband the Council of Ministers; (5) to establish a commission to investigate the anti-constitutional acts of the MVD, KGB and Procurator's Office during the crucial days following the *coup*; and (6) the implementation of this resolution to be entrusted to the Executive Committee of the National Chechen Congress.[3]

At a press conference in Moscow six weeks later, refering to Chechnia, the First Deputy Chairman of the RSFSR KGB, Vladimir Podeliakin, expressed outrage at an 'unconstitutional seizure of power by armed formations',[4] while Alexander Rutskoy, Vice-President of the RSFSR, vituperated on radio and television against Chechen 'bandits'. These bandits, it was revealed, had captured the buildings of the Council of Ministers, the KGB, the television and radio stations, and the telephone and telegraphic exchanges in Chechnia-Ingushetia. What could have happened to turn the erstwhile allies of the Russian democrats into 'criminal gangs'? The independent Groznyi newspaper *Svoboda* (30 August 1991) gave a lively account corroborated by descriptions from eyewitnesses.

News of the *coup* was heard on the radio, early in the morning of 19 August. All telephone links with Chechnia-Ingushetia were cut for some time. The leadership of the Republic was overtaken by 'mental paralysis'. The republican radio and television went silent, Doku Zavgaev was in Moscow, the acting chairman of the Supreme Soviet, Petrenko, went into hiding. Only the National Chechen Congress and the Vainakh Democratic Party led by Zelimkhan Yandarbiev reacted without panicking; they immediately set up operation headquarters in the former building of the *gorkom* and gathered all the democratic forces of the Republic under the leadership of the Executive Committee of the Congress. A plan of action was devised, messengers were despatched around the country, and contact with Moscow was re-established through leading Chechen figures such as Ruslan Khasbulatov, First Deputy Chairman of the RSFSR Supreme Soviet, and General Aslanbek Aslakhanov whose units were protecting President Yeltsin in the 'White House' against possible arrest. At 9.30 a.m. began the first rally of what turned out to be an unprecedented ten-week-long continuous demonstration.[5] Coordination was set up with the Ingush territory, Daghestan, Kabardino-Balkaria and Georgia as well as the main factories of Groznyi. The Ingush Popular Front, under the leadership of B.

Kotikov, was ready to take over control of the railway network. The same state of willingness to resist the *diktats* of the *coup* leaders was evident in the main urban districts of Gudermes in the east of Chechnia and Khasav yurt in Daghestan.

The government leadership of the Republic chose to adopt a 'wait and see' policy. Petrenko, the acting chairman of the Supreme Soviet, refused to convene an extraordinary session in the absence of Zavgaev. Asked whether he considered the *coup* constitutional, his reply was that he did not know. Among the government leaders of the Republic only G. Elmurzaev, First Deputy Chairman of the Council of Ministers, incensed by the actions of the junta, remained constantly at his post, followed the course of events in Moscow, and exchanged information with the National Chechen Congress. To its credit, the republican *Komsomol* took sides with the opposition.

At 4 p.m. on 19 August the text of Yeltsin's declaration condemning the *coup* was received by telephone and immediately distributed in the Republic. At 3 a.m. on 20 August, the militia attempted, unsuccessfully, to raid the headquarters of the National Chechen Congress. Later during the night, Groznyi garrison was put on the alert, and fresh troops and military hardware were brought in from the east and the west of the country. Some rural areas were occupied by the army under the pretext of helping with the harvest. When it became clear on 21 August that the armed forces in Moscow would not side with the junta, Zavgaev returned to Groznyi to call an assembly of the Supreme Soviet which duly condemned the initiative of Yanaev and declared that all was quiet in the Republic.

Post-putsch liberalism?

On 26 August 1991, Moscow Central Television transmitted the address of Nursultan Nazarbaev, the President of Kazakhstan, to the first session of the USSR Supreme Soviet after the failed *coup*. The speech resonated with the emotions which had built up during the traumatic three-day putsch, but Nazarbaev undoubtedly expressed the feelings of most of the non-Russians subjects of the empire regarding their future participation in the union. After acknowledging the debt owed by the cause of democracy in USSR to those who rebelled — the students of Alma Ata as far back as 1986, the victims of Tbilisi, Baku, Yerevan, Vilnius and Kishinev — he stated:

> 'For me it is obvious that the union can no longer be a federation. We have spent too long chasing after the past . . . You know that I

actively supported the speedy signing of the union treaty. I remain an active supporter. But the recent events have shown us how explosive and fraught with the danger of bloodshed the old scheme was . . .

'How do I envisage that future union? Having entered into contractual economic agreements among ourselves, we republics have in mind broad economic relations with everyone who agrees to that. It will not benefit any of the fifteen republics in economic terms to go their separate ways at present. Common union bodies retain certain functions. In my opinion these should be the protection of common borders, a supreme council for control over nuclear arms under a ministry of defence in which all members of the union would take part, controlling those who have their finger on the missile-launch button . . . As for the army in each republic . . . we would send the requisite number of servicemen to the union ministry of defence. If an external threat arises, the ministry would combine all our armed forces to defend the union . . . International relations should be shared only in working out general trends, including the problems of disarmament . . . Each republic must have its own ministry of foreign affairs regulating foreign political and economic activity and treaties with other states, with completely autonomous consular administrations so that our citizens do not have to depend on the USSR Ministry of Foreign Affairs to be allowed to travel abroad or to invite guests from abroad. We are used to the abbreviation "USSR". I propose leaving it and changing it to the "Free Union of Sovereign Republics".'

Significantly for the Chechens and the Ingush, Nazarbaev continued: 'By republics I have in mind all republics, including the autonomous ones which have declared themselves sovereign, and those which will want to do so . . . In other words, we are proposing that a confederative treaty be concluded. I am convinced that only then shall we attain genuine equality for the republics . . .' Nazarbaev, however, recognised the rights of the republics which did not want to be part of any union treaty: 'I call for an immediate solution to the granting of full freedom to the Baltic Republics, Moldava and Georgia, and to all that have expressed their aspiration for independence and autonomy by legal democratic means, without any settling of accounts or presentation of spurious claims for debts amounting to billions, because even one human life is invaluable and the peoples of our country have paid with enough lives for their love of freedom. And are these victims the last?'

In a reference to previous attempts to formulate union treaties before the putsch, he said:

'The "nine-plus-one" formula[6] is a thing of the past. . . . The tactics for the immediate future must comprise the urgent formation, not of a cabinet of ministers, but a transitional inter-republican economic council. In it, representatives of all the republics will work on an equal footing, joining in an economic community. But before that we must give those who have decided to leave the opportunity to exercise that right. All may join that interim council, including those who have decided to secede from the union . . .

'That is my view, in general terms, for the future union. To conclude I want to make clear to any one who harbours such illusions, that Kazakhstan will never be any region's underbelly or anyone's younger brother. We shall enter the union only with equal rights and equal opportunities.'[7]

The logical outcome of the failed *coup* is well known. In quick succession those federal republics that had not dared do so earlier, declared sovereignty and independence and tried to free their administration from the control of the Communist Party. Despite Nazarbaev's entreaties, however, this was not the case in the RSFSR. In the general euphoria brought by the dawn of democracy and freedom in Russia, the implications of an important statement went unnoticed: on 29 August, TASS published a terse note emanating from the parliaments of several of the 'autonomous' republics which form part of the Russian Federation. After proclaiming their support for Yeltsin and Gorbachev during the *coup*, the leadership of these republics declared, using a phraseology reminiscent of the stagnation days: 'Our republics are in favour of preserving the Russian Federation as a single and indivisible state, with its time-honoured traditions and famous history as a single multi-ethnic family of peoples. We consider it necessary to adopt emergency measures to stabilise the political situation in the [federal] republic, the basis of which can only be a union treaty elaborated with consideration for the situation which has arisen. We state that the union treaty should be signed in the name of the RSFSR by a united Russian Federation.' The statement asked for urgent economic reforms, unspecified, and concluded: 'We appeal to all citizens, to all peoples and national groupings within Great Russia at this difficult hour to come together and join forces to strengthen the unity and might of our homeland.' Looking even beyond the borders of the RSFSR, they added: 'We call for the unification and cohesion of the peoples from all the republics of the Soviet Union. Only along this path lies the guarantee that our country will occupy a worthy place in the world community.'[8] The signatories included ten of the sixteen autonomous republics of the Russian Federation — the Karelian, Yakut, Udmurt, Komi, Mordvan, Mari, Bashkir and, for the North Caucasus, the Kalmyk, North Ossetian and Daghestani Republics. Important among those that abstained, together with Buryatia, Tuva and Chuvashia, were Tatarstan (where the cleavage between the Russian and Tatar democrats is increasing), Kabardino-Balkaria and Chechnia-Ingushetia in the North Caucasus.[9]

Uprising in Chechnia?

On 27 August, the All-Union Radio monitored by the BBC reported an 'uprising' in the Chechen-Ingush Republic.[10] People were demonstrating, demanding the immediate resignation of the republican leadership which had 'betrayed its people during the days of the failed *coup*'; the airport of the capital, Groznyi, was blocked in order to stop the leaders of the Republic running away to Moscow; the television and radio stations, the telephone exchange and a range of other administrative government buildings were controlled by demonstrators; and the parliament was in permanent session to discuss the suspension of the Presidium's chairman, Doku Zavgaev. On 30 August, TASS from Groznyi reported that delegations from every town and village of the Republic were pouring into the republican capital to support the insurgents. The number of demonstrators ran to thousands, barricades were erected, and the centre of Groznyi was closed to traffic. On 1 September, the buildings of the Council of Ministers and parliament were seized by armed self-defence units of the National Chechen Congress. Russian Radio reported that the green flag of Islam was hoisted above these buildings, and commented that 'in the view of a number of local journalists, the events occuring the Chechnia-Ingushetia had been provoked by pro-Islamic nationalist activists who were opposed to joining and being subordinated to both Union and Russian authorities'.[11] On 3 September, the Presidium of the republican Supreme Soviet adopted a resolution to introduce a state of emergency — which it was unable to sustain — and to hold direct presidential elections a month later, on 29 September.

On 6 September, after two weeks of round-the-clock demonstrations, the mainly pro-communist Supreme Soviet was stormed while in session and disbanded by the National Guard units of General Dudaev. During the raid, the Russian chairman of Groznyi *gorkom*, Vitaly Kutsenko, threw himself out of a window and died. TASS and Russian Television reported a festive atmosphere in Groznyi while noting that armed formations of the National Chechen Congress, whose ranks were growing every day, were patrolling and occupying the centre of the capital. In an interview given to *Vesti* on 7 September, Ruslan Imranovich Khasbulatov welcomed the fall of Zavgaev — his longtime opponent — whom he accused of having been a subservient emissary of the central powers, of having mismanaged and destroyed the wealth of the Chechen-Ingush Republic, and finally of supporting the putsch. He expressed the opinion that the situation would stabilise in the near future.

From then on, however, the situation became more explosive and confusing. A parliamentary delegation from Moscow led by Gennady Burbulis, the RSFSR State Secretary, was dispatched to Chechnia to promote an agreement between the opposition and the remnants of the government in order that, to use Burbulis's words, 'the democratic content of the processes taking place in Chechnia-Ingushetia should be given a legal channel'. These 'processes' were not helped by the fact that Zavgaev stubbornly refused to recognise his defeat and resign. TASS stressed that although the disbanded parliament had not formally laid down its powers, the Executive Committee of the National Chechen Congress, 'around which all the democratic movements have united', had taken on the parliament's functions *de facto*. It was further reported that the National Chechen Congress agreed to allow the parliament to assemble once more 'but only in order to accept the resignation of the chairman of the Supreme Soviet, set a date for the presidential elections and announce the self-dissolution of the parliament'.[12] The critical state of two demonstrators on hunger strike in front of the parliament building had already prompted dozens of deputies to resign before the parliament held its final session on 15 September. Temporary executive powers were transferred to a Provisional Council (*Soviet*) of thirty-two headed by the forty-year-old Deputy Husain Akhmadov, close to the National Chechen Congress, with instructions to hold elections within two months. A provisional committee headed by another deputy, Lechi Magomedov, was elected earlier at a meeting held by the National Chechen Congress to work out proposals for new legislation, including the new structure of the state, laws on citizenship, and elections. These were to be submitted for the approval of the Provisional Council. One of the first acts of the Provisional authorities was to hand over the House of Political Education to the Islamic Institute. The same evening Ruslan Khasbulatov, arriving from Moscow, addressed the demonstrators and congratulated the nation on the triumph of the democratic forces.

Meanwhile the situation was far from quiet in the neighbouring republics. On 30 August 1991 the Supreme Soviet of the Kabardino-Balkar Republic, beset by demands from sixty-eight hunger strikers, announced after an extraordinary session that elections would be held in the Republic ahead of schedule. Two days later the parliament was effectively dissolved and the leaders and deputies of the Republic had 'gone'. On 19 September Russian Radio issued a statement to the effect that the Kabardino-Balkar Supreme Soviet had accepted the resignation of its chairman, Kokov, who was temporarily replaced by Karmakov, and that the deputies were prepared to relinquish their powers pending new elections.[13] The struggle which led to these upheavals has yet to be fully analysed. In Daghestan, the capital Makhachkala had witnessed almost daily demonstrations since June 1991, often motivated by religious demands such as those related to the pilgrimage to Mecca. A state of emergency was declared on 11 September in the Kazbek *raion*, when thousands of Chechens and Daghestanis flooded Lenin-Aul demanding an immediate re-allocation of the lands which had been confiscated after the deportation of the Chechens in 1944. A military column from North Ossetia driving into Daghestan on 14 September was blocked on a bridge in Gerzel aul on the Rostov-Baku highway. Hundreds of people, including many women and old people, closed the road and forced the column to turn back after word spread that the military had orders to crush the Chechens demonstrating in Lenin aul. On 15 September, a well-attended rally of Daghestan's combined national, democratic and religious movements was held in Makhachkala demanding early elections for a new supreme soviet, as in the Chechen-Ingush and Kabardino-Balkar Republics.

On 19 September, TASS announced that elections in the Chechen-Ingush Republic for a new president and parliament were set for 19 and 27 October and that the demonstrators had agreed to disperse. Life, it seemed, was returning to normal. Thereafter there was an almost complete news blackout for nearly two weeks, maybe due, if one wanted to be cynical, to the presence in Groznyi of the RSFSR Minister of the Press and Mass Information, Mikhail Nikiforovich Poltoranin, at the head of a Muscovite delegation.

At the end of September it transpired that the Provisional Council in Chechnia has split into radical and conservative sections, the radicals supported by the National Chechen Congress demanding speedy presidential elections as originally planned, no doubt in order to pre-empt any efforts by Moscow to stir muddy waters. The conservatives, for their part, were trying to postpone the elections until 17 November 1991 in the hope of re-grouping their dwindling forces. If nothing else, this fact alone is an indicator of the changing climate in the national republics after the failed putsch — until then it had always been the opposition groups that had pleaded for time to organise for elections.

On 30 September, Khasbulatov sent an irate telegram to Groznyi complaining about the interference of 'informal groups' in the work of the Provisional Council. The National Chechen Congress reacted immediately, condemning Russia for meddling in the affairs of the 'sovereign' Chechen-Ingush Republic. A week later the situation began to deteriorate dangerously. On 5 October TASS reported that barricades had been re-erected on Liberty Square in front of the Council of Ministers' building after thirteen members of the Provisional Council, allegedly supported by the KGB, had decided to replace its chairman Husain Akhmadov. Regarding this as an attempt by the local KGB bodies to usurp power, the National Chechen Congress announced the dismissal of the Provisional Council, arrested Alexander Pushkin, the Procurator of the Chechen-Ingush Republic, and blocked the KGB building.[14] Alexander Rutskoy, Vice-President of the RSFSR, headed for Groznyi purportedly on a peacekeeping mission. Rutskoy was a former Air Force colonel, a man with an impeccable military record and undoubted courage demonstrated during service as a helicopter pilot in Afghanistan, but his strong Russian nationalist profile did not make him the most suitable emissary for such a task. Neither were his colleagues on this assignment an auspicious choice — Andrei Dunaev and Viktor Ivanenko, respectively RSFSR Minister of Internal Affairs and Chairman of the KGB, two institutions which still symbolise repression whatever their proclaimed good intentions after the putsch may be. On his return Rutskoy compared the situation in the Republic with that in Nagorno-Karabakh, an irrelevant comparison on all counts. There are no irredentist claims on the Chechen territory by other Caucasian nations; the present demands for 'autonomy' by the local Cossack communities, the descendants of the vanguard tsarist troops during the conquest, can only derive legitimacy from the surviving colonial rule and dependent status of the North Caucasus — in contrast to the essentially territorial border war between Armenia and Azerbaijan. Rutskoy alleged that the unrest in Chechnia-Ingushetia was inspired by President Gamsakhurdia of Georgia — in the eyes of Russian public opinion, another ploy to discredit the Chechen opposition. He described Dudaev's supporters as a 'gang terrorising the population' numbering only some 250 men — a somewhat surprising assertion in view of the damage they had inflicted in such a short time to the political establishment of the Republic.[15] On Rutskoy's advice, the Russian Parliament voted a hard-line 'Resolution of the Presidium of the RSFSR Supreme Soviet on the Political Situation in the Chechen-Ingush Republic', which effectively condemned the Chechen-Ingush Republic to the pre-putsch *status quo ante* which denied the Republic the same rights to change which had been gained by the federal republics of the Union. Dated 8 October, this resolution was as follows:

Having listened to a report by Alexander Rutskoy on the political situation in the Chechen-Ingush Republic, and having examined an appeal by the Provisional Council and the conclusion of the Procurator's Office of the Chechen-Ingush Republic on the state of law and order in the Republic, the Presidium of the RSFSR Supreme Soviet expresses serious concern at the situation which has evolved in the Chechen-Ingush Republic . . . The escalation of violent actions on the part of illegal formations is continuing. State institutions are being seized and so are officials. Individual social formations are assuming the authority of bodies of power, and other anti-constitutional actions are being carried out. The life, rights and property of citizens of the Chechen-Ingush Republic are being subjected to growing danger.

Striving to promote the earliest normalisation of the situation and the restoration of constitutional order in the Chechen-Ingush Republic, the Presidium of the RSFSR Supreme Soviet resolves:

(1) that until a new Supreme Soviet of the Chechen-Ingush Republic is elected, the Provisional Council of the Republic, formed by members of the previous Supreme Soviet of the Chechen-Ingush Republic, should be regarded as the only legitimate body of state power on the territory of the Chechen-Ingush Republic;

(2) illegal armed formations should hand over weapons to the Internal Affairs bodies before 2400 hours on 10 October 1991;

(3) to propose that the Provisional Council of the Chechen-Ingush Republic, headed by comrade Bakhmadov,[16] should adopt all the

necessary measures to stabilise the situation in the Chechen-Ingush Republic and to ensure law and order unconditionally; that elections to the Supreme Soviet should be held on the basis of existing legislation.[17]

The last clause regarding legislation was viewed by the opposition as an attempt to emasculate the national movement, similar legalistic arguments having been used against the Baltic Republics during their first steps towards independence.

On 9 October 1991, the tone of Alexander Rutskoy's attacks on the Chechen opposition became more brutal. He gave a lengthy interview for Russian Television during which he accused the National Chechen Congress of having killed Kutsenko, the Groznyi CPSU chairman who died during the storming of the Supreme Soviet,[18] and once again labelled the members of the Congress' Executive Committee as criminals and brigands. He recommended that President Yeltsin should take 'specific measures to detain these criminals' under Article 218 of the Criminal Code regarding the illegal possession of arms, and Articles 67 and 68 on terrorism against the lawful authorities. The Presidium's Resolution and Rutskoy's declarations had a predictable effect locally. The situation took a sharp turn for the worse. Weapons requisitions in the past had always been followed by ruthless repression and deportation. The Chechens remembered this too well to comply meekly with such a demand. Furthermore, the ultimatum to submit to the decisions of the Provisional Council, staffed as it was by old-guard bureaucrats, together with the legislation clause, was deemed to be unacceptable interference in the Republic's internal affairs, and a clear case of double standards on the part of the democratic leadership in Moscow.

General Dudaev declared that the Presidium's resolution was 'virtually a declaration of war on the Chechen-Ingush Republic'. On 10 October 1991, the Chechen National Guards were put on heightened alert, and the Congress declared a general mobilisation of the Chechen male population aged between fifteen and fifty-five. In Groznyi 50,000 people demonstrated in support of Dudaev and seized the building of the Council of Ministers. Moscow's stance became increasingly threatening: Rutskoy reiterated his accusations against the 'criminal' Chechen Congress, although he admitted that the slogans which motivated Dudaev were 'to a certain extent democratic'. For the first time he showed concern that the Chechen crisis could spread and ignite the whole North Caucasus. He announced that he was empowered by the RSFSR

Presidium to declare a state of emergency, but pronounced himself against bringing in the armed forces. However, he stressed that the Ministry of Internal Affairs (MVD) of the Chechen-Ingush Republic was ready to take 'appropriate action' in order to stop the activities of the Chechen 'political clique'. He reminded people that 300,000 Russians living in Chechnia were at risk — always a strong emotional ploy — , and appealed to the Russian public to 'take measures', thus preparing the ground, if necessary, for military intervention by popular request. Khasbulatov backed Rutskoy's stand for 'very tough measures', repeating the allegation that the National Chechen Congress amounted to no more than 200–300 desperate terrorists. 'The people', he said, 'are unequivocal in expressing their commitment to being part of the Russian Federation, to being together, to living together, to tackling common problems together in this difficult predicament. That is what the people are saying. Naturally Dudaev and his associates are not the people, and they have nothing to do with the people.'[19] Another RSFSR parliamentary delegation was dispatched to Groznyi.

On 18 October 1991, General Dudaev urged the people of Chechnia-Ingushetia to prepare for war which he judged inevitable 'since hostile forces were massed in North Ossetia and Daghestan preparing to attack the Republic and strangle the revolution'. He stressed that 'any actions of the Russian centre aimed at undermining the democratic processes in the Republic' would be seen as 'a continuation of the genocide against the Chechen people'. He reported that 62,000 men had signed up for the ranks of the national guard and the people's militia. Meanwhile preparations for the elections of the president and parliament, set for 27 October, were in full swing, and delegations from neighbouring North Caucasian republics began to arrive in Groznyi to support the National Chechen Congress.

Background and slogans of the national movement

The National Chechen Congress had held its inaugural meeting on 23–25 November 1990 in Groznyi. Its purpose was that of a popular front — to unite all the republican political movements ranging from the liberal democratic opposition to the communist establishment. On 27 November, under pressure from the Congress, the Chechen-Ingush Supreme Soviet proclaimed the Republic's sovereignty. The aims of the nationalists were originally fairly modest, mainly to escape from the fold of the Russian Federation and to raise the status of their country from autonomous to union republic, which would have enabled them to sign a union treaty with the USSR on an equal basis with the other fifteen former union republics. At the time of its second convention, in June 1991, the position of the National Chechen Congress had hardened. A precise agenda was formulated, setting up conditions and a timetable for negotiations with Moscow. These were published together with a speech by General Dudaev in the Groznyi independent newspaper *Bart*.[20] In words boldly outspoken even by today's more liberal and uncensored standards, Dudaev hailed the fall of the colonial empire which had robbed the nation of its 'religion, language, education, science, culture, natural resources, ideology, mass media, leadership cadres, and rights to freedom and life'. The instruments of colonial oppression were pinpointed as the CPSU, the KGB, the MVD, and specifically the Procurator's office; their goal — to preserve the empire at any cost; their main method — to fight Islam, the only force able to unite the Caucasian nations and to resist foreign ideology and creeds; their tactics — to manoeuvre speedily in the face of a changing situation and balance of power. Rejecting any 'hybrid' version of sovereignty for the sake of economic stability, as advocated by the republican establishment and the Supreme Soviet in Moscow, Dudaev eloquently argued that 'the price of genuine sovereignty is so great that to expect to achieve it cheaply is as absurd as to presume that the Chechens will ever be reconciled with their present miserly colonial freedom . . . There is only one question to raise today: do we want to be free or shall we willingly sell our future into serfdom? The time has come to make our choice.'

In the name of the Executive Committee of the National Chechen Congress, Dudaev made the following proposals to the Chechen-Ingush Supreme Soviet, aimed at rapidly changing the political structure of the Republic:

(1) to elect a legislative body which would have plenary powers from the electorate until new elections the following month — the elections to be supervised jointly by the republican Supreme Soviet and the National Chechen Congress;

(2) to adopt a new constitution and law on citizenship — this in order to prevent Moscow using the argument that independence is not possible because the Ingush wish to remain within the RSFSR. (The situation of the Ingush is particularly difficult. They number some 300,000, with approximately one-third of the population living outside their nominal territory. They are in conflict with North Ossetia over some of their

ancestral lands apportioned to North Ossetia during the Second World War deportation, which they have not yet been able to repossess. They are also threatened by the Cossacks of the Sunja region of Ingushetia who are presently striving to set up an autonomous Sunja Cossack district. Because of this, the Ingush have been cautious in their demands for sovereignty and have so far elected to remain within the Russian Federation.[21])

(3) the population to decide on its citizenship before 15 August 1991;

(4) to hold presidential elections before 15 September 1991,

(5) to hold a referendum before the end of November 1991 to determine the status of the Republic and its citizens *vis-à-vis* the centre;

(6) to ask the Ingush to choose their own state system and determine by referendum their relations with Chechnia, their decision to be formalised by a pact between the Chechen and Ingush nations.

It was stressed that no treaty could be signed with either the USSR or the RSFSR before these measures had been taken. Besides, specific conditions had to be fulfilled beforehand:

— the unconditional recognition of the right of the Chechen nation to sovereign independence;

— the signing of a peace treaty as a logical outcome of three centuries of uninterrupted warfare (to wit: the Russian wars of conquest of the eighteenth and nineteenth centuries, the 1920–1 war 'fought on irreconcilable positions', the elimination of the Mountain Republic recognised by Great Britain, France, Germany and Turkey, the deportation under Stalin and subsequent annihilation of one-third of the Chechen population);

— the trial of those guilty of crimes of genocide against the Chechen nation in the Soviet period;

— payment of compensation for the crimes against the nation and the return of the national patrimony;

— establishment of a proper government structure based on democratic principles.

Noting the present paucity of contacts among the nations of the North Caucasus, Dudaev advocated a strong pan-Caucasian stand: 'We must not forget that we bear a responsibility for the fate of our sister-nations in the Caucasus. The union of all the Caucasian nations on an equal basis is the only possible way for the future. As we hold a central geopraphic, strategic and economic position in the Caucasus, and have the necessary human potential, we must be the initiators of this future union.' He stated that the National Chechen Congress was ready to propose a blueprint to re-establish the Mountain Republic, which had been 'one of the most important efforts to create a common Caucasian home' in the past. Furthermore he urged the creation of a national defence system and demanded that Chechen youths perform their military service in their homeland. 'Despite all the aggressiveness and dangers which have always faced the Chechens, we must learn the lesson that a slave who does not wish to free himself of his chains deserve his slavery.'

Negotiation or confrontation?

On 19 October 1991, the political conflict between the National Chechen Congress and Moscow escalated with the intervention of Yeltsin himself. The Russian president ordered the Chechen opposition to submit unconditionally, within three days, to the Resolution of the RSFSR Supreme Soviet. He warned that if the opposition did not comply, all measures provided for in the laws of the Russian Federation would be employed to normalise the situation and ensure the protection of the constitutional order. His ultimatum was dismissed out of hand by Deputy Husain Akhmadov on Chechen television as the 'last belch of the Russian empire' and 'an evident desire to throttle democratic forces in the Chechen Republic'.[22]

On 23 October, the RSFSR Procuracy in Moscow issued the following statement:

> Under the law that is in force, citizens are subject to criminal liability for public appeals for the overthrow or forcible change of the state and public system, for violating the integrity of the RSFSR, whipping up national or religious hatreds or differences, incitement to mass disturbances, pogroms, resistance to the authorities, blocking transport communications, encroaching on the normal operation of institutions. The mass media may not be used for these purposes. For such offences they are liable under due legal process even to the point of stopping an edition coming out or closing down publications. The activity of any associations of citizens, including political parties, public organisations or mass movements, aimed at incitement to national hatred or underlining differences, the use of force or violation of the integrity of the territory of the Russian Federation is against the law and, if a court so decides, may be banned. In some republics forming part of the RSFSR, national guards and other armed formations are being set up whose activity is not regulated by legislation, and this is unlawful. Procurators

of republics, *krays* and *oblasts* have been told by the RSFSR Procuracy to take measures in response to all instances of violation of the law.[23]

This statement makes depressing reading. If one dismisses the legal niceties of the text — 'under the law that is in force', 'due legal process', 'if a court so decides' — and remembers that the Soviet Union was always cautious about giving its oppresive measures a legal framework, one is left with the same basic tenet that the Russian communists have striven to apply since they first came to power — unquestioning compliance in thought and action with a dogma imposed from above; previously this was communism, now it is Moscow's own interpretation of democracy. From Kalinin's dream to give everyone in the USSR 'the psychology and ideals of a Russian industrial worker from Petrograd' to the later hybrid *Homo Sovieticus*, the Soviet nationalities have been expected to fit within a mould acceptable to Russia. The North Caucasians are still expected to conform, notwithstanding any 'differences', for the sake of Russia, for the 'integrity of the territory of the Russian Federation'.

Since late August 1991, much has been done by Moscow to vilify the Chechen opposition and to distract attention from the main issue at stake, that of a colony aspiring for freedom as plainly expressed by General Dudaev. The methods used by Moscow were not novel; if anything they showed a distinct lack of fresh inspiration: counter-rallies organised by the local *nomenklatura* to protest against the 'unconstitutional behaviour' of the opposition, letters to Moscow newspapers complaining about the 'undemocratic' and 'unconstitutional' behaviour of the National Chechen Congress, possibly provoking a mutiny in the main prison of Groznyi in order to label the opposition as 'criminals', playing on ethnic, national and clanic differences with only moderate success, and above all encouraging the warlike ambitions of the Cossack colonies — all manoeuvres redolent of the old pre-*perestroika* days. (It is noteworthy in this context that some of the Cossack *stanitsas* of Chechnia-Ingushetia, in Naurskii district, which are vociferously demanding their re-attachment to Russia, have taken up the protection of the Lenin monuments.)

Nonetheless the elections went ahead, and on 27 October 1991, beating three other candidates, General Dudaev was elected president of Chechnia by an overwhelming majority according to the National Chechen Congress.[24] Only two contradictory comments were available at the time of writing: Ruslan Khasbulatov (himself elected chairman of the RSFSR Supreme Soviet on 28 October) claimed that the elections contradicted the norms of democracy, while observers from the International Committee on Human Rights did not think that any violations of such norms had occurred (Russian Television, 1800 GMT, 29 October 1991). Significantly, one of the first decisions of the National Chechen Congress following the election of Dudaev was to set up a Caucasian Independence Party[25] — a move intended to sponsor pan-Caucasian unity. The party was to be formally proclaimed at a congress of the Mountain Peoples of the Caucasus due to be held in Sukhumi, capital of Abkhazia (in the Republic of Georgia), in November 1991.

Alexander Rutskoy's fear that the rebellion in Chechnia could ignite the whole North Caucasus is not far-fetched. Already in August 1991, shortly after the putsch, the newspaper *Svoboda* had published the following message from the president of the Assembly of the Mountain Peoples of the Caucasus, Musa Shanibov, to the National Chechen Congress:

> We are thrilled with the political awareness and courage of the Chechen nation. You have given an example to all the free nations of the Caucasus. Demonstrations have already begun in Nalchik [capital of Kabardino-Balkaria] in support of our Chechen brothers. I know that Abkhazia is ready to give you whatever help you need. We are even thinking of holding a session of the Assembly in Groznyi in the near future. The centre of the political struggle in the region has moved to Chechnia-Ingushetia. The fate of the Caucasus is being decided in Chechnia. All the republics and member nations of the Assembly of the Mountain Peoples of the Caucasus fully support the activity of the Executive Committee of the National Chechen Congress and its chairman Dzhokhar Dudaev.[26]

Besides the political shift in the Kabardino-Balkar Republic mentioned earlier, other nations which provided the Caucasian legions resisting the Russian conquest in the eighteenth and nineteenth centuries, are now 'on the move': the Lezghins and Avars in Daghestan have held national assemblies (12 October 1991) following the example of the National Chechen Congress; the Adyghe Congress has demanded that seats for deputies representing their region in the Supreme Soviet in Moscow be reserved for their indigenous population (21 October 1991); the Cherkess Congress ended with the proclamation of the Republic of Cherkessia (24 October 1991). It was the first time that the Cherkess peoples were able to take political initiatives in Russia since the forced exile to Turkey in the nineteenth century which left their ranks decimated.

None of these nations will be willing to give up their newly-claimed freedom for the benefit and greater glory of Russia. Furthermore, there were signs that the Sufi *tariqat*, which had been sympathetic to the national movement in Chechnia but have taken no active part in the political debate, have rallied vigorously around the National Chechen Congress after Yeltsin's ultimatum. Calls for *Ghazawat* were heard. For most Chechens it remains, even today, a compelling duty whether they are active members of a *tariqat* or not. The chief of staff of the Chechen Congress, Iles Arsanukaev, has warned that any use of force against the Chechen liberation movement would lead to another 'Caucasian war', and that the resistance would automatically adopt the tactics of Shamil's *murids*.[27] A commitment from the *tariqat* will ensure that the independence movement started in Chechnia will rapidly acquire a pan-Caucasian dimension and spread to neighbouring North Caucasian republics, since the religious Sufi brotherhoods' loyalties often cut across ethnic and clanic divisions. Undoubtedly Daghestan, which has been in the grip of religious demonstrations since June 1991, will be drawn towards a more defiant political stand than it has expressed so far. It is probable that the first casualty would be the Daghestani republican leadership which has so subserviently voted in favour of remaining part of an 'indivisible Russia' — a particularly absurd notion in view of that country's history.

On the basis of the scarce information available,[28] the leaders of the Chechen opposition appear true to the fine Caucasian tradition, which has been so rich in heroic figures. Their position seems as irreconcilable with Moscow as that of the Sufi Naqshbandi resistance against the Bolsheviks in 1920. There is nothing to indicate that they would be willing to compromise. All information indicates that much groundwork had been done long before the August 1991 upheaval, especially in organising self-defence — the example of Azerbaijan and Armenia having shown that the former Soviet nations that want to assert their statehood and sovereignty must be able to show some minimal level of military preparedness and ability to defend their borders without resorting to Moscow's arbitration. Thus if a compromise is to be found it will have to come from Moscow. On the face of it, there should be less difficulty for the RSFSR leadership in granting independence to the North Caucasian republics than to Tatarstan, which is also deeply engaged in a struggle for independence but situated nearer the Russian heartland. A precedent has already been set by the neighbouring Transcaucasian republics, which are rapidly becoming independent states *de facto* as well as *de jure*, although their disputes and internal political problems will ensure that they are unable for some time to come to present a common front which could pose a challenge to Moscow. However, the three-stage programme of the National Chechen Congress — independence first, confederation second, and federation of the Mountain Peoples of the Caucasus third — which will no doubt find many echoes among other North Caucasians, raises the spectre of a strong Muslim, oil-rich and by no means friendly southern bloc in an area which Russians have long considered as 'their Caucasus'. Furthermore a future North Caucasian confederation or federation on the model of the former Mountain Republic would entertain strong economic ties with Azerbaijan, and would naturally look for alliances with Turkey, Iran and the Middle East, gradually escaping from the Russian sphere of influence, and possibly changing the balance of power in the region. Thus one cannot dismiss the possibility that the Russian leadership intends to be as ruthless as the tsarist and Soviet administrations in its effort to safeguard its political and territorial interests.

Whatever the outcome of the present crisis — whether Dudaev remains in power or not — the objectives of the National Chechen Congress will be achieved sooner or later, but Moscow's handling of the situation to date could ensure that Russia will lose whatever modest goodwill it has enjoyed so far. Short of military intervention, Russia's options are limited. With the benefit of hindsight one can say that all the strategies applied in the past — assimilation, cooptation of élites, colonisation, deportation, anti-Islamic campaigns — have failed. What Moscow can do is to foment unrest and even incite local warfare: to encourage and arm various clanic and tribal factions in Chechnia opposed to Dudaev — according to TASS, this is already happening; to fuel Cossack militancy; and to sponsor a secessionist Ingush stand favourable to union with the RSFSR. In the Caucasus as a whole, conflicts could easily flare up at the smallest provocation between North Ossetia and Chechnia-Ingushetia over Vladikavkaz and the territories ceded to Ossetia during the Chechen and Ingush deportation in 1944, between Chechnia and Georgia over the Abkhaz question, or between Georgia and Daghestan over the expulsion of the Daghestani population from the Georgian border regions. In short the path to unity, so necessary before the Caucasian people can at long last enjoy the fruits of their independence, may be fraught with dangers. Moscow's gain in such a scenario would be merely psychological — to be able to adjudicate in border disputes between the republics, thus perpetuating Russia's disposition for playing policeman. But whatever the outcome, there is probably no future in the North Caucasus for 'one indivisible Russia' as advocated by Denikin.

March 1992

NOTES

1. In Russian *Obshchenatsionalnyi S'ezd Chechenskogo Naroda*.
2. Published by the weekly independent newspaper *Svoboda (Marsho)* (Freedom), Groznyi, no. 1 (28), 30 Aug. 1991, 10,000 copies, formerly called *Novaia Gazeta*.
3. *ibid.*
4. V. Martynov for Central Television, First All-Union Programme, 2100 GMT, 8 Oct. 1991, SWB SU/1199 B/4, 10 Oct. 1991.
5. This first rally was addressed by Yandarbiev who was promptly arrested at 2 p.m. and the meeting dispersed by the militia. He was released later in the day but only after General Dudaev had warned the Supreme Soviet that Petrenko would be held personally responsible for Yandarbiev's arrest. Dudaev himself was under threat.
6. 'Nine-plus-one agreement' signed on 23 April 1991 by Gorbachev and the leaders of nine Soviet republics wishing to remain part of the USSR.
7. Central Television, First All-Union Programme, 1300 GMT, 26 Aug. 1991, excerpts from the BBC SWB SU/1162 C1/7, 28 Aug. 1991.
8. TASS World Service, 0908 GMT, 29 Aug. 1991, as quoted by SWB SU/1165 B/6, 31 Aug. 1991.
9. According to Radio Liberty *Report on the USSR*, vol. 3, no. 36, 6 Sept. 1991, p. 101, representatives of the Karachai-Cherkess Autonomous *Oblast* were also absent.
10. SWB SU/1163 ii, 29 Aug. 1991.
11. SWB SU/1168 ii, 4 Sept. 1991, quoting a Russia's Radio report of 2 Sept. 1991.
12. Personal communication to the author from Groznyi, confirmed by TASS World Service in Russian 0815 GMT, 13 Sept. 1991, quoted by SWB SU/1178 B/2, 16 Sept. 1991.
13. Russia's Radio 1330 GMT, 19 Sept. 1991.
14. SWB SU/1196 i, 7 Oct. 1991.
15. Russia's Radio, 2100 and 2200 GMT, 8 Oct. 1991, SWB SU 1199 C1/1, 10 Oct. 1991.
16. Baudi Bakhmadov, a procurator, was chosen as the new chairman of the Provisional Council to replace Husain Akhmadov, probably considered to be too favourable to the National Chechen Congress.

17. TASS World Service in Russian, 1920 GMT, 8 Oct. 1991, SWB SU/1199 C1/2, 10 Oct. 1991.
18. This particular accusation, whether true or not, will be seen by the Chechens as a particular act of hypocrisy. Indeed it is common belief in Russia that the three putschists who committed suicide — Pugo, Akhromeev and Kuchina — were in fact killed.
19. Rutskoy: All-Union Radio, 1730 GMT, 10 Oct. 1991; Khasbulatov: Russian Television, 2123 GMT, 10 Oct. 1991, SWB SU/1201 B/5–9, 12 Oct. 1991.
20. *Bart*, no. 6, June 1991. Published in Groznyi since September 1989, editor S. Yunusov, distribution 2000 copies.
21. An Ingush Congress held on 20 June 1991 in Nazran proclaimed the establishment of the 'Ingush Republic within the RSFSR', see *Svobodnaia Gruziia*, 5 July 1991. On 8 Oct. 1991 the Ingush Congress meeting in Groznyi adopted the decision not to separate from Chechnia, at least not until the issue of the Ingush territories in North Ossetia has been settled.
22. TASS World Service in Russian, 1856 GMT, 19 Oct. 1991, report by S. Asuev, SWB SU/1208 B/5, 21 Oct. 1991.
23. TASS and Russia's Radio, 1800 GMT, 23 Oct. 1991, SWB SU/1212 B/4, 25 Oct. 1991.
24. The other candidates were R. Gaytemirov, leader of the Green movement; M. Sulaev, a state farm agronomist, chairman of the World Democratic Movement; and B. Umaev, of whom no details are known.
25. *Partiia Nezavisimosti Kavkaza.*
26. *Svoboda (Marsho), op. cit.*
27. SWB SU/1208 i, quoting TASS, 23 Oct. 1991.
28. We know that General Dudaev graduated from the Tambov Higher School of Pilot-Engineers and the Gagarin Air Force Academy. He served in Siberia and the Ukraine. Recently he was commander of a large Air Force formation in Estonia.

BIBLIOGRAPHICAL NOTE

ON SELECTED WORKS PUBLISHED IN RECENT DECADES IN WESTERN EUROPEAN LANGUAGES

The Caucasian wars

Allen, W.E.D. and Paul Muratoff, *Caucasian Battlefields: A History of the Wars on the Turco-Caucasian Border*, Cambridge University Press, 1953. A comprehensive work covering the period 1828–1922.

Baddeley, John Frederic, *The Rugged Flanks of the Caucasus*, Oxford University Press, 1940.

——, *The Russian Conquest of the Caucasus*, London: Longmans, Green, 1908.

These two books remain the most valuable historical works written to date on the nineteenth-century Russian wars of conquest.

Bennigsen, Alexandre, 'Un mouvement populaire au Caucase au XVIIIe siècle. La *"Guerre Sainte"* du sheikh Mansur (1785–1791), page mal connue et controversée des relations russo-turques', *Cahiers du Monde Russe et Soviétique*, vol. V, no. 2, April–June 1964. Reassessment of the first North Caucasian *jihad* and the personality and role of Sheikh Mansur, based on previously unknown documents found in the Ottoman archives by Professor Bennigsen.

Blanch, Lesley, *The Sabres of Paradise*, London: John Murray, 1960. A very readable, historically accurate, but somewhat romanticised portrait of Shamil by a talented novelist.

Henze, Paul, 'Circassia in the Nineteenth Century. The Futile Fight for Freedom', in C. Lemercier-Quelquejay, G. Veinstein and S.E. Wimbush (eds), *Passeé Turco-Tatar, Présent Soviétique. Etudes offertes à Alexandre Bennigsen*, Louvain and Paris: Editions Peeters and Editions de l'Ecole des Hautes Etudes en Sciences Sociales, 1986, pp. 243–73.

——, 'Fire and Sword in the Caucasus: The 19th-Century Resistance of the North Caucasian Mountaineers', *Central Asian Survey*, vol. 2, no. 1, July 1983, pp. 5–44.

——, 'Marx on Russians and Muslims', *Central Asian Survey*, vol. 6, no. 4, 1987, pp. 33–45.

The first of these two works put the North Caucasus in the international context of Great Power rivalry and deal with the resistance of the Cherkess tribes to the Russian conquest of the north-west Caucasus. The third comments on Karl Marx's letters and articles on the 'Eastern Question'.

The twentieth century — history, demography

Bammate, Haidar, *Le Caucase et la révolution russe*, Paris: L'Union Nationale des Emigrés de la Republique du Caucase du Nord, 1929. Revolution and civil war in the North Caucasus and Transcaucasia. Some of the problems raised in this short book remain topical today. The author was Minister of Foreign Affairs of the North Caucasian Mountain Republic.

Bennigsen, Alexandre, 'Muslim Guerilla Warfare in the Caucasus (1918–1928)', *Central Asian Survey*, vol. 2, no. 1, July 1983, pp. 45–56.

—— and Hélène Carrère d'Encausse, *Une république soviétique musulmane: Le Daghestan*, Paris: Paul Geuthner, 1956.

Conquest, Robert, *The Nation Killers: The Soviet Deportation of Nationalities*, London: Macmillan, 1970. The standard work on Stalin's deportation during the Second World War of the North Caucasians, as well as the Volga Germans, Crimean Tatars and Meskhetians.

Kolarz, Walter, *Russia and her Colonies*, London: George Philip and Son, 1952. One chapter is devoted to the North Caucasus peoples.

Swietochowski, Tadeusz, *Russian Azerbaijan, 1905–1920: The Shaping of National Identity in a Muslim Community*, Cambridge University Press, 1985. Useful reading which helps set the history of the last great Daghestani uprising of 1920–1 against the background of political events in the neighbouring Transcaucasian republics.

Historiography

Bennigsen, Alexandre, 'Les limites de la déstalinisation dans l'islam soviétique', *L'Afrique et l'Asie*, no. 39, 1957, pp. 32–40.

Henze, Paul, 'The Shamil Problem' in Walter Z. Lacqueur (ed.), *The Middle East in Transition: Studies in Comtemporary History*, New York: Praeger, 1958, pp. 415–43.

Tillet, Lowell R., *The Great friendship: Soviet Historians on the Non-Russian Nationalities*, Chapel Hill: University of North Carolina Press, 1969.

——, 'Shamil and Muridism in Recent Soviet Historiography', *American Slavic and East European Review*, vol. XX, 1961, pp. 253–69. The standard works on the conflict over the interpretation of Caucasian *Muridism* in Soviet historiography.

Traho, Ramazan, 'The "Rehabilitation" of Imam Shamil', *Caucasian Review*, no. 1, 1955, pp. 145–62.

Wolfe, Bertram D., 'Operation Rewrite: The Agony of Soviet Historians', *Foreign Affairs*, vol. XXXI, no. 1, October 1951, pp. 39–57.

Linguistics

Dumezil, Georges, *Documents anatoliens sur les langues et les traditions du Caucase*, Paris: Institut d'Ethnologie, Musée de l'Homme, 1965. This monumental work provides Ubykh texts on the history of the Russian wars, the Ubykhs' exile and re-settlement in Turkey, their literature and folklore. It is thanks to Professor Dumezil's work that the language of the Ubykh has been recorded and therefore not become totally extinct. The introduction 'Notes pour un centenaire' gives a poignant history of the Ubykhs' last stand against the Russian army on the beaches of the Black Sea.

Islam

Bennigsen, Alexandre, 'Sufism in the USSR: A Bibliography of Soviet Sources', *Central Asian Survey*, vol. 2, no. 4, 1983, pp. 81–108.

—— and Chantal Lemercier-Quelquejay, *Le soufi et le commissaire. Les confréries musulmanes en URSS*, Paris: Seuil, 1986.

Bennigsen, Alexandre, and S. Enders Wimbush, *Mystics and Commissars: Sufism in the Soviet Union*, London, C. Hurst, 1985.

The two latter works deal with Sufism in Central Asia as well as in the Caucasus. The French version is more complete and includes archival material and letters from Shamil.

Bennigsen, Alexandre, and Chantal Lemercier-Quelquejay, 'Lieux saints et soufisme au Caucase', *Turcica*, vol. XV, 1983, pp. 180–99.

——, 'L'"islam parallèle" en Union Soviétique. Les organisations soufies dans la République tchetcheno-ingouche', *Cahiers du Monde Russe et Soviétique*, vol. XXI (1), January–March 1980, pp. 49–63.

Bryan, Fanny E.B., 'Anti-religious Activities in the Chechen-Ingush Republic of the USSR and the Survival of Islam', *Central Asian Survey*, vol. 3, no. 2, 1984, pp. 99–116.

——, 'Anti-Islamic Propaganda: *Bezbozhnik*, 1925–1935', *Central Asian Survey*, vol. 5, no. 1, 1986, pp. 29–48.

Lemercier-Quelquejay, Chantal, 'Sufi Brotherhoods in the USSR: A Historical Survey', *Central Asian Survey*, vol. 2, no. 4, 1983, pp. 1–36.

Longuet Marx, Frédérique, 'Tradition et Modernite' à travers l'analyse des fêtes et rituels au Daghestan', unpubl. doctoral thesis, Institut National des Langues et Civilisations Orientales, Paris, 1991.

Bibliography

Gammer, Moshe, 'Shamil and the Murid Movement, 1830–1859: An Attempt at a Comprehensive Bibliography', *Central Asian Survey (Special North Caucasus issue)*, vol. 10, no. 1/2, 1991, pp. 189–247.

Tatlock, T., 'The Centenial of the Capture of Shamil: A Shamil Bibliography', *Caucasian Review*, no. 8, 1959, pp. 83–91, 101–2.

Traho, Ramazan, 'Literature on Checheno-Ingushes and Karachay-Balkars', *Caucasian Review*, no. 5, 1957, pp. 76–96.

Journals — Special Issues

Central Asian Survey has published two issues specially dedicated to the North Caucasus:

— vol. 4, no. 4, 1985, contains a section entitled 'Shamil: New Documents and Correspondence', and two articles: 'Aul Yulan: An Episode of the Caucasian War' by Mohammed beg Hadjelache', and 'Crisis and Response in Soviet Nationality Policy: The Case of Abkhazia' by Darrell Slider.

— vol. 10, no. 1/2, 1991, contains among others:

Ramazan Traho, 'Circassians', pp. 1–64. A comprehensive history of the Cherkess, from antiquity to the Soviet period.

Franco Venturi, 'The Legend of Boetti Sheikh Mansur', pp. 93–102. An essay on the Italian legends concerning Sheikh Mansur.

Michel Tarran, 'The Orthodox Mission in the North Caucasus: End of the 18th — Beginning of the 19th Century', pp. 103–18. Russian Orthodox missionary work among the Ossetians and Abkhaz.

Vassan-Giray Cabagi, 'Revolution and Civil War in the North Caucasus: End of the 19th — Beginning of the 20th Century', pp. 119–32. An account by a participant in the events of this period. The author was Minister of Finance of the North Caucasian Mountain Republic.

Michael Rywkin, 'The Communist Party and the Sufi *Tariqat* in the Checheno-Ingush Republic', pp. 133–46. Based on rarely available newspaper sources from Groznyi.

Paul Henze, 'The Demography of the Caucasus According to 1989 Soviet Census Data', pp. 147–70.

INDEX